In Freud's Tracks

New Imago: Series in Theoretical, Clinical, and Applied Psychoanalysis

Series Editor
Jon Mills, Canadian Psychological Association

New Imago: Series in Theoretical, Clinical, and Applied Psychoanalysis is a scholarly and professional publishing imprint devoted to all aspects of psychoanalytic inquiry and research in theoretical, clinical, philosophical, and applied psychoanalysis. It is inclusive in focus, hence fostering a spirit of plurality, respect, and tolerance across the psychoanalytic domain. The series aspires to promote open and thoughtful dialogue across disciplinary and interdisciplinary fields in mental health, the humanities, and the social and behavioral sciences. It furthermore wishes to advance psychoanalytic thought and extend its applications to serve greater society, diverse cultures, and the public at large. The editorial board is comprised of the most noted and celebrated analysts, scholars, and academics in the English speaking world and is representative of every major school in the history of psychoanalytic thought.

Titles in Series:

Desire, Self, Mind, and the Psychotherapies: Unifying Psychological Science and Psychoanalysis, by R. Coleman Curtis.

In Freud's Tracks: Conversations from the Journal of European Analysis, edited by Sergio Benvenuto and Anthony Molino

In Freud's Tracks

Conversations from the Journal of European Psychoanalysis

edited by
Sergio Benvenuto and Anthony Molino

JASON ARONSON
Lanham • Boulder • New York • Toronto • Plymouth, UK

A JASON ARONSON BOOK

ROWMAN & LITTLEFIELD PUBLISHERS, INC.

Published in the United States of America
by Rowman & Littlefield Publishers, Inc.
A wholly owned subsidiary of The Rowman & Littlefield Publishing Group, Inc.
4501 Forbes Boulevard, Suite 200, Lanham, Maryland 20706
www.rowmanlittlefield.com

Estover Road
Plymouth PL6 7PY
United Kingdom

British Library Cataloguing in Publication Information Available

Library of Congress Cataloging-in-Publication Data

In Freud's tracks : conversations from the Journal of European Analysis / edited by Sergio Benvenuto and Anthony Molino.
p. cm. — (New imago: series in theoretical, clinical, and applied psychoanalysis)
ISBN-13: 978-0-7657-0630-0 (cloth : alk. paper)
ISBN-10: 0-7657-0630-X (cloth : alk. paper)
ISBN-13: 978-0-7657-0632-4 (electronic)
ISBN-10: 0-7657-0632-6 (electronic)
1. Psychoanalysis. 2. Psychoanalysts—Interviews. I. Benvenuto, Sergio. II. Molino, Anthony, 1957– III. Journal of European Analysis.
BF173.I425 2009
150.19'5—dc22 2008034418

Printed in the United States of America

∞™ The paper used in this publication meets the minimum requirements of American National Standard for Information Sciences—Permanence of Paper for Printed Library Materials, ANSI/NISO Z39.48-1992.

CONTENTS

Preface 7
Anthony Molino

Introduction 11
Sergio Benvenuto

I WINDOWS ON HISTORY **25**

Life and Times, Values and Visions 27
Johannes Cremerius

Freudianism in France 47
Elisabeth Roudinesco

Psychoanalysis in America 61
Otto Kernberg

The 'Impossible' Training of Analysts 77
Elvio Fachinelli

Into Fiction, Through Catastrophe 95
Christopher Bollas

II PSYCHOANALYSIS, PHILOSOPHY AND POLITICS **107**

The Emergence of the Unconscious in Western Thought 109
Michel Henry

Freudian Models of Language 123
Julia Kristeva

Psychoanalysis and Sacrifice 139
René Girard

The Psychoanalyst's Narcissistic Wound 159
Isabelle Stengers

Of Autonomy, Individualism and Psychoanalysis 169
Cornelius Castoriadis

III CLINICAL PRACTICE AND SOCIETY **183**

The Mirror's Child 185
Françoise Dolto

Masochism and Sexuality 201
Jean Laplanche

Narcissim: The American Contribution 209
Otto Kernberg

Group Analysis Today 219
Diego Napolitani

Psychoanalysis and Homosexuality 227
Elisabeth Roudinesco

Contributors 245

About the Editors 247

PREFACE

Anthony Molino

'Each clinical and theoretical development, each case presentation, is about the survival and development of the analyst, though the detail of it is usually kept secret, private, unacknowledged, unconscious… and this makes it hard to know what we, readers and listeners, have heard or read, and who we are in relation to it. But when we can exchange something of our autobiographies, and hold one another's difficulty as we do with our patient, we have some basis for a meeting, for some mutual understanding, and for possible transformation through the immediacy of contact with another's survival and development'. So write Gershon Molad and Judith Vida in a paper titled 'The Autobiographical Dialogue between Analysts' (See *Relational and Intersubjective Perspectives in Psychoanalysis*. J. Mills, ed. Aronson, 2005). Readers familiar with my earlier collections of interviews, *Freely Associated* and *Culture, Subject, Psyche* primarily, will easily fathom the extent to which I share Molad and Vida's appreciation for the transitional spaces and objects, for the I-Thou bridges, that are evoked and established in the *temenos* of the actual human encounter between any two 'subjects of analysis' (Ogden).

When the subjects, however, that trace and inhabit that *temenos* are analysts themselves, or figures who have for a lifetime passionately engaged the elusive restlessness of the unconscious, then that sacred space invites, and indeed demands, a particular kind of respectful violation. (The Greek τεμενος means field, estate, but also sacred ground, sanctuary, temple.) There is no space for a reader's reverence or adulation, no distance safely kept, no sense – ultimately – to any transferential mystification of the parents or gods such figures will summon. For any such outcome, any such approach, can only signify the failure of our encounter, as readers, with the pairs that inhabit books like *In Freud's Tracks*. A sublimated voyeurism, if you will, or, more simply, the desire to know the other, to partake of the logics and vagaries of another's thinking *and* suffering, is essential to the destruction of the intimacy generated in the field of the *temenos*. Only then, with vertices joined, is a genuine triangle – and thus a community – realized; only then is dyadic intimacy made fruitful. Only then, one might say, does that peculiar version of the Freudian pair that is the autobiographical interview, or conversation, truly *en/gender* and come to life.

* * *

Readers familiar with my earlier books will understand just how and why the *Journal of European Psychoanalysis* came to appeal to me years ago. As anyone who has ever attended an international congress will know, the privileged link of psychoanalysis to spoken language does not necessarily facilitate communication among analysts and psychotherapists of different mother tongues. The *Journal of European Psychoanalysis* – published since 1995 – has long sought to overcome these linguistic barriers. Traditionally, it has introduced English readers to important European authors, as well as to authors of Latin American countries whose paradigms are close to European 'styles'. More importantly, however, freed of the editorial and political constraints that often govern the 'official' organs of schools and institutions, *JEP* has, for many years, regularly featured conversations with some of the most prominent and brilliant figures in contemporary psychoanalysis: highlighting debates and trends within psychoanalysis and related fields while remaining ever-sensitive to the practical, ethical, and theoretical implications of clinical practice. And while these conversations were not always refulgent gems of style, their occasional imperfections only added to the reasons for someone like myself – long devoted to the genre, and a stickler for getting pleasurable *texts* to preserve the memory of such precious encounters – to want to compile, smooth and polish where possible the wealth of material known, in all likelihood, to but a select few worldwide. For the *Journal of European Psychoanalysis* has survived, until now, with hardly any distribution and thanks mostly to the support of fervid friends and subscribers. But its resilience is attested to by the vitality of the encounters here presented, most of them sought and spurred over time by my co-editor Sergio Benvenuto, founder of the journal and promoter of an enduring labor of love whose efforts, I hope, will long spill over beyond these pages. And that vitality, I might add, is even evidenced by the undying wisdom and inquisitive fire that issue still from the conversations with colleagues no longer with us: analysts like Françoise Dolto and Johannes Cremerius, Elvio Fachinelli and Cornelius Castoriadis, whose blazing, lifetime commitments to the *temenos* of psychoanalysis have not yet ceased to impassion, educate and inspire. Indeed, my bet in compiling *In Freud's Tracks* is that their pedagogical impulse is far from extinct. And with that bet comes the hope that while their writings are practically unknown in English (as is the case with Cremerius, Dolto, Fachinelli and others), their presence here will compel some daring translator or publisher to want to stake a bet of his own…

* * *

In Freud's Tracks collects – across three balanced but, to some degree, invariably overlapping sections – some of the most engaging and provocative of the conversations hosted over the past decade by the *Journal of European Psychoanalysis*. These conversations manage, in my view, not only to trace a recent history of psychoanalytic thought, but they do so while insisting happily upon the discipline's vital and vibrant connections with the fields of politics and social policy, science and philosophy, cultural studies and the social sciences. Here convened, in a longstanding international forum at the frontiers of psychoanalytic inquiry, are thinkers and clinicians as esteemed and diverse as Christopher Bollas, René Girard, the late Michel Henry, Otto Kernberg, Julia Kristeva, Jean Laplanche, Diego Napolitani, Elisabeth Roudinesco, Isabelle Stengers, together with the cited Castoriadis, Cremerius, Dolto and Fachinelli: researchers whose controversial perspectives and practices have looked to link and transform the contemporary proliferation of partial understandings that all-too-often relegate psychoanalysis at the margins of scientific discourse. It is my hope that in partaking of the same independent spirit as *Freely Associated*, *In Freud's Tracks* will likewise celebrate, for years to come, the promise and freedom that inhere in any genuine psychoanalytic enterprise.

* * *

In closing, my thanks to Trevor Brown (Free Association Books), Sergio Benvenuto, Renato Parascandolo (RAI – Radiotelevisione Italiana), Marie-Martine Serrano (Editions Payot & Rivages), Marion Colas (Presses Universitaires de France), Ilaria Angeli (FrancoAngeli Editore), Christopher Bollas, Mihaela Farcas, Claudia Vaughn, all those interviewed and their estates (when called upon), as well as the interviewers and translators who have helped make possible both the *Journal of European Psychoanalysis* and *In Freud's Tracks*. Finally, I would like to take this opportunity to dedicate *In Freud's Tracks* to the memory of three formidable analysts and teachers – all three great conversationalists – whose work never made it into the journal or the book: to Armando B. Ferrari, who before he died gave a wonderful interview to two Italian colleagues which I hope someday to translate into English; and to Marie Coleman Nelson and Nina Coltart, two grand old ladies of psychoanalysis whom I did have the good fortune of knowing and interviewing many years ago and who – each in her own generous, no-nonsense way – taught me much about becoming transformed 'through the immediacy of contact with another's survival and development'. May some such transformations also be visited upon the readers of *In Freud's Tracks*.

Vasto, Italy
August 2008

INTRODUCTION

Sergio Benvenuto

The authors interviewed in this book – be they psychoanalysts, philosophers or essayists – come to psychoanalysis in different ways. The analysts themselves, moreover, descend from different psychoanalytic lineages. This feature in itself marks a rarity in psychoanalytic publishing, since every school and tradition tends most often to stake an exclusive claim to primacy in the field, usually ignoring or marginalizing contributions from other schools. But this *is* the history of psychoanalysis which, rather than unifying the many, splits the One into many. I believe, as a result, that it might prove useful to provide something of an overview – especially for the non-specialist reader – of the State of the Art of psychoanalysis, so that the contributions gathered here, in their basic heterogeneity, can be situated and understood.

1 Resisting Globalization

Psychoanalysis has found diverse 'sanctuaries' over its century-long life. The first psychoanalytic generation (running roughly from 1900 to 1938) spoke mainly German: Vienna, Berlin and Zurich were the cradles and capitals of the New Science. The second generation (from World War II to the mid-1960s) was mostly Anglophone: the hegemony of London and New York went unchallenged, although the two were incompatible, and conflicting theories – those of Melanie Klein in Great Britain and of Ego Psychology in the United States – dominated the era. The third generation (from the late 1960s to the late 1980s) witnessed a Latinization of psychoanalysis, including the expansion of the very same Anglophone masters into mostly Latin regions: Paris, Buenos Aires and Sao Paulo became the swinging capitals of psychoanalysis. (This is the generation which worshipped the French Lacan and Derrida, the Chicagoan Kohut, and the Bion of the Brazilian lectures)[1]. It is still difficult to get a picture of the fourth generation. Today, while we witness a decline

[1] Completely or partly Latin countries, such as Switzerland, Argentina and France, have the highest number of psychoanalysts per inhabitant; the United States and Great Britain follow.

of psychoanalytic practice in most Anglophone countries, there is in Eastern countries (including as far east as Russia and China) a burgeoning interest in psychoanalysis, which seems to go hand-in-hand with the introduction in such countries of a market economy.

Generally speaking, different analytic tendencies prevail in certain specific areas – *soft* psychoanalysis, unlike hard sciences, is aligned along cultural-linguistic coordinates. Ego Psychology, which was conceived by German and Austrian analysts who emigrated to the United States around World War II, has prevailed to date in the United States and in German-speaking countries. In Great Britain and Italy – and extensively in Brazil and Argentina as well – the Klein-Bion-Meltzer line, England's autochthonous creation, prevails. Lacanian doctrine prevails in Francophone countries and in Latin America. Indeed, Latin America's complete rejection of American 'brands' of psychoanalysis is but a corollary of the fundamental hostility of Latin-American intellectuals towards everything *gringo*. Unlike the sciences – homologated in the Standard English of the international scientific community – psychoanalysis is still entangled in the historical and political moods of the countries and cultures in which it struggles and sometimes prospers.

Analysts living outside Anglophone countries tend to resist the use of English as *lingua franca:* everyone writes in the language in which they practice. This is not a marginal detail: the decline in psychoanalysis' prestige is also linked to its resistance to accommodating itself to Standard English. A cognitive scientist at an Italian research institute once remarked to me: 'Psychoanalysis can't be a science. Otherwise you analysts would write in English, the language which all scientists use today'. Instead, psychoanalytic practice is linked to the language, history and specific traditions of each country. Wherever you go, that's the psychoanalysis you'll find. Psychoanalysis today appears closer to literature and cinema than to sciences precisely because of this character which Antonio Gramsci would have called *national-popular*. Crossing a European border, one has the impression of entering another psychoanalytic world. In Great Britain, one finds the Kleinian School and what is today called object-relations, but little or nothing of Ego- and Self-Psychology. By contrast, in a German-speaking country one finds analysts with strong connections to American schools, which in France – with few exceptions – are ostracized. In France, Lacanism, as well as autochthonous schools influenced by Klein and Winnicott, flourish. And so it goes for every linguistic-cultural area.

Even within international scientific communities certain divisions exist, yet most members of a particular disciplinary community share some basic and generally unquestionable paradigms: what Kuhn (1970) called *normal science* prevails across the board. Psychoanalysis has instead existed for over a century in what Kuhn called a state of *extraordinary science*. In fact, psychoanalysts do not constitute a single community, since they often disagree on the very basic foundations of their discipline (and often even disagree on how to interpret basic Freudian tenets). They divide themselves up into schools or trends just as easily and readily as philosophers or literary critics do.

Every linguistic area not only ends up developing its own vernacular psychoanalysis, but having a particular image of psychoanalysis *in toto*. Having studied in both France and Italy, I can say that beyond the enormous differences between the two countries, young people in both were from the start permeated by this basic assumption: 'Anna Freud completely misunderstood her father's thinking, American psychoanalysis has degenerated and betrayed the true psychoanalytic spirit, succumbing to the American Way of Life. True psychoanalysis is European...' And in France, one would go on to say, '... Sigmund Freud is the Absolute Master and Lacan is His Prophet', while in Italy people would maintain that 'Klein and Bion represent *true* psychoanalysis'.

In taking exception to this divisive and parochial state of affairs, *In Freud's Tracks* – in line with the decade-long tradition of its intellectual matrix, namely the *Journal of European Psychoanalysis* – takes this plural and extra/ordinary character of psychoanalysis not only as its limit, but as its richness as well.

2 The Times They are a Changin'...

Many of the conversations in this book – and especially those in the section titled ***Psychoanalysis, Philosophy and Politics*** – point to the mutations that psychoanalysis has undergone over the last twenty-five to thirty years, changes more clearcut in the United States than in Europe. Psychoanalysis has been largely abandoned by psychiatrists and in general by the 'sciences'. Biological organicism and the cognitive sciences dominate psychiatry today, and as a result psychoanalysis is taught less and less in Western medical schools. Not only: even psychology departments tend to displace it, favoring coursework in cognitive sciences, neurosciences and evolutionary psychology. In short, psychoanalysis has lost a good deal of its academic and scientific respectability. In Anglophone countries, however, it has not been completely marginalized, and has even become a strong reference point for the Humanities. Disciplines as diverse as history, art history, the history of cinema, comparative literature, cultural studies and anthropology, women and gender studies, gay and queer studies, art, communications all grapple with and are critically engaged by psychoanalysis. In short, psychoanalysis has less and less to do with psychiatrists and psychotherapists and more to do with literary critics, feminists, Continental philosophers, historians of cinema and cultural fashions, and hermeneutical anthropologists. Even in Latin countries, psychoanalysis is now taught more in departments of philosophy[2], humanities, art and literature, communications, etc. than in psychology or psychiatry.

Accompanying all of this is a change in the ethical-existential function of the analytic cure. One goes to the psychiatrist or psychotherapist hoping to be cured, quickly, of a symptom. Instead, one starts a long analysis when wanting to go along the path of what Paul the Apostle called *metanoia*: that is, of a spiritual conversion or reconversion of one's being-in-the-world, of 'transformation'. It is not true what journalists often write, that the psychoanalytic cure has been supplanted by the Prozac culture. As a matter of fact, analysands often take prescribed drugs, a secret not well-kept of the collusion between modern-day psychopharmacology and psychoanalysis. What we see then, in the West, is just how psychoanalysis goes about trying to transform itself: from its own self-cultivated ideal as a highly specialized and sophisticated form of therapy into a supportive modality, a lifestyle aide not very different from the portrayals seen in so many Woody Allen films.

Thus, the analyst is less and less a doctor and more and more a psychologist and, in Anglo-American countries, more and more a social worker (a figure completely absent in Latin countries). And, more often than not, a woman[3]. The analyst is increasingly more a *maternal* figure than a *paternal* one: greater spiritual-affective support and less 'medical' technique, more *holding* and *care* than *treatment* and *cure* are the rule. Furthermore, in many countries, analytically oriented therapists are less linked to a specific School or Association; she follows her own very personal formative path, and increasingly practices in an eclectic, freelance mode, free of rigid and/or prestigious institutions.

This three-pronged tendency of analysis – de-medicalization, socialworkerization and de-institutionalization – is best expressed by the success of certain theories and psychoanalytic styles. Consider, for example, Kohut's Self Psychology, 'narratology' and the hermeneutic or intersubjective vogue. These approaches tend to cancel that certain technical – or technocratic – severity of early psychoanalysis, making it in a wider sense an intersubjective relationship, somewhat indefinable and imprecise, where, in the end, 'the heart' is more important than the 'brain'. The right theories, one might say, for the

---

2 Philosophy departments in Anglophone countries teach almost exclusively analytic philosophy or the philosophy of science and of mind. European-Continental faculties privilege classic philosophy, which in the United States and United Kingdom is instead a mainstay feature of comparative literature or history departments. One joke in the United States today goes, 'if you analyze a rat's vertebra, you are doing philosophy; if you analyze Hegel, you belong to CompLit' (Žižek & Daly 2004, p. 52).

3 In psychoanalysis the female contribution has been no less decisive than the male. Lacan used to say that women were better analysts because they grasp better than males how weird humans are. This feminization has probably pushed psychoanalysis to concentrate on the 'fusional' or 'symbiotic' – in any case, primitive – relations between mother and child, and to increasingly marginalize the role of the father (which Freud, instead, had deemed crucial).

present-day, 'average' middle-class therapists and clients.

Self Psychology, which gives maximum weight to the empathy between analyst and analysand and to the adjustment of the Self, was adopted mostly by American social workers. The narrativist trend tends to assimilate the analytic process ever more to the aesthetic or critical-literary creation: it is no longer important whether an interpretation or reconstruction is true, but that it helps the subject to tell a 'happier' story for herself. Psychopathology would consist in being the victim of unhappy stories about oneself, and the cure would lie in succeeding to tell a better story – and believing it.

The hermeneutic reinterpretation of analysis rejects the 'scientistic self-misunderstanding' (Habermas) of psychoanalysis and leads it back to an existential activity of *Bildung* (formation), in the full romantic Germanic tradition. Analysts no longer analyze dreams but 'texts of dreams', no longer slips of tongue but 'slips in the discursive tissue' – the unconscious comes down to what is linguistic and intersubjective. Terse Freudian language tends to be replaced by new buzzwords which smack of hermeneutics: *relation*, *comprehension*, *narration*, *being-with*, *communication*, *relationship*, *relational field*, *intersubjectivity*, *dialogue*, *lived experience or Erlebnis*, *conversation*, *desire*, *text*, *pietas*. In this way, psychoanalysis climbs back into bed with humanistic *consolationes*. Psychoanalysis, a discipline forever suspended on the borderline between 'scientific' and 'humanistic' cultures, is today slipping decisively towards the latter.

Still, there are those analysts who do not renounce the ideal of scientific respectability, and thus publish in official journals ever more arid and concise articles in Standard Scientific English, which imitate the impersonal writing style of scientists. This task – above all stylistic – of 'scientificity' aims at bringing psychoanalysis back among the 'respectable' disciplines, in short, to make analysis a branch of the wider international scientific community. The trouble though is that analysts, even those most inclined towards rigorous scientific protocols, in order to remain analysts must believe in the unconscious – in practice, they need to attempt interpretations. Here, the plausibility of psychoanalysis as a science becomes problematic, since modern science tends to give no place to interpretation. The sciences can admit that unconscious psychic processes exist, but they cannot accept the idea that 'unconscious discourses' or 'unconscious thought' are brought to consciousness through interpretive reconstructions. They tend to reject the consideration of dreams or parapraxes as metaphors. This is why analysts who, driven by scientific respectability, prefer to call themselves psychotherapists, and tend to abandon the interpretive method.

3 New Analysts, New Patients

In 1985, four American psychologists filed a class-action lawsuit against the American Psychoanalytic Association and some of its institutes, charging that they had conspired to establish a monopoly of MDs in psychoanalysis in violation of Federal antitrust law. (The APA was the only analytic organization in the world which exclusively accepted medical doctors.) The lawsuit was settled in November 1988, with the institutes promising to no longer discriminate against psychologists or other 'non-medical candidates'.

Analogous legislation was implemented in Europe (for example, the 1988 Ossicini Law in Italy) whereby even non-MDs can officially call themselves *psychotherapists*. (National legislations usually regulate 'psychotherapy', and psychoanalysis is rarely mentioned.) In short, this legislation acknowledges what is already taking place – that MD psychiatrists are increasingly abandoning analytic practice.

Today, the mindset of a typical psychiatrist is informed and structured by the so-called DSM: the long-globalized and official Anglo-American psychodiagnostic manual, presently in its fourth edition. Drug prescriptions are his specialty, as psychotherapies and psychologies are left mostly to those dealing with matters of socio-psycho-pedagogical concern. Psychoanalysis' longed-for dream of respectability – to be accepted as a legitimate member of the exclusive club of Medical Science – seems to have been just that, a dream. More so than ever, the psychoanalyst appears to say, like Groucho Marx, 'I wouldn't want to belong to any club [of scientists] that would have me as a member'.

Coupled to this change in the analyst's identity is an analogous change in the *typical client*. For analysts who follow IPA norms, any real analysis necessarily involves four to five sessions a week of forty-five to fifty minutes each over many years; anything less is only a less prestigious, second-class 'analytically directed psychotherapy'. Today, classical analysis is made up almost exclusively of students in training – a sign that psychoanalysis, at least in its classical form, tends to become self-referential, a practice of analysts only for analysts. All of this seems to give credence to Fred Crews' invective (Horgan 1999) by which Freudian analysis is not a therapeutic method: a Freudian forms other Freudians, like a vampire creating other vampires...

But beyond this vampire-like strategy, analysis is becoming more and more a form of intermittent, sporadic support for those who need quick, tangible results, or who require some kind of support in a 'critical phase' of their life. Naturally, older analysts – nostalgic for the good old times, when psychotherapists were few and far between – consider these barbarian invasions. But what we are dealing with is probably a sub-product of a change in subjectivity in the West. The type of transference on which early twentieth-century analysis was based – produced by the illusion of the analyst as the 'subject supposed to know', as Lacan said – seems to unfold less and less, and is less amenable to technique. The analyst has lost his original gift of authority, and needs increasingly to conquer the analysand's consent and complicity, in a flexible and open context. According to what so many analysts claim, patients today are more cultured, more disenchanted, and thus have defenses that are more entrenched than in the past. Defenses seem more entrenched because patients today believe ever less in the power of speech. The criticism against that supposed-to-know authoritarianism – a criticism psychoanalysis promoted and helped spread in the Western lifestyle – at a certain point rebounded in part against the authority of psychoanalysis itself. The transferential illusions and classical interpretations of yesteryear are less persuasive today, compelling more attuned analysts to work to invent new forms of analytic ties which might again (or for the first time...) make twenty-first-century subjects susceptible to the power of speech.

4 New Psychopathologies

Changing psychopathologies have also contributed to modifications in psychoanalytic function and technique. For many decades analysts resorted to the original diagnostic categories of psychoanalysis: hysteria, obsessive neurosis, perversion and psychosis. In recent years, increasing numbers of patients complained of symptoms reflecting narcissistic personalities and pathologies, whereby theory and technique (from Kohut to Kernberg) moved over time to focus on narcissistic 'disorders' and syndromes. The conversation with Kernberg here illustrates precisely this shift in interest towards narcissism.

Furthermore, Anglo-American psychiatry, by now almost completely severed from any psychoanalytic influence, went on to compile the various editions of the DSM. Confronted with the new DSM standardization of psychopathology, analysts opposed to this trend went on to adopt diagnostic outlooks and attitudes linked to the cultural traditions of their countries. Some have even completely rejected the new DSM classification and remain linked to the Kraepelinian and Freudian categories in which they were trained. Others, anxious for psychoanalysis to gain access to the dominant scientific culture of psychiatry, use the DSM to classify and conceptualize their clients – going so far as to even abandon the very concept of hysteria (because the DSM ignores it), from whence psychoanalysis took its first steps. Still others, perhaps the majority, sought or are still seeking a sort of eclectic language which includes Kraepelinian, Freudian and DSM aspects, often depending on schools, cities and languages.

Whatever the moods and trends, however, it goes unquestioned that psychoanalysis contributed significantly to a shift towards what Foucault (2001), referring to ancient Greek culture, called 'the care of oneself'. In the West, increasing demands for psychological help are met with an analogous increase in the supply of psychologists and psychotherapists. As a result, and aside from its own contemporary 'crisis', psychoanalysis can only meet in small part today's growing need for 'self care/cure'.

Moreover, the injunction to 'know thyself' in the century of psychoanalysis often burst into a narcissistic cult of one's own psyche. In this day and age, people increasingly tend to give psychological interpretations to their own disasters or misfortunes: i.e., they give increasing importance to one's own subjective responsibility. For example, Castoriadis, in his conversation here, attacks the idea, expressed by some American analysts, that unemployment is a pathological symptom: unemployment, exclaims Castoriadis, is an economic problem, not a psychological one! In reality, problems are hardly ever confined to a determined sphere, and every problem has many facets: sociological, psychological, biological, ethical-political, etc. Unemployment, for instance, surely fluctuates according to certain economic cycles, although, if one is psychologically fragile (and thus 'inefficient'), that person will likely be the first to be fired in an unfavorable economic climate.

By way of example, more and more people seek help after suffering a loss: any reaction to an objective loss is lived increasingly as a subjective flaw, 'if I am suffering so much, it is because something is not quite right with me'. This 'psychologization' is also a form of 'narcissisation'. But this narcissistic psychologization of our problems is also an effect of psychoanalysis' historical success.

While psychoanalysis has brilliantly described narcissism, it has also indirectly favored narcissism's cultural primacy. Lacan expressed this when he insisted that psychoanalysis is itself a *symptom* of our times. It can be seen in today's language, especially among cultured classes. A young mother no longer says 'how wonderful it is to have a child!', but rather 'the *experience of maternity* is really important to me'. Many no longer say to an invasive guest, 'I wish you would go away', but '*I fantasized* that I kept you out of my home'. As psychoanalysis teaches, stylistic preferences are never innocent, and in this case signal the narcissistic tropism of our culture. 'Having a child is wonderful' is a transitive expression, the impulse goes entirely towards the object, the child. To say, instead, 'my experience of maternity' means cancelling this transitivity and electing *my* experience as the true object: like in the mirror, I see my feeling myself a mother, or fantasizing myself aggressive, as objects of my contemplation. In a mirror, I see myself, not what I look at. As T.S. Eliot might have put it, between power and the act... falls the shadow of psychological reflection.

Paradoxically, this 'psychologization' of life has had a boomerang effect on psychoanalysis. It is precisely the narcissistic triumph of the self-cure – so that the psychological metaphor filters my being-in-the-world – that creates growing difficulties for the analytic cure. In so far as he becomes increasingly narcissistic (that is, ever more imbued by the analytic culture), the early twenty-first-century analysand slips, so to speak, 'off the couch'. Analysis in effect functions not only because it concentrates the gaze on the subject himself, who thus recognizes himself as the maker of his own destiny (even if he is unemployed during a 'bearish' phase of the economy): it functions also to the degree in which, through transference, the analyst's authority acts. But this transcendentality – in the philosophical sense of the term – is hardened today by the solipsistic idea that 'only *my* psychic processes matter!' Is it any surprise that so many analysts working today decry that analysands nowadays are too narcissistic?

Recently, the huge success of the notion of narcissism – and the theory according to which our Western culture is becoming ever more narcissistic – has ended up painting everything somewhat the same color: narcissism, everywhere in view, has become a bit, as Hegel said, the night in which all cows are black. Moreover, certain *new pathologies* have come into play: as in Kristeva's (1995) 'new maladies of the soul', or what the Lacanian Recalcati (2002) calls 'pathologies of the void' (i.e., eating disorders, depressive syndromes, drug addictions, certain psychosomatic disturbances). These new pathologies challenge the classic psychoanalytic technique because they appear devoid of any metaphoric dimension, and in short mostly escape the analyst's interpretive *insight*: symptoms are opaque, devoid of symbolic valence, more pure behaviors or heavy experiences than signifying acts. As the American analyst Bass (2000, 2006) underscores, what he calls 'concreteness' – the resistance to interpretation – today generally prevails. We are speaking of clear 'anti-hermeneutic' pathologies, with little or nothing to interpret.

Faced with this, the efforts of classical analysis – to interpret as sign or discourse something which right off presents itself with the opacity of the symptom, of the 'non-thought' – appears futile. Furthermore, cognitive psychotherapies, which reject the idea of the unconscious and thus of interpretability, are more comfortable treating these pathologies which seemingly do not refer back to anything particularly 'profound'. So psychoanalysis is betting its cards for its own survival and eventual re-launch on the treatment of these new pathologies (a claim Kristeva herself puts forth in her conversation here). In particular, the psychoanalyst is challenged to relinquish his interpretive tool (of the symptom or transfer) and to give greater weight to its *enactment*: the analyst is called upon today to be increasingly active, and less silent and passive, as was the case in classical technique.

5 Psychoanalysis and Philosophy

In Freud's Tracks presents the thinking of some important philosophers – or parttime analyst-philosophers – on psychoanalysis. There is no space here to go into the state of relationships between philosophical and psychoanalytical inquiry today. Psychoanalysis has often aroused the interest of philosophers, albeit an extremely polarized interest. Some philosophers (among whom Habermas, Althusser, Derrida, Lyotard, Castoriadis, Žižek) have celebrated psychoanalysis in very positive terms, even making it the revolutionary paradigm of a new type of knowledge and practice. Others instead (among whom Popper, Grünbaum, Bouveresse, Crews, Borch-Jacobsen) have decisively attacked it as a 'false science', 'scientifically unproven theory', 'modern type of mythology', 'imposture', etc. It is as though philosophers were incapable of arriving at a balanced, or 'grey', opinion with regard to psychoanalysis: they either exalt it or revile it.[4]

Even here significant differences among national cultures emerge. In effect, the relationship between psychoanalysis and philosophy is particularly problematic in Anglophone countries, where the official philosophy is analytic (linguistic), the philosophy of science, or the philosophy of mind/body problems. With some exceptions (Donald Davidson, Richard Rorty), analytic philosophy is hostile towards psychoanalysis and tends to discredit it. On the other hand, the growth of psychoanalysis across Europe (outside of Britain) occurs in a cultural climate pervaded by 'Continental' philosophies (phenomenology, post-structuralism, hermeneutics), better disposed – even enthusiastic – towards psychoanalysis. For thirty to forty years now, the drama of Anglo-American psychoanalysis has been its increasing distance from the philosophical (and not only philosophical) climate of the environment in which it dwells – apart from the post-modern fringe – while Latin and Euro-Continental psychoanalyses operate on a far more favorable cultural terrain.

Finally, even Continental Europe is witnessing a recent change in the philosophical climate, a change from which psychoanalysis might be able to draw new sap. Here too, it is a crisis of what Rorty has referred to as the *linguistic turn*: that is, a preference for language, for the symbolic, for interpretation and communication. Now, philosophical interest seems to be shifting towards the general terms of biological life (the *nuda vita*, 'bare life', as Agamben [1998] calls it), of biotechnologies, of the confusion between virtual and real, of the animal dimension of man (Derrida 1999), and what Foucalt called *biopoli-*

[4] This positive and negative polarity actually lives, in a sort of ambivalent screeching, within the same philosophy: thinkers as diverse as Ludwig Wittgenstein and Gilles Deleuze, for example, have nourished in the course of their careers somewhat contradictory attitudes in its regard.

tics. It is a change in perspective that could perhaps favor a reflective return to what, in terms of fact, were the 'biological' and 'neurological' origins of Freudian thought.

6 Three Perspectives

The first part of *In Freud's Tracks*, ***Windows on History***, presents conversations which illustrate the development of psychoanalysis above all in the two countries, France and the United States, which play or played a leading role in psychoanalysis today. **Elizabeth Roudinesco** – generally recognized as the most important historian of French psychoanalysis – holds an eminent position from which to speak about Freudianism in France. **Otto Kernberg**, former Secretary of the IPA, brings to his revisitation of the development of American psychoanalysis his own varied experience as an Austrian Jew who first emigrated to Latin America and ultimately settled on the East Coast of the United States. Both Roudinesco and Kernberg thus provide a view from 'within' the psychoanalytic histories and traditions of which they speak: Roudinesco, herself a psychoanalyst, is deeply influenced by the Lacanian approach, while Kernberg's eminent status is recognized throughout and beyond Anglo-American psychoanalysis. A view not from 'afar', and thus detached, but 'from inside', participant and militant.

The conversations with two analysts who are no longer in our midst – the German **Johannes Cremerius** and the Italian **Elvio Fachinelli** – assess, in often strongly polemical tones, the question of analytic training and the state of psychoanalytic institutions in general. Both were members – albeit critical members – of the IPA, and it is significant that while coming from widely different traditions (Fachinelli was influenced mostly by the Frankfurt School and by French post-structuralism, while Cremerius belongs to the tradition of German-speaking psychoanalysis), both end up articulating converging doubts, criticisms, arguments and dissatisfactions with the actual state of psychoanalytic institutions.

Finally, the section closes with what is to date the most recent conversation published in *JEP*. In 'Into Fiction, through Catastrophe', the Anglo-American analyst **Christopher Bollas** provides an *apercu* onto the insidious 'catastrophes' that permeate both present-day history (i.e., the rise of Islam in revolt against the West) as well as the thinking of segments of the profession (or the consumer-culture 'thinking' of which analysts often partake). In so doing, Bollas takes sides, unequivocally, in the century-old debate concerning the reaches of the analyst's supposed 'neutrality'.

The section ***Psychoanalysis, Philosophy and Politics*** collects contributions of a philosophical nature – but with ethical and political implications

– from authors from widely diverse fields. Some (Kristeva and Castoriadis) are analysts as well as essayists and theorists; two (Henry and Stengers) are philosophers but not analysts; another (Girard) is a theoretician of literature and anthropology. The fact that all of these contributions come from French-language authors – even if Girard has resided and taught in the United States for decades – is a sign of the impassioned character and persistent vitality of the debate surrounding psychoanalysis in French-speaking areas.

Here, **René Girard** outlines his personal anthropological conception, articulating his well-known theories on mimetic desire, the role of the 'scapegoat', and on the relationship between violence and the sacred. The late **Michel Henry**, esteemed French interpreter of phenomenological philosophy, brings the Freudian discovery back to the European philosophical tradition whose point of arrival it marks: a tradition starting with Descartes and continuing with Schopenhauer and Nietzsche. **Julia Kristeva**, as a semiologist, resumes here her original reading of Freud in relation to language. Kristeva, while profoundly influenced by Lacanian thought, views the role of speech and language in ways that differ significantly from Lacan.

Isabelle Stengers – the philosopher of science known mainly for her studies in thermodynamics with the Nobel Prize for Chemistry Ilya Prigogine (Prigogine & Stengers 1984) – in her conversation summarizes her still-evolving attitude towards psychoanalysis, without blunting her criticisms of the cultural politics of certain Francophone psychoanalytic institutions. Lastly, the analyst-philosopher of Greek origin, the late **Cornelius Castoriadis** – well known in France and elsewhere especially for his criticisms of Marxist orthodoxy – synthesizes his own iconoclastic thinking via a harsh critique of Lacan grounded at once in both his own personal practice as an analyst and in his philosophical and political work.

The book's third section, ***Clinical Practice and Society***, looks at cutting-edge figures and developments in the recent history of psychoanalysis. One such figure is French psychoanalyst **Jean Laplanche**, universally known especially for his *The Language of Psychoanalysis* (co-authored with Jean-Baptiste Pontalis), which has become a standard encyclopedic reference. In his conversation here, he deals with an especially crucial problem in psychoanalysis: the relationship between masochism, sexuality and pleasure. Laplanche's thesis – which highlights the primacy of the Other (i.e., the adult) in the formation of every infant's unconscious – is an eloquent example of the present psychoanalytic approach, which links more and more every subject's psychic history to her relations with the significant others from early childhood.

Alongside Laplanche, **Otto Kernberg** offers an overview of contributions from the American school to the theory and cure of narcissistic personalities and disorders. In also reviewing his own work, Kernberg testifies to what he calls the *expansive* phase of psychoanalysis: a time when it became necessary to show that the analytic tool – with adjustments – could be made to function even with narcissistic patients who, according to early formulations, were beyond the reach of psychoanalytic treatment. In a completely different key, the Italian psychoanalyst **Diego Napolitani** illustrates his contribution to group psychoanalysis. A daring figure who counts among his influences certain aspects of Bion's thought, philosophical hermeneutics, and theories of complexity, Napolitani is a prime example of the kind of thinker the *Journal of European Psychoanalysis* has sought, over the years, to bring to the attention of its Anglophone audience. On yet another plane, **Françoise Dolto**'s conversation with **Juan-David Nasio** – which opens this section – explicates her approach to working with children. Dolto, a European pioneer in child psychoanalysis starting in the 1930s, focuses above all on the narcissistic dimension and unconscious image of the child's body.

Finally, **Elisabeth Roudinesco** analyzes, polemically and along mostly ethical and political lines, the charged issue of homosexuality in psychoanalytic institutions. Today, although there are no longer explicit norms or directives excluding aspiring analysts who happen to be homosexual (political correctness precludes such actions), the situation is such that in many psychoanalytic societies homosexual candidates continue, *de facto,* to be excluded. The position taken by Roudinesco – who does not consider homosexuality a pathology to be cured, or a sign of psychic immaturity to be denounced – squarely takes on and challenges the widespread prejudices that still lurk in many psychoanalytic communities around the world.

In closing, it would no doubt be foolish of me to suggest that the interlocutors here convened – and convened by *the Journal of European Psychoanalysis* over the years – somehow share or converge upon a homogeneous vision of psychoanalysis. But the fact that they have been convened at all does attest to what has been a longstanding 'philosophy' of *JEP*: namely, that the future development of psychoanalysis, if indeed it is to develop at all, will depend upon its capacity for *dissemination.* Upon a capacity to disseminate fruitfully not only its divergent and at times fractious theories and paradigms, but the variety of techniques and styles that get deployed in the trenches of clinical practice. In short, what I think we need is something like a psychoanalytic Big Bang which, far from fleshing out the supposed 'good' brands of psychoanalysis from the 'bad', will instead help propagate multiple forms of thinking into a galaxy ready, and yearning, to be revitalized.

Bibliography

Agamben, G. (1998) *Homo Sacer: Sovereign Power and Bare Life*. Stanford University Press, California

Bass, A. (2006) *Interpretation and Difference. The Strangeness of Care*. Stanford University Press, California.

– (2000) *Difference and Disavowal. The Trauma of Eros*. Stanford Univ. Press, California.

Derrida, J. (1999) 'L'animal que donc je suis'. In M.-L. Maller, ed., *L'animal Autobiographique. Autour de J. Derrida*. Editions Galilée, Paris.

Foucault, M. (2001) *L'herméneutique du Sujet*. Seuil/Gallimard, Paris.

Horgan, J. (1999) *The Undiscovered Mind*. The Free Press, New York.

Kristeva, J. (1995) *New Maladies of the Soul*. Columbia University Press, New York

Kuhn, T.S. (1970) *The Structure of Scientific Revolutions*. University of Chicago Press, Chicago.

Prigogine, I. & Stengers, I. (1984) *Order out of Chaos: Man's New Dialogue with Nature*. Flamingo Press, London.

Recalcati, M. (2002) *Clinica del Vuoto. Anoressie Dipendenze Psicosi*. Franco Angeli, Milano.

Žižek, S. & Daly, G. (2004) *Conversations with Žižek*. Polity, Cambridge (UK).

I

WINDOWS ON HISTORY

LIFE AND TIMES, VALUES AND VISIONS

Johannes Cremerius

FOLLOWING WORLD WAR II, German-born Johannes Cremerius (1918–2002) entered psychoanalysis before leaving for the United States as part of a postwar 're-education' program for German anti-fascists. During his time in America, he got to know some of the most important psychoanalysts of his day, many of whom had been exiled from Europe for political and racial reasons: among them, Alexander, Kris, Loewenstein, Horney, Rado and Deutsch. To aid him upon his return to Germany, the Rockefeller Foundation funded a psychosomatics department at the Polyclinic of Munich, where he worked for several years. He then went on to teach at the universities of Giessen and Freiburg, at a time when psychoanalysts with university posts were strongly committed, in line with the ideals of the Frankfurt school, to promoting a genuine spirit of criticism and democratic activism against all residual authoritarianism. Throughout the years, this libertarian spirit continued to animate all aspects of his work, as Cremerius remained fiercely committed to the freedom that inheres in and defines the psychoanalytic enterprise. It is, furthermore, a spirit largely evidenced by his rich and diversified contributions to fields ranging from history to sociology, from clinical practice to theory, education, literary criticism, aesthetics and the professional training of analysts. This output, however, remains largely untranslated into English, save for some scattered articles and one book: an edited collection titled, aptly, *The Future of Psychoanalysis* (London: Open Gate Press, 1999).

In this conversation with Marco Francesconi, Cremerius discusses his life, from his escape to Italy to avoid conscription in Nazi Germany to his formative experiences in the United States to the beginnings of his psychoanalytical practice in a Germany finally free of Nazism and beyond. He also illustrates various features of his psychoanalytical methodology and practice, and comments extensively on aspects of psychoanalytical theory, as well as on his approach to Freud – of whom he could be daringly critical. Finally, Cremerius attacks the compromises, exclusiveness and corruption of psychoanalytical societies and makes an impassioned defense – in the best Enlightenment tradition – for upholding the essential values of human life and liberty.

The original interview with Johannes Cremerius, which took place in Milan on 11 November 1999, was first published in the *Journal of European Psychoanalysis* n. 14 (2002). It is reprinted here, in an abridged version, with the permission of Marco Francesconi and the widow of Dr. Cremerius, Annemarie.

* * *

Marco Francesconi

When and why did you come to Italy for the first time?

Johannes Cremerius

That was in October 1939, because I wanted to avoid military service. My father was an anti-fascist. Someone helped me to find a room at the University College of Pavia, where I was in hiding and where I studied medicine. Then, when the Germans occupied Lombardy, and later the whole of Italy, someone in Milan let something out about there being a German in Pavia, so I was forced to leave. I didn't get shot, but they told me I would have to leave immediately for the Russian front, luckily as a medical doctor, so I wouldn't have to shoot anyone.

In previous years I had moved from one university to the other so that there would have been no trace of me: from Giessen to Lipsia, from Lipsia to Marburg, from Marburg to Giessen, from Giessen to Freiburg, always stopping for just one semester. If I had stayed longer, I would have been asked why I wasn't fulfilling my military duties. I stayed in Freiburg for one year, until October 1944. During that time I met my future wife, whom I married in September of the following year.

When did psychiatry and psychoanalysis enter your life?

In Pavia I had become fascinated by a famous psychiatry professor, Dr. Berlucchi. He was already rather old, very cultured, very human. I began work in his hospital. On the front I practiced surgery, realizing that the surgeon's life could never have become my life. That's when I thought: I'll take up psychiatry. But all the psychiatrists I had met until then had contributed to the elimination of mental illness sufferers for the 'good' Hitler. It was quite a tough situation. But the director was very humane, and chose me as his teaching assistant.

I then obtained my qualification and went to Munich, because I already understood that I didn't want to do only psychiatry. It was something I felt as too 'scientific', too distant. So I opted for psychoanalysis. In Düsseldorf I had already gone to see Viktor von Weizsäcker, a famous neurologist and psychiatrist, the first German professor to have already read Freud's works during the Nazi period. During the war he had opened a psychosomatic medicine department at the University of Heidelberg and had published an excellent book on psychosomatic psychoanalysis.

I arrived in Heidelberg with my uniform still on. The only thing I knew about von Weizsäcker was that he smoked a pipe and, since at the time tobacco was as valuable as gold, I bought him a pouch of tobacco. So, I arrived at the institute with my pipe and some tobacco. The institute was in ruins. There was an underground entrance and I found him in the basement, working with his gloves and overcoat on because of the cold. When I met him I handed the tobacco over to him. He was extremely kind, very interested. He told me what path to follow to learn about psychoanalysis, what to read.

At the time there was one institute in Berlin, traditional, and one in Munich, not as traditional, not as sealed off, somewhat eclectic. Adler, Jung and Freud had taught there. As I couldn't go to Berlin, because I couldn't find a job that paid well enough, my wife Annemarie waited for me in Munich, where I found an internal medicine clinic directed by someone who at the time was undergoing analysis, an old communist. When he heard my story he welcomed me and told me I could start work the following day. He wanted to introduce psychoanalysis to his clinic. We went there in the winter of 1948 with forty deutschmarks each, all we had.

What about your training as a psychoanalyst?

Under the Nazis psychoanalysis had been banned; some time after their downfall, in 1950, a group of classical analysts was formed in Berlin. In 1947 I got in touch with von Weizsäcker, and at the end of 1948 I went to Munich to begin my training, and there I found an IPA analyst with whom I began a training psychoanalysis. At the same time I worked as an assistant in this internal medicine clinic, and in 1950 I was chosen, with a group of anti-fascists, to go to America for a Program of Re-education for Germans. The Americans had this strange idea of taking young German scholars from various faculties to America to learn democracy but also to study their own subjects (in my case psychoanalysis, psychotherapy and psychiatry), to take all this back to Germany and to 're-educate' the Germans. I spent this half year or so in America pleasantly, going from one psychoanalytic-psychotherapeutical institute to another, in clinics which already had a psychosomatic medicine department – but unfortunately without my wife. There I got acquainted with Franz Alexander, Helene Deutsch and her husband, Frieda von Reichmann, Küby, Rado. I was very impressed by Eissler, for whom I wrote an obituary in 1999.

When, in the fall of 1950, I came back from America, I was able to open a psychosomatic medicine department, a strictly analytic one, within the internal medicine clinic. The Americans gave me two hundred thousand dollars to set it up, buy the couch, some books, a bookcase. I was able to pay two trainee doctors and two psychologists, one full time and the other part time. I worked until 1960, when I failed my university teaching qualification test.

I participated with a paper on diabetes, the result of research which led us to discover that diabetics have a specific problem of object relation. Closed as they are in their system of syringes, they end up in a kind of symbiosis with their mothers, and this gives them relational difficulties. Medical theory at the time was that diabetic patients suffered from erectile impotence, a disorder of the hormonal system. During our research we asked these people who had complained of impotence how things went with masturbation. We found there were no difficulties there. That's what I wrote in my university qualification paper. As it had to go through the faculty before being accepted, the other internist who held the chair invited me to discuss my thesis, and told me: 'My dear doctor, what you have done lacks any common decency. A well-mannered doctor does not ask such questions'. The referring psychiatrist was outraged – he was hostile to psychoanalysis – and I was rejected.

At forty-two, after fifteen years of university, I had to leave. It was a tragedy, it seemed everything was over for me. It was partly my fault too: I had this missionary impulse – the 'flag' of psychoanalysis against 'inhuman' medicine – which the faculty wouldn't allow. I hadn't been a realist in relating to the institution. With a touch of diplomacy, of strategy, things may have gone differently. But my way of doing things was already somewhat 'Cremerius'. In my life I've always had a 'flag' to wave: anti-fascism, anti-medicine, today anti-institutionalized psychoanalysis – not against psychoanalysis but against the institution.

After this affair a friend told me that in Switzerland there was a mental asylum I could work in, because the director was an analyst, and I could carry out research on the analysis of serious psychotics. It had, and still has, a famous institute of psychoanalysis, with teachers like Morgenthal, Parin and other great personalities. With an older analyst of the Swiss Association, Bally, I did a second analysis in order to work on this theme of the 'flag': my own self-destruction, this trait of 'going against' which I had assimilated from my father, and which had caused my family so much suffering.

I had really idealized this father of mine who seemed so strong, 'one man against the rest of the world'. I wanted to be big and strong like him. Mine had been a Protestant family since 1580, converted only sixty years after the Reformation. This had been my father's other 'flag': our being 'original Protestants', waving a flag against the Catholics. My elementary education was in an extremely Catholic school; there was no alternative to going to that school. The young teacher became very fond of me. Mine was a village of ignorant peasants who couldn't read, but I could already read and write before even attending school, because my mother had taught me.

The teacher couldn't believe that she finally had someone she could do something with. She gave me small portraits of saints and, as I felt I had a kind of 'secret' relation with her, I kept them hidden because I felt she was my first love. One day my mother found them and said: 'My God! You know this is horrible! *They* have saints, for *us* there is only Jesus Christ!' She spoke about it with my father. What was to be done? Leaving this school was impossible, so they told me to stop accepting these presents and to keep the flag flying high. But I was so much in love with this teacher! Seventy years have gone by and I can still remember her name, the clothes she wore, the perfume on her body. She carried on giving me these gifts. We had our own house in the garden – to have a bit of shade in the summer we built a sort of pavilion – that's where I hid these gifts away.

When I was ten we left the village because dad had found a job in a town that was half Catholic and half Protestant, which also had an extremely 'pure' Protestant school. I went there for one year before joining a non-confessional high school in a nearby town. I graduated from there in 1937, with a strong preference for German language and literature, history and religion, whereas I felt mathematics, chemistry and physics to be very distant from me.

Did you get more from your analysis in Zurich with Bally or from the previous one?

Yes, my analysis with Bally saved me. The first analyst had really ruined me: I felt full of hate, disturbed, and had real difficulties in my ability to relate to people.

How long did the first analysis last?

Three years, but in those days you only did two hours a week. In Switzerland I did three, and at the same time I repeated a complete training at the Institute of Psychoanalysis, a classic IPA institute. I went to Zurich in 1960, and I published two or three essays on the psychoanalytic treatment of psychotics.

I then received an invitation from the University of Tübingen: here a psychiatrist wanted to found a psychoanalytical-psychosomatics department within psychiatry. I proposed myself, presenting a detailed report, and I was accepted. I liked being in the team. I was a guest in the psychiatrist's house, an orthodox Protestant. Before meals we stood up and prayed, and I gathered that he wanted an eclectic kind of psychoanalysis, one that would preserve the teachings of religion. I realized that I could not go along with it, because after the war, with my experiences with the various churches, I had abandoned religion. It had cost me a lot of pain, because my father's Protestantism had certainly given me a lot. The pope had signed the concordat with Hitler and the Protestant church had done the same. What's more, while I was a doctor in the infantry battalion I met a priest, a coward: he drank our wine, ate our food, and blessed our weapons against the Russians. He spoke of Hitler's great victory. I found him utterly disgusting. After the war, when I read up on the matter – the betrayal of the pope and the archbishops – I asked myself: 'So, what's the point of the church?'

My development mainly followed the Kant, Hegel, Schopenhauer line, then the Enlightenment idea, which is difficult to reconcile with the Christian religion. For me Freud is one of the great Enlightenment thinkers. My father went through a lot of suffering because of this abjuration of mine, but eventually he came to understand it some. However, it did represent a problem between the two of us until his death. After four hundred years of flying the flag, the only remaining son – my brother died in Stalingrad, so I'm the last in Germany to bear my father's name – had abandoned the faith.

After the war I followed psychoanalysis not so much as a therapy, but more as an Enlightenment idea, an 'enlightening idea'. I never accepted the Tübingen offer because I felt we wouldn't have got along on the religious issue. At the same time an offer came from Richter for Giessen. He was looking for an analyst to do training analysis and supervision with assistants. My qualification was guaranteed. I accepted and in 1963 I went to Giessen, where I became qualified in 1967 with a study on changes in functional disorders in the absence of therapy. We were interested in understanding what becomes of these disorders if they aren't cured.

By 1970 I had built up an intense publishing activity. I became famous in Germany and received a great many offers from Universities. Since 1960, by law, every medicine faculty had to have an autonomous tenure in psychosomatic medicine – not like in Italy, where this is subordinated to psychotherapy – a real clinic, with beds, surgery and an autonomous university chair. So, faculties were looking for people who could fulfill these roles, and between 1960 and 1970 nearly all these chairs were filled by psychoanalysts. I accepted an offer from Freiburg, where my wife owned the house I had spent my childhood in, where we have been living ever since.

Do you see yourself as having an actual theoretical method of your own? Or do your concerns lie primarily within the sphere of technique, of which you've written extensively?

I am a psychoanalyst of the research current, and I think psychoanalysis can only be defined starting from its method. There are several theoretical paths: those of Freud, Ferenczi, Abraham, Jung – all interesting attempts. But psychoanalysis itself can only be defined starting from its method, in the same way as with the natural sciences. This therefore means that two people meet in a room, on the basis of specific fixed conditions that must remain the same: this is the *setting*. They usually stay there for one hour and meet regularly for a determined number of weekly sessions, not less than three, generally four, and with an *open end.*

For the patient it's a question of learning to accept the rules of the game, to learn that the analyst's position implies neutrality, because when the analyst speaks he is not speaking about himself, he is speaking of the patient's problems. We may define the basic *interaction*, not between people, otherwise we would be dealing with an 'interpersonal' dimension, but rather with that which is equivalent to *Übertragung*, *transference*. Essentially this has to do with the interior object, and the analyst deals with the patient's interior world, the interior world that the patient transmits to the analyst during the session.

Psychoanalysis, therefore, is an operation on behalf of the analyst, who works using three technical means: *interpretation*, *confrontation* and *construction.* This is the basis. The rest is speculation or in-depth investigation, things that don't interest me. Everything, except method, is extremely speculative. Theories should not break into the session hour; all that's needed is to be perfectly awake, with eyes, ears and nose – I stress the nose too – paying careful attention to what's going on: how the patient comes in, says hello, lies or sits, whether he moves his arms or legs, how and when, if he speaks in a low or loud tone of voice, if he pauses, if there are long silences… All this is a re-enactment of an interior situation in the presence of the analyst. All that the patient says and does has to do with the 'other'.

Freud's assistants have stressed different aspects of his theoretical construction. Ferenczi, for example, interpreted it in a very original way, but I don't think he really altered the Freudian model. All the representatives of the different tendencies – followers of Klein, Winnicott or Kohut – do in any case draw steadily on this model (involving the *setting*, the role of the analyst and the interpretation) through three means: interpretation, confrontation and construction. Variations are significant only once you go beyond the boundaries set by Freud for treatment, i.e., when working with children, adolescents, drug addicts, criminals, alcoholics and borderline patients. In these cases the traditional setting cannot be kept; it is very likely that even the need to abandon total abstinence or neutrality will arise.

In my view, there are three possible forms of therapy: *pure psychoanalysis*, *analytic psychotherapy* and *focal analytic psychotherapy*. Pure analysis assumes that the patient has a certain degree of intelligence, enough to allow him to understand processes that may even be quite complex. Freud explained this very well: 'They must come from a family of readers'. If you read you are also able to talk about what you read. And what you read about is always the history of human beings. There are no books that *don't deal with relationships*: between parents and children, between children, between mother and father, between lovers, between husband and wife, between one generation and another. Ever since people began to write – since the earliest writings, Mosaic or Egyptian – there has been only one theme: the science of humans. And those who grow up reading learn psychology. But those who grow up in families of non-readers, where 'human issues' are never discussed, will have difficulty in explaining things like why they cry, why they're feeling sad, or why they can't get enough sleep. Parents who never ask 'what's wrong?' limit the development of introspective or self-reflective abilities. In such situations you grow up in a world that you don't learn to understand, an *animal* world, where drives, aggression, libido and needs dominate. In such cases – lacking the tools for thought – it may turn out that a 'pure' analysis shouldn't even be proposed. In a pure analysis, what you say to the person is: 'This is the method to adopt. It's up to you whether you accept it or not. The question cannot be solved in two sessions'; and it's no good if patient and analyst live too far away from each other, because regularity is a *conditio sine qua non*. In countries like Italy another condition is for patients to have the means to pay; they have to have some sort of bourgeois stability, otherwise after six months or so they'll say: 'I have to stop because I can't afford it anymore' or 'I have to go abroad for several months'. In these cases we find ourselves in the situation of the patient who, already on the operating couch, says 'Not now'.

So, there are two rules regarding both the situation and the method, as well as the disposition of your approach and the level of the patient's internal process…

Not every moment is ideal to begin...

Exactly. It is very important for the analyst to make clear that there are preestablished conditions to follow, of the spatial, temporal and economic kind. Furthermore, the situation needs to be stable enough to allow the operation to take place over two or three years.

Another important aspect is that psychoanalysis does not have an univocal objective. We do not work with the predetermined target of relieving someone's suffering, nor with that of healing anyone. *The way is the aim and the purpose*. You can hope for the patient to learn to discover himself, but it is not properly a concrete and predetermined target. I don't push anyone to follow any particular path, since it's up to the person to decide. It could be a doctor who decides to join the circus and be a clown: that's fine as far as I'm concerned. I make the effort not to have any particular objective. There are many ways of being happy and healthy.

This is very romantic indeed: 'the aim is the journey'…

Yes, Freud is very romantic as far as this is concerned… The second method is analytic psychotherapy. This may be chosen by those with a limited cultural level, who don't necessarily satisfy all the conditions – who can't come four times a week, who can't always pay, with whom it is possible to work only two or three times a week and with whom you have a limited objective. The aim there is not radical change. In these cases there are many more directions to follow compared to the psychoanalytical sphere. But the analyst does continue to keep a neutral position, without intervening in the patient's existence, only interpreting, comparing and reconstructing, only with a more active technique. What may even happen in an emergency – when the patient's life itself is in jeopardy – is that the analyst may talk with a close relative or anyone else who has a significant relationship with the patient.

The third method is focal analytic psychotherapy, which would be ideal, say, for a female medical student I'm following in supervision. A young colleague of mine presented me with the case of a third year female medical student who can no longer sit exams. The colleague had begun analysis with this young woman, but this might not have been indicated, as hers is not a closed situation: there's a difficult situation, she's blocked, but apart from this she's by no means psychotic, nor is she depressed. In cases like this you can concentrate on the *hic et nunc* of the problem. In a case like this the analyst should say: 'We'll meet for ten or fifteen hours and try to sort out why you can't sit exams'. This particular type of psychotherapy aims at making the patient's interior fantasies come out only in relation to the symptom. Pure analysis is a very painful job: many, after beginning, would like to escape. Many find excuses, saying that their father and mother are against it, that there are too many difficulties, anything to avoid talking about the only important issue at the root of the symptom. So, if the patient accepts, focal therapy can lead to analysis. For all mono-symptomatic neuroses a brief therapy should be offered at first, a focal therapy. This should focus on a single and acute symptom – for example, a person who has been suffering from asthma for ten years.

There is then a sub-group of the third method, i.e., for people who were damaged as young children, who didn't have normal experiences from a human point of view in the first three years of their lives. A paradigmatic case in this sense is that of a female patient whose mother put her in playpen every morning for the first three years of her life and then went to work and came back in the evening. Those who have suffered similar damage are very disturbed, and the central problem is represented by object relations. These cases usually involve personalities with strong autistic connotations, and they try to solve their problems by resorting to dissociation. They make use of splitting and lies to survive society. At times they dissociate themselves so much as to behave differently according to the situation. As long as they are conscious of their dissociation, everything is fine. In Protestant countries there is more freedom: in America you can say what you like, whilst in Catholic countries you have to turn to falsification to avoid suffering punishment.

In these cases the analyst has to make use of a very flexible technique, and it's important for him not to defend neutrality too strictly. This is where he must act. If it is a very young person suffering from this disorder, then the parents, or whoever else may live in close contact with the patient, must be involved too and co-operate, with the patient's consent. There are also conditions to be made, and these must be filled with content. The patient may also be asked to carry out specific tasks. It's almost like a re-education. This is the technique for borderline cases as defined by Kernberg.

Can the analyst judge a patient? Should he? Freud once suggested to Weiss not to take on a patient because he was 'a rogue'...

When someone's a liar, analysis becomes impossible. The same goes for a criminal. Honesty and sincerity are indispensable premises on which to work. When patients lie, manipulate, or fail to pay their fees, or when they don't come to sessions regularly, then the indispensable premises of the relationship are no longer there. It's not a question of judgment, it's a question of *instructions*: the same goes for when a patient needs an operation, but suffers from a heart disorder. In such cases the operation cannot be carried out.

For me ethics is an *upright professionalism*: I am responsible for the profession I have chosen. For me there is no other ethics aside from the profession. I have no religious, bourgeois or national ethics. I am solely responsible for the profession I practice, in the same way as surgeons are: when these are required to carry out an operation they are no longer Christians, bourgeois or Germans. They are solely responsible for the profession they practice. For them, therefore, there is only one thing that's important: to carry out the operation optimally. For example, they can't drink alcohol before an operation. When I worked, I never once went to a party the night before, getting drunk until two in the morning. That would have been impossible, because I had sessions the next day and needed to be absolutely sober.

Ethics, in any profession, means a sense of responsibility for what you have to do. I never judge any of the patient's wishes.

Is it sometimes difficult? Are you never faced with dilemmas?

Yes, from time to time. But in these cases the problem is mine. I find it very difficult, for example, to bear a patient who tells me how he mistreats his four-year-old daughter; but I have to understand and work on why they need to do that. If I consider this an aspect of a pathology, then I have to succeed in treating it as such and not from any moral standpoint. Occasionally you find yourself in situations that are hard to bear, but this is part of the profession too: training, personal analysis, should prepare us to distinguish between pathology and judgment.

But if, after a period of analysis, I realize that a patient is a criminal, I may naturally have to interrupt the sessions. If, for example, they say that they steal, that they're going to kill someone or anything of the kind, I may be obliged to say: 'We have to interrupt our analysis'. When patients commit actions that endanger themselves or society, their analyst has to understand them, and this can create the conditions for carrying on with the treatment, but also for putting a stop to it. In the end *tolerance* is the decisive point.

This is a tolerance that may shock the bourgeois world – it is difficult to be tolerant when faced with particular perversions. For example, I have never taken cases like these into analysis, because I couldn't have stood them. Fortunately when you're financially independent you can choose who to take into care. Sadly not all analysts enjoy this financial independence. Usually analysts live off their patients, but when you're employed by the state – as in my case, when I earned a salary from the university – then you don't need your patients' money. I, for example, could use it to make some extra purchases or to travel, but I didn't need it to live on – except in my early years, when things were difficult. This condition has, therefore, almost always allowed me to choose whom to take on.

For some pathologies I've quite simply said: 'They're not my type of thing'. For example, pathologies with aggressive manifestations towards other people, or perversions. Another disorder I couldn't deal with effectively was masochism – women who let someone beat them like dogs. I never wanted such cases. The more you grow, the better you realize what kind of cases make up your 'field of action'. Then you only choose patients you feel you can work with, the ones you perceive a kind of *rapport* with, as well as those who give you the feeling you can come to a solution. For three, four, five years… every day… this type of therapy fills a huge portion of the analyst's life and, as life is short and precious, I've always thought: 'In these years I can't only give; I also need to receive'. So the patient has to interest me, and I have to feel that something can develop.

There has to be *a light at the end of the tunnel*; if I don't see it, I don't take on the job. It would be slave labor otherwise. I'm not a masochist. I live according to the pleasure principle. I have discovered that analysis is a creative process for the analyst, and to be creative you have to feel well. It's essential for the analyst to feel joy. A patient, for example, has to be charming, lively, interesting, or he has to have an interesting problem from a scientific point of view. He could also be a subject that I perceive as interesting for the journey he may take in the future: in these cases, I will happily accompany them.

It's exactly the same for a painter who cannot paint a picture if he is not inspired by the subject.

What about writing? You've spoken of the creative process, and of your own creativity...

I have been very interested above all in problems of technique: what to do, and when to do it, with a particular type of patient; or when patients don't talk, or when they talk too much or when they say 'I can't think of anything'; when they turn up late, when they can't lie down. Young inexperienced analysts lose themselves in the simplest things: if, for example, a patient always turns up twenty minutes late, you have to be able to change the situation. I've always been interested in how to conduct an analysis so that the analyst will feel joy and the patient will understand more and more as time passes.

At one point I began to understand that the International Psychoanalytic Association doesn't always live according to the rules of psychoanalytic doctrine. This is something I've always fought against with a certain degree of anger, having also written several feisty articles against my own psychoanalytic society. If analysts follow their training, they must be inspired by a philosophy of truth, correctness, sense of responsibility, and guided by the principles of the Enlightenment. I can do analysis only if I continually have self-enlightenment as a driving principle. I cannot in any way support a society, nor be part of a society, that sells self-enlightenment for a few pennies or has the preservation of its own power as an aim.

Always, since the earliest days of the Christian communities, whenever a church was founded, Gomorra began too: the search for power. With the earliest popes corruption began too. When you organize something, the desire for power always arises along with it. The same happened for psychoanalysis. After World War II there were forty psychoanalysts in Germany: they all knew each other, they spoke among themselves, and there was no organization of any kind. Towards the end of 1929 there was a larger group of analysts in Berlin, most of whom were intellectuals. There were none of the power struggles we find today, at least not until the analytic institution was set up, and with it corruption arrived. At the same time two classes were created, one taking advantage of the other. If you earned more money than the others, you held more power. There was an interest in having as many analysts as possible in an institute: more aspiring analysts also meant more power. You had your own clan. I threw light on this, and thus became the black sheep of the association.

But back to your writing: how do you go about it?...

Freud was a pioneer, like the early radiologists who lost their fingers through exposure to rays. All pioneers bear their sacrifice. Freud sacrificed himself, at times he didn't manage particular patients well, he did make mistakes, but the radiologists, through their mistakes, realized how dangerous X-rays were, by paying with their own skin. I cannot criticize Freud. Darwin, Marx and Freud were the three great personalities to come after Kant. This has been Freud's century, just like the nineteenth century was that of Darwin and Marx. Our century is Darwinist too: no one at this moment in history can be non-Darwinist, just as you cannot be non-Christian. I'm an agnostic, but I cannot be a stranger to Christianity, because all of my education is a part of me. Christianity provided me with a way of thinking: *the theory of love.* 'Love and Honor'. And the analyst cannot set the theory of love aside.

As far as the way I write is concerned, I'm interested in history, and I want to explain how psychoanalytic theory and how the psychoanalytic movement and association evolved, how Freud worked. I'm interested in technique and, finally, in the critique of analytic institutions. These are the three issues I've dealt with, as well as psychosomatics, of course, but that was never a passion of mine. My passion has always been pure psychoanalytical technique. I delight in criticizing, my adrenaline levels rise considerably, I feel intense, angry and very much *alive* when I can attack.

Then, when I write, the thing I enjoy the most is *making the sentence*: subject, object, verb. I struggle endlessly to achieve a sentence. At high school my Latin teacher would always say: 'Cremerius! Despite your Latin name, your Latin is absolutely awful! You must learn to understand Latin phraseology!' Twenty years later these words came back to me and I understood that the ideal is to make a sentence as the Latins would have made it, with a clarity that remains unmatched still today.

It takes a huge amount of strength to make a sentence, everyone who writes knows that. This was my greatest pleasure, but in the last two or three years I have no longer had the strength to do it, and it causes me great suffering.

What about literature? Has it helped or inspired you in any way?

Yes. I like the great writers, who have a clear, concise style and who can talk about human beings in a way that is never banal. Flaubert, Conrad: what power that Pole had! Everything he wrote was in English, a second language for him. For me his was a truly special style; it could be compared to Proust, Thomas Mann or Flaubert's *Madame Bovary*: what a book! I love it when I feel that an author gives us *insight*, when an author dares to approach something forbidden, not tolerated. Remember that Flaubert was accused of having dared too much, like the real pioneers, who put their lives in jeopardy for the sake of writing.

Freud's life too was one of persecution: he never became a permanent professor, nor could he give regular university lessons. The pioneers were often mad geniuses, with only a few disciples, with no rules or training, who came from impoverished Jewish families, from countries like Rumania: adventurers like Ferenczi, someone of surprising genius. These are the kinds of people who have opened the way to important discoveries – often recognized, as in Ferenczi's case, only many years later. Einstein was surrounded by people like this. The only one who was definitely more normal was Darwin: he came from a wealthy family and made his discoveries in a totally quiet and relaxed environment; he didn't have to go through great suffering when the church complained about him. He felt tremendously safe because of his Protestant family. He founded no 'International' of any kind, something that Marx and Freud did – both had a great fear of transience, something Darwin never feared. He had the following conviction: 'I've made a great discovery that will persist beyond my death. I don't need an international organization to defend my ideas'. Freud was always afraid of a 'hereafter'. As his was the philosophy of a Jew, it could have been persecuted and thwarted like so many others begat by his race.

So, was it this need not to be forgotten that led Freud to set up such a fideistic structure? And how can the reality of psychoanalytical societies be managed today?

They have to change, otherwise they will soon end. In Germany the Societies are nearing their end, because they practice a kind of 'monotherapy'. The type of therapy they do is no longer carried out according to the principles of analysis: it's more of a psychotherapy. Above all they have abandoned the idea that Freudian analysis is a philosophy as well as a technique. Freud always said that you can use philosophy to do therapy, but to 'cure' was not his main objective. He found the enlightening function of psychoanalysis to be essential, and enlightenment is only possible when it is hidden – because no one wants to be enlightened. A psychoanalytic society doesn't want to be enlightened, it only wants to be founded, recognized and accepted. Whoever says 'this is not the way it should work' is attacked. This was the case for Kant, Marx and Freud. In his time Kant was seen as a rebel, because his idea of the moral obligation of knowledge was revolutionary thinking; until Kant appeared Christian tenets did not get questioned. Then this little man from Königsberg came along and said: 'It is possible to discuss anything, to investigate anything'.

Freud did something even worse: he explored the field of sexuality, which is extremely delicate, because no one is free from some kind of sexual problem, either 'technical' or moral (fears, feelings of guilt). Freud knew that by delving into this field he would have the whole of society against him: but there was no alternative. If you uphold certain ideas you're also aware of the fact that you'll be making lots of enemies... it's inevitable. Psychoanalysts gave up on this enlightening and revolutionary aspect long ago; today they feel they've 'achieved success'. They've come a long way: in Germany they've become government officials, they receive their wages every three months, so much per patient. But in exchange for this they have to love the state, they can't attack it, and they accept things as they are, so that they'll have money and power. Therefore psychoanalysis is no longer visible in society. In Germany anyone who has undergone psychoanalytical training can call himself a 'psychoanalyst'. And on the nameplate on any door of a Jungian, Kleinian, Adlerian or neo-analyst, you read: *Psychoanalyst.*

On the other hand, only those who have penetrated Freudian philosophy have a right to be recognized as analysts: therefore those who have struggled for freedom, who have fought anti-Semitism or the oppression of the weak, who have fought for the rights of children, of women. Someone who fights for these causes is therefore not well-accepted. I have enjoyed this role of the black sheep, but I've never suffered because of it. My wife has always agreed with me. I've had friends who've fought alongside me – few, because money is important, and everyone has a family to support. So, many are often willing to betray Freud and the philosophy of emancipation. In the church it's the same thing: this pope goes to South America and says: 'the church forbids the use of condoms', so women there have to undergo an abortion once a year. It's disgusting to use the theory of love to kill women.

During fascism, in Germany, every Sunday priests prayed for the wellbeing of Hitler, for the victory of the fascist armies. So, I just said to myself: 'These churches no longer represent Christianity'. I have my own Christianity, but the church now accepts any compromise to preserve its power and riches. In Germany priests are paid by the state, with a life-long salary of three thousand dollars a month, and they also have a free house and car as well as free health care. When you accept all this, you can't fight the state. They all prayed for Hitler. If every Sunday every priest had said: 'I cannot pray for an inhuman system', then Hitler would definitely have had an early downfall, because Germany still had and still has the Protestant tradition.

My father fought the system and my family lived in total isolation until 1945. When I returned to Germany in 1943, I visited my parents. In Protestant families you pray standing behind your chair; the father of the house says his prayer addressing God with the informal '*Du*': 'My God, I thank you for this day, because you have let us awaken in health, and have given us our daily bread'. And every morning, throughout the war, my father would say: 'I pray for the victory of the Allies'. During Nazism my mother was depressed, and cried continuously; my father had a stomach illness and could no longer eat. Some youths in the streets even attacked him. But he never stopped praying for an allied victory. This mental attitude is part of my life, and because I am a Freudian, I am against any psychoanalytical association that lies and stoops to compromises.

What's the best way to train and select analysts?

The main change should occur in training: instead of doing training analysis *during* training, you should do a personal analysis *before* training. In IPA societies you do 'training analysis' during training: it can't be a true analysis, because the training analyst is an analyst and at the same time he holds a powerful position as a member of the institute. Therefore it is faked. Anna Freud had said so: this is not analysis.

So, for twenty years I went round Germany like John in the desert preaching reform. What I suggested was that personal analysis should precede and be separated from other aspects of the formal training, while also allowing for total freedom in the choice of one's analyst. 'This guy is someone I feel I can trust, I'm sure it can work between us'. For two or three years two hundred young people in Germany fought with me, but then they realized that if they continued to follow me down my road they would never get to the top, because the society says: 'Do things your own way if you really want, but don't count on us for certification'. So they all went back to the fold on their knees, and now they are good analysts who accept all the compromises you would care to imagine.

I suggested also to open up the ghetto of IPA institutes; they are closed to the world, they make no contact with the other human sciences, and they don't have the guts to integrate themselves in the universities and discuss their issues there. Psychoanalysis has many issues that are still open, regarding, for example, the need for explanations as regards terminology: there are still many concepts that can be understood at an intuitive level but that haven't yet been explained at a scientific level. It would be much better to do this job together with philosophers, sociologists, educators, instead of staying inside the ghetto where a single paranoid language is spoken and where everyone just worries about one thing, that the sacred image of Freud isn't touched. It's just like in the church.

If in a city you get patients through the association, then you're in shackles, no longer independent. In addition, during training you're committed to obtaining your certificate, and then most want to be training analysts, because training analysts earn 40 percent more than others; and the training analysts also have guaranteed patients on their couches for years. With analysts who have no training tasks, patients come and go; they interrupt analysis for long periods or give up altogether, they're difficult to deal with, and they attack the analyst. Moreover trainee candidates – the patients of the training analyst – are sheepish, they always have more or less realistic fears, because of their shackles; if they want their certificate, it is risky to attack their analysts. Anna Freud had already described all this before World War II, but no one cared to listen.

With personal analysis, and the opening up of the institutes to the human sciences and universities, training analysts would cease to exist, and there would no longer be a caste, but rather a scientific society, people who do the same thing together and ask the same questions, without anyone necessarily being worth more than anyone else. Even in an association of chemists there are those who hold particular positions: you can be a professor and then the chairman for three years, but basically the members are all equal. It could be that one knows or understands more; but in this case what distinguishes him is a scientific criterion, not one of power. In the International Psychoanalytical Association, instead, there are two classes: those who have power and those who don't.

Furthermore, there must be the freedom to ask anything, even when it may appear to be questioning Freud himself. Some colleagues and I, for example, analyzed three of Freud's cases, arguing these should not be used as models during training, because all three are failures: *Dora*, *The Wolfman* and *The Ratman*. How might they be used instead? They could be used to teach what *shouldn't be done*. Only then will it ever be possible to understand what happens when mistakes are made. But after World War II they were presented to us as ideal teachings; we've been trained on the basis of erroneous didactic material, simply because people didn't want to study Freud in a critical way.

So for me the important points are the German sentence, the Latin sentence, my passion for the sentence, my passion for criticism and my criticism of the system. At the root of all this we find the Enlightenment, Kant, Freud and Protestantism. Luther was an Enlightenment thinker, as was my father, but this tradition never stopped me from reading Kant and Freud critically. Today I can even look at my father critically.

What is the future of psychoanalysis?

Reform of the institutions, of training, opening up to universities, to the sciences: dialogue, from a methodological point of view. A return to Enlightenment sciences, the courage to speak the truth, to criticize society – to say, for example, that the war in Kosovo was intolerable, that it is outrageous that the victims of fascism haven't been compensated yet; that gypsies, for example, haven't yet been refunded for what they suffered. We are not given the opportunity to criticize our system of government, for the voting system is such that it is almost impossible to influence the government. In Germany we don't have the Swiss system of referenda. We analysts could be the only ones capable of helping others and understanding why they need this system, or why no one is capable of protecting children, or why no one wants women to occupy important posts. We're the only ones who could criticize and help to understand. Communists only criticized, since they just needed another religion to replace the existing one.

We want to help to understand why we behave as we do, or why we can't manage certain things. Why are men afraid of women? No one can understand this without psychoanalysis. Why in Germany do the rich become richer and the poor ever increasingly poor? It is also possible to explain why people need money, and if someone realizes that the money he has is too much for him, then he may ask himself why he needs it: is it because he doesn't know how to enjoy anything else? Then perhaps we could come to change society. This person might understand that his life with his partner is miserable, because he only thinks about money and has no time for his wife and kids.

We should also ask ourselves what will become of the family if no one reads books anymore. My father would read out aloud every evening, when I still couldn't read very well. And there was no radio: Protestants couldn't have a radio. So, after dinner we would read a book and talk about it. But who does that nowadays?

Couples are doing badly. It must be said that the monogamous couple is humanly impossible. But if, after all is said and done, we still seem to want and defend marriage, that's probably because it's the only form by which human beings can develop – I have to admit to that after fifty-four years of my own marriage. My own marriage hasn't been a piece of cake: we've had our share of contrasts, quarrels, arguments. But basically marriage is the only form man and woman can produce, if they're sincere, and this implies the defense of a pact. If I go away and pick up another woman, I won't learn anything, I won't be able to understand the problems that can arise between men and women. If you say that you don't want to try and understand, then you split up. The same goes for having children. Who wants to take on such a responsibility?

It must be constantly admitted that being married or having children is an *impossible task*, but all great tasks are impossible. It's impossible to be a great surgeon, a good analyst, a good teacher. I've taught for a lifetime with the feeling that my lessons weren't quite what they should have been; I should have better formulated my explanations in order to be really understood. Everything is impossible in the end and is never perfect, and you have to try reformulating pleasure, the enjoyment of life, again and again, otherwise you're already dead and buried by the age of nineteen!

The Enlightenment failed because in 1933 Europe lost all reason, not only in Germany. The French too collaborated. We all became guilty. It was the defeat of the Enlightenment, but nothing is perfect. The idea of Christ's love is violated every day too, even if it should be understood how wonderful it is to try to love each other, to create something as a couple, to have happy children, a family nucleus open to other people. One ought to be a model in a politically corrupt society that is destroying itself.

Every time I struggle for the Enlightenment I'm told: 'But just look: it's been totally defeated!' I reply: 'I don't give a damn!' Everything suffers its defeats, and if the Enlightenment had had no defeats it wouldn't have been the Enlightenment. If the Christian religion hadn't had its defeats, then the theory of love couldn't be defended and supported, and it would just be an orthodoxy. The Enlightenment has to be a risk; otherwise it would become a habit. *Habit* is the enemy of our life. You see, I'm passionate about the Enlightenment, and I can handle defeat. For I, too, have had my share.

FREUDIANISM IN FRANCE

Elisabeth Roudinesco

ELISABETH ROUDINESCO, historian, psychoanalyst and writer, was born in 1944. She was a member of Jacques Lacan's Ecole Freudienne de Paris (1969–1981), and presently teaches history at the University of Paris VII and at the Ecole des Hautes Etudes en Sciences Sociales. Vice-president of the International Society for the History of Psychiatry and Psychoanalysis, she is also a frequent contributor to the major French daily, *Le Monde*.

Following publication of her famed *Jacques Lacan & Co.: A History of Psychoanalysis in France, 1925–1985*, Roudinesco here describes – in a 1994 conversation with Sergio Benvenuto – the development of Freudian thought in France from its beginnings into the 1990s. Placing that development in the contexts of both surrounding political events as well as of prevailing philosophical, literary and artistic movements (such as surrealism), she pays particular attention to relations between the French philosophical tradition – inspired essentially by phenomenology – and the psychoanalytic debate at-large. Prof. Roudinesco then goes on to describe the crucial role played in France by Lacan and his Ecole Freudienne in establishing psychoanalysis in that country's intellectual and popular circles.

The following interview with Elisabeth Roudinesco, excerpted from a longer conversation originally published in Italian in the *Enciclopedia Multimediale delle Scienze Filosofiche*, first appeared in the *Journal of European Psychoanalysis* n. 3–4 (1997) under the title 'Freudianism in France'. It is here reprinted courtesy of RAI – Radiotelevisione Italiana.

* * *

Sergio Benvenuto

Were philosophers much interested in psychoanalysis during Freud's lifetime?

Elisabeth Roudinesco

Apparently not. Edmund Husserl ignored Freud, although his disciples would soon discover an analogy between Husserl's phenomenology and

Freud's approach to the unconscious. In fact, Husserl's new reading of Descartes questioned the Cartesian 'cogito', as well as the principles of thought spanning this entire century, starting with the crisis of science. Although not clearly defined by the philosophers themselves, there is a relation between the questions raised by Freud and those raised by twentieth-century philosophy. Although Freud ignored Nietzsche, both posed questions of genealogy.

What was Freud's response to his pupils when they pointed out the resemblance between some of his theories and those of Nietzsche?

He ignored them, as he was not at all interested in reading philosophy with the exception of Schopenhauer, for whom he claimed an affinity. He did not even read Spinoza, although references to Spinoza's philosophy emerge in the Freudian theory of desire. Kant influenced his theory of dreams. And although Freud did not explicitly acknowledge these influences, his successors did.

Phenomenology, specifically Ludwig Binswanger's psychiatric school, would link Freud and philosophy. A German-speaking psychiatrist working in Switzerland, Binswanger attempted one of the first, great post-Husserlian syntheses. Through Heidegger's philosophy in particular, Binswanger created what has been called 'existential psychoanalysis', a melding of Heidegger's and Freud's thought in order to re-think madness. Binswanger, while maintaining his friendship with Freud, nevertheless developed his own thought.

Apart from the psychiatric trend in Germany and Switzerland, it is France that was to play an important role in linking phenomenology and psychoanalysis, albeit through literary and intellectual channels rather than through the psychoanalytic movement. Between 1914 and 1930, the surrealist milieu and the *Nouvelle Revue Française* took an interest in Freudian thought. The surrealists inherited from Rimbaud and Mallarmé the exigency to change life, language, everything, to see things from another side of consciousness, thus creating a new approach to the subject: '*Je est un autre*' ('I *is* an other'), Rimbaud wrote to Izambard in a letter dated May 13, 1871. Thus, in France the ground was laid for intellectuals, and above all for poets, to appropriate Freud's ideas in order to change consciousness. Freud, who was then still alive, did not fully grasp that movement. In fact, when André Breton, the founder of surrealism, met Freud in 1919, he was disappointed by Freud's interest in minor writers, such as Henri Lenormand, whose names today are all but forgotten. Freud showed more interest in classical literature or in the contemporary literature fashionable at the time than he did in the avant-garde.

Yet Freud admired Dali...

True, but they met later. Only after Dali had painted Freud's portrait, did Freud recognize his genius. In fact, he more readily recognized genius in painting than he did in the literature of his time. And yet he was a great reader; all his references were literary, ranging from Greek tragedy to Shakespeare and the novel. He read much less philosophy, because his insights lay somewhere between science and literature; and although he was aware of the importance his discoveries had for the history of philosophy, he did not formulate them in philosophical terms.

Was it just the French avant-garde that showed an interest in Freud?

No, in France even classic writers such as Romain Rolland or Pierre-Jean Jouve were interested. However, although that interest was more or less international, in France it was ongoing. In England it began with the literary environment of Virginia Woolf and the Bloomsbury Group. In Austria, at the very moment psychoanalysis was taking shape and among so-called twentieth-century writers (Karl Kraus being perhaps the most noteworthy), there were debates on whether to oppose or defend psychoanalysis. France, however, was more sensitive owing to the 'Dreyfus Affair', which galvanized the French intellectual class into an avant-garde.

Why was the 'Dreyfus Affair' so important to French culture?

The Dreyfus Affair – France's second great step after the French Revolution – caused a dramatic split among intellectuals and divided France between conservative rightist thought, represented by Barrès, and leftist writers. For the first time, the word *intellectuel* would substitute for *écrivan*, writer: an 'intelligentsia' formed around Zola to protest not just against the charges against Dreyfus, but against anti-Semitism, conservatism and traditional Catholicism as well. It was the first great mobilization of intellectuals as a class which, in France alone today, still has a great importance.

Freudian ideas would soon saturate the French intellectual environment, although philosophers, Georges Politzer in particular, would later become interested. Politzer, not yet a communist when he became interested in Freud, produced an important work on the foundations of psychology which showed clearly the bearing of Freud's work on the philosophical question of the subject. But it would be Jacques Lacan – with his 1932 thesis in medicine on *De la psychose paranoiaque dans ses rapports avec la personnalité* – to provide the first philosophical framework for Freud's thought. Lacan, who was trained not in philosophy but in psychiatry, became a psychoanalyst in the 1930s. In 1932 he made a Spinozan interpretation of Freud; he was linked to the surrealists and had a special interest in female madness. Moreover, Lacan also had ties with the phenomenological legacy of Freud, which was taken up in France by Eugène Minkowski. Binswanger, Husserl and Heidegger were also being read in France at that time, so that Lacan, embracing this trend, was initially a phenomenologist.

Was not Minkowski also influenced by Henri Bergson's thought?

True. Minkowski was the first in France to read Husserl and to create a psychiatric phenomenology, thus deeply influencing Lacan and that entire generation. Minkowski was as important for France as Binswanger was for Switzerland.

Was Minkowski directly influenced by Freud?

Yes, all psychiatrists at that time made Freud their reference point for renewing nosology. Minkowski had read both Freud and Husserl. At the beginning of the century, views on mental illness had completely changed. Before 1900, or thereabouts, mental illness was considered hereditary or organic, what would today be called genetic. With the Freudian discovery, the genetic theory of mental illness was shelved for approximately eighty years, although today it is being reconsidered. In any case, the primacy of psyche-dominated mental illness was thought to derive both from the subject's problems relating to his environment, as well as from the division existing within consciousness itself: madness lying both within and without. New treatment methods for madness brought about the dismantling of traditional nineteenth-century insane asylums; this had started with Pinel during the French Revolution, and continued in 1911 Switzerland with Eugen Bleuler, with whom Freud would later make contact. (It was Bleuler who introduced the notion of schizophrenia.) Minkowski, and later Lacan, emerged from the legacy of Eugen Bleuler, Carl Gustav Jung and Binswanger – in short, 1911 Zurich.

The second major encounter in France between Freud and philosophy took place before World War II, between 1933 and 1939, when Lacan met the Russian émigré Kojève, whose seminars on Hegel were followed by a great part of the Parisian 'intelligentsia'. Thus, during that period, Hegel's thought was rediscovered from the perspectives of Heidegger and Husserl.

And thanks to the research of Alexandre Koyré, Kojève's contemporary, André Breton, Jean-Paul Sartre and Jacques Lacan discovered a new Hegel. I consider Koyré even more important than Kojève; although familiar with Freud's work, he, like Husserl, did not find psychoanalysis useful. Koyré was an historian of science and a philosopher and historian of religions whose concerns lay far from Freud's. Despite their being contemporaries, Koyré was one of Lacan's masters, and Lacan subsequently applied Koyré's philosophical teachings to his interpretation of Freud.

The writer and philosopher Georges Bataille also played an important role in the diffusion of Freudian ideas; he read Freud, and attended both Koyré's and Kojève's seminars. Although Bataille was at the edges of philosophy, his thought must today be placed in the context of European philosophy. Lacan was influenced by Bataille, who was the first in France to make a connection between Nietzsche and Freud.

And Hegel as well…

Certainly, but Bataille was concerned above all with Nietzschean nihilism, as he oscillated between Hegel and Nietzsche. Nietzsche, because of his sister, was considered anti-Semitic in France at that time. There were two traditions of Nietzscheanism in France: a leftist trend represented by Charles Andler, who read Nietzsche in the perspective of the Enlightenment and progressivism; and a rightist trend, which, drawing from his (surely misunderstood) notion of 'Superman', linked Nietzsche with anti-Semitism, identifying him as a precursor of Nazi thought. A new reading of Nietzsche developed around Pìerre Klossowski and Bataille's two journals, *Documents* and *Acéphal*e. Bataille lashed out against this 'rightist' reading of Nietzsche, and sought to reveal Nietzsche's hidden role as an Enlightened thinker. He was more interested in Nietzsche's Dionysian philosophy of the sacred. The Nietzsche of Andler was much more Apollonian, to use Nietzschean terminology. (Andler, basically a socialist, had produced a voluminous work on Nietzsche in the midst of the war, in 1914.) Bataille, rediscovering a buried Nietzsche, would read Freud in the same vein. Bataille and Roger Caillois were to found the *Collège de Sociologie*. A 'philosophical college', frequented also by Lacan, it provided a meeting point for philosophers, whether Nietzschean or Freudian. It helped Bataille and his generation to conceive a new form of the sacred, which they discerned in the rise of fascism. Bataille was particularly interested in Freud's 1921 text, *Group Psychology and Analysis of the Ego*, wherein Freud theorized on mass identification with a leader and, above all, with an army or church, with every subject in relation to a leader understood as an Ego-ideal. Freud, who wrote this text before either fascism or Nazism existed, was thus thinking rather of socialist masses or perhaps of communism, although he did not state this clearly. Bataille made an enlightening interpretation of this text, showing how well it clarified the nature of fascism. In the irrational tie which unites the exalted crowd to its fascist leader, Bataille detected the rise of the *part maudite*, the 'cursed side' – that is, of the sacred, of the unexplainable or unnamable, of pure horror. In short, Lacan was much influenced by Bataille's reflections on Freud and the sacred.

Was the rise of existentialism in France in the 1940s a refusal of, or an attempt at dialogue with, Freudianism?

The great synthesis would occur in 1943 with the publication of Sartre's *Being and Nothingness*. Sartre had always been considered anti-Freudian, despite his being an extraordinary interpreter of Freud, as this text already demonstrates. He criticized Freud, but at least he'd read him, unlike Heidegger or Husserl, who refused to consider his thought. However, Sartre, faulting Freud's mechanicism and biologism, chose Binswanger's existentialist analysis over psychoanalysis. He justly criticized Freud's rootedness in biologism in *Being and Nothingness*, thus anticipating Lacan, who would attempt to detach Freud from the biologism of his time and make him a theoretician of purely psychic activity. Lacan's theory of the imaginary initially relied on phenomenology, and later on linguistics, with which he supplanted the idea of a biological substratum with an 'unconscious structured like language'.

In *Being and Nothingness*, Sartre attempted a more phenomenological reading of Freud. He later became not so much anti-Freudian as more markedly anti-psychoanalytic, in particular, against the guild of psychoanalysis. But, had Sartre not read Freud, *Being and Nothingness* would not have been the same.

Sartre even wrote a film script on Freud…

Yes, a magnificent, unfortunately little-known work, published posthumously as *The Freud Scenario*. The film director John Huston – intending to make a film on the beginnings of psychoanalysis and Freud's relationship, around 1896, with Wilhelm Fliess – had asked Sartre in 1955 to write the script, which he did, drawing inspiration from the then just-published biography of Freud by Ernest Jones. Unfortunately, because it would have required eight or nine hours of film time, Huston was unable to use it. However, the portrait of Freud which Sartre drew bore no resemblance to that of Jones. Sartre's Freud was a typical scientist of the history of science *à la française*: that is, a scientist who, because he is riddled by doubt, goes from error to truth, a character who could have been created by Thomas Mann, but one also close to Cavaillès and Canguilhem.

Jean Cavaillès and Georges Canguilhem, a French philosopher of mathematics and a French philosopher of the history of science, respectively, were Foucault's teachers. Canguilhem, who is now ninety years old, left his mark on the entire structuralist generation; his famous thesis on *The Normal and the Pathological* was published during the Occupation. Neither was a philosopher of *engagement* (commitment); both were much less influenced by Husserl, or by the theory of the subject, than was Sartre; they were not phenomenologists, but pure theoreticians of the history of science. And yet, in June of 1940, it was oddly enough these two philosophers of science who would become involved in the Resistance, and not Sartre, Lacan, Merleau-Ponty or even Bataille. Sartre was certainly not a collaborator, and was involved in the Resistance for a few weeks, but he failed to fully understand the real significance of the situation, and consequently never became a militant. That entire generation would later elaborate the philosophy of *engagement*, commitment, but it arose from a guilty conscience. Simone Beauvoir, in her *Mémoirs*, reflected that at the war's end none of them had really grasped what had taken place. This reflection, begun in 1943–1944, gave birth in 1945 to the journal *Les Temps Modernes*, headed by Sartre and Maurice Merleau-Ponty, which questioned the responsibility of intellectuals, albeit in retrospect. That entire generation had failed to take a stand.

The great historian Marc Bloch did take part in the Resistance – both he and Cavaillès lost their lives – yet they did not proclaim the intellectual's commitment. Many of the self-proclaimed, *committed* writers of the 1930s embraced not armed commitment, but a commitment to ideas. The French intellectuals who took on important roles after 1945 had been exclusively ideological supporters of the Resistance.

Did Freud's thought generally influence more the thinkers of the Left or of the Right?

Inevitably of the Left, because the French Right wing has always been strongly marked by Catholicism, and Freud was profoundly critical of religious ideology. He had labeled religion a neurosis in *The Future of an Illusion*, so it was logical for Catholicism and the French Right to find his thought unacceptable.

Yet Freud did not consider himself as belonging to the Left, and in Austria he had always voted liberal, for Center-Right policies.

Yes, but it is also true that one's vote and one's thought are quite different matters. In the history of Western thought, the Freudian discovery is perceived as part of a greater, progressive trend (whether with him, or against him, as in the case of the feminist movement). It matters little whether Freud was conservative or not. But because his thinking induced questions concerning sexuality, his entire theory automatically became scandalous for conservative thought. Psychoanalysts from the extreme Right were rare.

Secondly, Freud and nearly all of the founders of psychoanalysis were Jewish, and thus subject to Nazi persecution. The majority were to emigrate from central Europe and settle in the United States. The International Psychoanalytic Association represented for many a refuge from persecution. Thus, the history of psychoanalysis is indelibly linked to the extermination of the Jews, and to the Diaspora that represented their salvation. In the United States, those Jews would embrace the idea of adaptation to the American way of life, and in some aspects thus became conservative. However, as Jews persecuted by a fascist dictatorship, it was only natural that they align themselves along progressive lines.

An exception in France was the psychoanalyst Edouard Pichon – one of the founders of the French psychoanalytic movement (he died in 1940) – who was a member of *Action française*, the monarchist movement inspired by Charles Maurras. *Action française* brought together all the rightist Catholic tendencies, uniting Roman Catholicism with a return to ancient, classic values and ideas, with the idea of bringing to power in France everything that goes under the name of 'pétainisme'. In 1940, half of this group was to join the Resistance (as a result of anti-German sentiments), while the other half was to collaborate with the Nazis. But the marked Germanophobia of *Action française*, along with its desire that the West rediscover its Latin roots, would eventually create internal contradictions that resulted in its dream of an alliance with Italian fascism against Nazism. Yet Pichon, although a student of Maurras, was not anti-Semitic – on the level of ideas, everything is possible – while *Action française* was.

What about the 1960s, when there was a renewed interest in Freud, especially in France?

This renewal was part of the tradition of which we are speaking. After 1945, French thought – first of all Merleau-Ponty, and, subsequently the anthropologist Claude Lévi-Strauss – took Freud into consideration. Lacan played a considerable role, drawing from Freud all the philosophical implications. In the 1960s, interest centered around structuralism, that is, on the simultaneous reading of Saussurian theories on speech and language by Lévi-Strauss on the one hand, and of Freudian thought on the other. In France, all post-war philosophers, starting with Sartre, read Freud – which was not the case in other countries – because after 1920 Freud was viewed in France as an intellectual and a theoretician of the unconscious, and not merely a physician. In short, he was not read exclusively by psychoanalysts. And Lacan, who was both the leader of a psychoanalytic movement and a thinker, would later unite Freud the intellectual with Freud the psychotherapist.

Strangely, in English-speaking countries, psychoanalysis is viewed above all as a therapy and leaves the intellectuals indifferent, while in France it was especially the intellectuals who were drawn to it, although it did not take off as a therapy until the end of the 1960s. It was around that time, in fact, that Paul Ricoeur published Freud and Philosophy, *a book in which he presented a hermeneutic reading of Freud...*

Ricoeur is also closely related to Merleau-Ponty and interested in Freud, as were all French philosophers. His personal hermeneutic interpretation marked the culmination of phenomenology in the 1960s. But Ricoeur is anything but a structuralist, to the point of conflicting with Lacan on this point.

The second and more interesting wave is represented by Michel Foucault, Jacques Derrida, and Gilles Deleuze, among others. It matters little whether they are anti-Freud, pro-Freud or anti-Lacan: they nevertheless read both. Derrida read Freud, although his reading of Freud began with a criticism of Lacan's work.

Foucault is not Freudian. His 1961 *Histoire de la Folie – Madness & Civilization* in English – outlined the limits of Freud's work. Yet, without the Freudian idea of a beyond consciousness, and without the idea of a division (*coupure*) imposed by Freudian thought, he would never have been able to write it, thus revealing precisely the need for a history of madness, and not of psychiatry. In *Madness & Civilization* he is fairly Nietzschean, and takes up Bataille's idea that madness is the 'cursed part' within the subject, subsequently situating Freud in this line. In a wonderful page from his book he absolves Freud from the accusation of having been one of the oppressors of madness, placing him instead among the discoverers of the depths of the Unconscious.

Guattari, instead, was a psychiatrist in the famous La Borde clinic near Orléans…

Guattari, a psychoanalyst analyzed by Lacan, was linked to what came to be called in France the Movement of Institutional Psychotherapy, which grew out of La Borde clinic and became the equivalent of the anti-psychiatric movement in Italy and England (Basaglia, Laing, Cooper, etc.). He and Deleuze were to promote a critical reading of the later Lacan and of Freud. *Anti-Oedipus* is a criticism of Freudian dogmatism, and reconsiders certain theses of Reich. Wilhelm Reich, of Austrian origin, was a disciple of Freud and one of the representatives of Freudian-Marxism in the 1930s. From 1920 on, all German and Austrian psychoanalysts were concerned with social problems: how to adapt psychoanalysis to the masses, rather than use it exclusively to treat the rich bourgeoisie. Many – particularly from the psychoanalytic Left, represented by Otto Fenichel and Wilhelm Reich – were Marxists, although not necessarily communist party militants. Their motto was: 'Freud wanted to change the individual, Marx wanted to change society, but both wanted to change Man'. At that time, the revolutions of the subject and of society were being questioned. Reich, who attempted to unite the two, was excluded both from the psychoanalytic movement in 1933 for deviationism, and from the communist party, which led to his ultimately giving primacy to biology. His tragic destiny was madness. There was no Reichian trend in France, Deleuze being the only representative. Reich was discovered late, in a way characteristic of the French. In *Anti-Oedipus*, subtitled 'Capitalism and Schizophrenia', Deleuze and Guattari assert that madness in its pure state is a contestation of capitalist society, because madness consists of surges of desire – Deleuze is a Spinozan – which implies an opposition to all systems. Deleuze reconsiders Reich; Reich, however, spoke from a Freudian-Marxist, and later biological, point of view. It was only forty years later, in *Anti-Oedipus*, that his ideas were taken up in philosophical terms. And it was only after 1968 that Reich's work was finally translated in France.

Anti-Oedipus *was published during a 'radical' cultural climate in France, rendered even more electric by the political protest movement…*

Yes, it came out against a background of worldwide protest, the last great shudder of Marxism before the end.

In France, Marxism entered into crisis with the so-called new philosophers…

Yes, there was a general criticism of Marxism. The emerging discovery of the Gulag and of the tragic effects of communism, promoted by critical communists, would be the last wave. There was a simultaneous protest against traditional psychiatry. Thus, *Anti-Oedipus* was both a contestation of traditional psychiatry as well as a Leftist criticism of Marxism.

But in the 1960s, and even earlier, there was a reading of Freud with Marxist overtones by the Frankfurt School, in particular by Marcuse and Habermas. What influence did this have in France?

None. That movement passed directly from Frankfurt to the United States, through emigration. In the 1930s, prior to Nazism, the Frankfurt School had been linked to the Freudian left. When Otto Fenichel founded the Psychoanalytic Institute of Berlin in the 1920s, he had ties to the Frankfurt School and to Adorno in particular. They would eventually emigrate to the United States, without ever passing through France. Thus that entire trend had a German-American background, with no effect in France.

Not even when, in the late 1970s, Habermas became a world famous philosopher?

Habermas is certainly well-known in France. But the way in which Habermas was appropriated does not have the same importance in France today as the appropriation of Hegel, for example. For this to happen, a noted philosopher in France would have to take it upon himself to teach the Frankfurt School in the same way that Kojève taught Hegel.

And what happened in the 1980s?

Most importantly, Lacan died (in 1981), which marked the end of an entire era. This epoch was characterized by a rebirth of the 'human sciences' in France, and by an ultra-criticism of the recent past – although in general there was a return to a form of conservatism. The dogmatic excesses of Lacanism were seen in the same light as those of Maoism or Marxism. Lacan appeared as a dictator who, like Lenin, began well and ended badly, opening the way for a general criticism of his entire work.

In the United States, this phenomenon took the form of revisionism (as represented in particular by Frank Sulloway) and, after 1970, the evolution of Freudianism led to a harsh criticism of Freud. The period of the Freudian cult was followed – with typical American faddishness – by a period during which Freud was said to have invented nothing, to have concocted legends all of his own, and to have proclaimed himself inventor of the unconscious, which instead had existed long before. A philosophy of 'science as a continuum' was established, according to which Freud was nothing more than a scientist of his time. I do not share this opinion: there are some breaks in science, and some, at a certain moment take a decisive step. One of these was taken by Freud. Sigmund Freud is not Pierre Janet. But this 'American'-style criticism exists even in France.

Represented by whom?

By Gauchet, by Raymond Aron's students, and by the neo-Kantians. This trend radically criticizes Structuralism as an obscurantist philosophy developed by Nietzsche through Freud to Foucault opposed to human rights and to liberalism. And it criticizes the idea that what determines consciousness pertains to Heidegger or Nietzsche, and not to Enlightenment philosophy. In my opinion, this criticism is false; I do not consider either Foucault or Lacan to be unconditionally Nietzschean, even though French thought at that time may have been strongly influenced by Nietzsche, Hegel and Heidegger. But it all depends on how it was influenced. If doubting the liberty of man means obscurantism, and if this doubt is countered with the benefits of a liberal society in which the subject is free – which is the thesis of Aron's followers – then it is hardly interesting. Thinkers such as Foucault, Lacan or Derrida may be critics of the subject's freedom (the subject is determined by his Unconscious, by coercions beyond his control), yet they certainly are not irrational or obscurantist. They are thinkers of what might be termed the 'obscurity of Enlightenment', the obscure *Aufklärung*, because they meld the two trends of the Enlightenment. There exist no pure genealogies in the history of thought.

Yet Freudianism is inherent to the tradition of the Enlightenment and progress. Psychoanalysis, the very moment it becomes part of the history of progress, questions progress itself. For example, Freudian thought, which is critical of liberalism, took root only in democratic countries.

Freud did not believe in progress…

Freud did not believe in a cumulative conception of progress, although, despite his personal reticence, he is part of the history of progress. He believed that madness was an illness and not a form of divine possession, and that women should have equal rights with men; but he too believed in an eternal return, that progress was not an irreversible process. I agree: even within a religion of progress lies the possibility that the worst horrors of humanity might return. Psychoanalysis and Freudian thought have always been persecuted under dictatorships, whether communist or Nazi.

The last time was in Argentina in the 1970s…

Yes, even then, which further proves that the theory of non-freedom of the subject cannot be practiced freely in countries where democratic freedoms are suspended. For the Western subject to doubt the freedom of his consciousness, he must have the freedom to do so. Even a freedom from religious restraints is necessary, which explains why psychoanalysis has never been introduced in Islamic countries. Recently, an Algerian psychiatrist was assassinated by the Algerian Islamic Front because he had been treating women, hysterics in particular. Integralist-type religions, or dictatorships, preclude psychoanalysis. Psychoanalysis may be inscribed in the history of humanity's progress, but it is an inscription which is both critical and obscure.

Selected Bibliography

For What Tomorrow...: A Dialogue with Jacques Derrida. Palo Alto: Stanford University Press, 2004.

Why Psychoanalysis? New York: Columbia University Press, 2003.

Jacques Lacan. New York: Columbia University Press, 1999.

Madness and Revolution: The Lives and Legends of Theroigne De Mericourt. London: Verso, 1993.

Jacques Lacan & Co.: A History of Psychoanalysis in France, 1925–1985. Chicago: Chicago University Press; London: Free Associations Books, 1990.

PSYCHOANALYSIS IN AMERICA

Otto Kernberg

OTTO F. KERNBERG was born in Vienna in 1928. He emigrated with his family to Chile in 1939 to escape Nazism, and there studied biology, medicine and psychiatry before training as a psychoanalyst with the Chilean Psychoanalytic Society. He first went to the United States in 1959 on a Rockefeller Foundation fellowship to study and do research with Jerome Frank; he later joined, and then became director of, the C.F. Menninger Memorial Hospital and, in due course, of the Menninger Foundation's Psychotherapy Research Project. In 1976, two years after being appointed professor of clinical psychiatry at the College of Physicians and Surgeons of Columbia University, he became professor of psychiatry at Cornell University and director of the Institute for Personality Disorders of the New York Hospital-Cornell Medical Center. Past president of the International Psychoanalytical Association (1997 to 2001), Dr. Kernberg's principle contributions have been in the fields of narcissism, object relations and personality disorders.

In this conversation with Raffaele Siniscalco and *JEP* editor Sergio Benvenuto, Otto Kernberg looks at the history of psychoanalysis in the United States. Among the themes discussed are the links between American and British psychoanalysis, the influence on American psychoanalysis of establishment psychiatry, and the now-famous dispute between the American Psychoanalytic Association and American Psychological Associations over the exclusive right to train psychoanalysts. Originally published in Italian in the *Enciclopedia Multimediale delle Scienze Filosofiche*, the conversation with Dr. Kernberg appeared in the *Journal of European Psychoanalysis* n. 5 (1997) under the title 'Psychoanalysis in America'. It is here reprinted courtesy of RAI – Radiotelevisione Italiana.

* * *

Benvenuto/Siniscalco

Can you give us a brief outline of American psychoanalysis?

Otto Kernberg

American psychoanalysis very much identified with Ego psychology, an approach which dominated things from the 1940s through the 1960s. This approach came from Anna Freud and those closest to her, and was represented in the United States by the giants of American psychoanalysis: Hartmann, Kris, Loewenstein, Rapaport, Erikson, and later on by Jacobson and Mahler. Isolated psychoanalysts working in this country were influenced by the British schools of Balint, Winnicott and Fairbarn, the so-called *middle group*, on the one hand, and by the school of Melanie Klein, on the other. The latter constituted an opposite polarity to the school of Anna Freud, and the 'middle group' was so called because it fell between the two. But, beyond these isolated influences, Ego psychological thinking in the United States had a near-monopoly. The strong animosity in England between the school of Anna Freud and that of Melanie Klein was transplanted to the United States, where Anna Freud's group dominated totally.

This changed under the influence of Heinz Kohut, who originated 'Self psychology', which questioned many of the tenets of the theory and technique of Ego psychology. Despite the fact that his approach has always been in the minority, his influence was very important because – in contrast to earlier divisions within psychoanalysis in this country, which led to a total separation of certain schools from the Ego-psychological mainstream – Heinz Kohut's group remained within the American Psychoanalytical Association (APA). The largest association of psychoanalysis in the United States, the APA grouped between thirty and forty psychoanalytic institutes and societies in various cities, and was also almost exclusively medical. This resulted from the decision in 1938 of the International Psychoanalytic Association (IPA) to give the APA the exclusive rights for training in the United States; a right which was practically restricted to physicians.

When, in the 1970s, Kohut's Self psychology remained within the APA, a monopoly was no longer possible. Other important currents started to develop, and American psychoanalysis became multi-centered. Ego psychology, although still dominant, has since begun to incorporate some of the tendencies from other emergent schools. In the United States a culturalist psychoanalytic school centered around the teachings of Harry Stack Sullivan also existed – one that gathered important psychoanalysts like Otto Will, Harold Searles, Frieda von Reichmann, Edith Weigert, Karen Horney and others. This group bore different degrees of closeness or distance from the American mainstream, but nevertheless constituted a separate influence for many years.

In the 1970s, the ideas of culturalist psychoanalysis began to enter the psychoanalytic mainstream, and there now exists a so-called interpersonal psychoanalysis, an important current rooted in the culturalist psychoanalytic school, but influenced also by Ego psychology, and by British theories. The latter have entered this country under the broad terminology of 'British object relations theories', which include both the schools of Melanie Klein and of Winnicott. So there now exists in American psychoanalysis a theoretical and technical opening to all these orientations.

French psychoanalysis is still relatively absent or little known. This regards both the Lacanian school and the French psychoanalytic societies that, unlike Lacan, remained within the IPA and, in reaction to Lacan, developed a very special 'French' approach. This approach, despite some influences from the British schools, is mostly centered around its own distinguished French theoreticians and clinicians (i.e., Didier Anzieu and Jean Laplanche), but is still quite unknown in the United States. Exceptions are the works of André Green, of Janine Chasseguet-Smirgel (who has contributed to the study of the ego ideal, perversion and early development), and of Joyce McDougall. The American attitude demands clarity and precision, hence the very strong criticism and rejection in general of Lacan's ideas and writings, which are almost purposefully obscure. But, in my view, some of his ideas are very interesting, particularly his early contributions, which contain less of the willful mystification found in his later work.

So, the general tendency in American psychoanalysis today is toward a greater theoretical openness, with a willingness to learn from differences rather than insisting on the dogmatic discussions of the past.

With which of the trends originating in England does American psychoanalysis have a special link?

During the last decade or so the Kleinian approach – which was totally rejected by Ego psychology, and used to be considered un-American – has enjoyed increasing interest, as have the ideas of the independent group, inspired by Fairbairn and Winnicott. Winnicott is widely accepted today, and through his contributions to child analysis, object-relations theory has come to be integrated into American psychoanalysis. The Kleinian approach still has rather small roots and few contributors, although some Kleinian ideas have come to be incorporated, particularly by those American psychoanalysts working with sicker patients with severe personality disorders, whose serious regression in the transference illustrates some of the primitive mechanisms that Melanie Klein and her school explained and taught. The ideas of authors such as Wilfred Bion, Herbert Rosenfeld, Hanna Segal and Betty Joseph are now beginning to enter the United States. Increasing contacts with the international psychoanalytic community has made object relations theories, and European and Latin-American psychoanalytic thinking in general, better-known.

Italian, Spanish and Portuguese psychoanalytic contributions, with very few exceptions, are almost unknown, because these languages are affected even more than French by the language barrier. One exception is the important Italian study by Jacqueline Amati Mehler, Jorge Canestri and Simona Argentieri, *The Babel of the Unconscious,* on the influence of polylinguistic capabilities on the psychoanalytic process. But the interest in this study is almost an exception that confirms the rule. Another important contributor, Ignacio Matte Blanco, from Chile (but who emigrated to Italy), claims a small but dedicated group of followers in this country. Important contributions from Scandinavian, German speaking and Latin-American countries are generally hardly known.

So, psychoanalysis in its development has suffered from these linguistic barriers. English has been more than a *lingua franca,* it has been really a monopolistic language. And one of my intentions as future president of the IPA is to foster translations from other languages into English, to strengthen the presence of European and Latin American psychoanalytic thinking in North America.

In scientific fields, English is the language that everybody uses. Why is this not so among psychoanalysts?

The large majority of psychoanalysts have been professionals in private practice, and only a minority have been actively involved in academic or research centers, where this function of English is understood. Thus, many psychoanalytic publications operate only in the original language, and many psychoanalysts don't speak English. But another major problem is a certain reluctance on the part of English-speaking psychoanalysts to learn foreign languages. This is changing, but not fast enough.

A very influential opinion among European psychoanalysts accuses American analysis of being politically conservative, aiming as it does to adapt patients to their social environment, to conformist ideals. Is this accusation justified?

It is partially justified: the early generation of Ego psychologists of this country (in particular Hartmann) insisted, theoretically and technically, on adaptation to the environment, on psychoanalysis becoming a general psychology, on the adaptive functions of the psychic apparatus for the individual, and on the adaptive functions of defensive operations. Psychoanalysis became very fashionable in the United States, sweeping through the universities and the departments of psychiatry in the 1950s and the 1960s; this produced a conservative atmosphere within psychoanalytic institutes, and a tendency to adjust to the cultural norms of society.

But the accusation is only partially true. Some American psychoanalysts strongly criticized this tendency, and were concerned with the revolutionary nature of the knowledge of the unconscious. There were counter-currents, in theory and technique: Margaret Mahler, Edith Jacobson, Otto Fenichel and Hans Loewald (from a different existential viewpoint) all criticized this adaptive quality of American psychoanalysis. Today the approach is less conformist: interpersonal psychoanalysis, in particular, questions conventional adaptation, accenting the importance of subjectivity and intersubjectivity; and Kleinian psychoanalysis insists on the importance of the primitive manifestations of libidinal and aggressive drives. So, conservatism never was as absolute and complete as, for example, you find in the Lacanian or in the counter-culture critique of 1968.

Since the 1930s, what has been the relationship between American psychoanalysis and psychiatry? Has psychiatry's shift toward a biological and neurological approach influenced the practice and theories of analysts in this country?

There have been important shifts in the overall psychiatric climate. American psychiatry has always tended to focus on the psycho-social aspects of psychological functioning and psychiatric illness. Pure neuropsychiatry, the organistic tradition of Europe, never became firmly established here because of innate American optimism: the possibility to change people, the determinacy of the environment, all of which was signaled by the psychobiology of Adolf Meyer and his followers.

Psychoanalysis built upon this and 'invaded' the United States in the 1930s, becoming very strong in university, psychiatric and cultural circles of the 1940s and 1950s. This was the result not just of its emphasis on the unconscious to the detriment of biological determinance, but also because of its emphasis on subjectivity, on the existential approach to psychological illness, and on its early links to surrealist anti-objectivist currents dominating both European and American culture at the end of World War II. Psychoanalysis strongly influenced American psychiatry to the extent that in the 1960s, the leading psychiatric institutions and departments of psychiatry – Harvard, Yale, UCLA and even Johns Hopkins under John Whitehorn – all had a strong psychoanalytic orientation. At one point, the Menninger Foundation, a private psychiatric institution that represented the very core of Ego psychology psychoanalysis, trained 8 percent of all the psychiatrists in the United States. So, most departments of psychiatry were under the leadership either of psychoanalysts or psychiatrists very favorable to psychoanalysis.

This changed in the 1970s, slowly at first and then dramatically, and the pendulum swung towards the other extreme in the 1980s and early 1990s. Now, a few years later, we are returning to a more balanced view and the pendulum is already swinging back toward the center.

A first major reason for that change: psychoanalysis exaggerated its claims regarding knowledge and therapeutic success. Psychoanalysis focused on symptomatic neurosis, on character pathology, on the relatively milder psychiatric illnesses, while not being of fundamental help to the more severe, chronic psychotic, and mentally retarded patients who constituted a large number of inmates in state institutions.

Moreover, the development of biological psychiatry, and in particular of psychopharmacology — due to the positive results obtained with the psychopharmacological treatment of chronic schizophrenic illness, of manic depressive psychosis, and later of depression and anxiety at all levels – brought about the possibility of putting thousands of patients back into the community. The developments of biological psychiatry have excited departments of psychiatry, and gained a strong ascendance among researchers. In addition, psychoanalytic institutes became very conservative, rigid and dogmatic, isolated themselves from the university, and took on a kind of adversarial role with relation to biological psychiatry. This initially made it difficult for biological psychiatry to gain acceptance, but when it eventually did triumph, it led to an isolation and rejection of psychoanalysis, which by the late 1980s was practically eliminated as a major force from most departments of psychiatry in this country. At the same time, psychiatric residencies and training leaned ever more toward biological psychiatry, losing interest in psychoanalysis. So, the combination of new discoveries in psychobiology, the nature of the patient population not covered by psychoanalytic efforts, and the conservatism of psychoanalytic institutes in those years, all led to a gradual decrease of the influence of psychoanalysis within the university and the world of psychiatry.

At this point, the situation has reached an equilibrium: the best psychiatric training centers are aware of the fact that you cannot neglect psychodynamics and normal psychological functioning. In my view, neurobiology and psychoanalysis are two basic sciences of normal and abnormal psychology, and they are mutually enriching; eliminating one altogether impoverishes the field. The boundary between the mental and the physical is the most interesting aspect not only of psychology but also of psychiatry. And so, psychoanalysis is now gradually being recognized as a highly specialized aspect of normal and abnormal psychology, and not as an overwhelming science that can incorporate all others; the same is true for neurobiology.

Another consequence of this shift in psychiatry has been a decrease in the interest of psychiatrists in psychoanalytic training. So, following the enormous interest in psychoanalytic training in the 1950s and 1960s, there was a dramatic decrease in the number of psychiatrists entering psychoanalytic training.

Until a few years ago, the American Psychoanalytic Association accepted only medical psychiatrists for its own psychoanalytic training; only following a court sentence was the APA forced, in 1989, to open its doors to non-MD analysts. Do you think the old politics, which aimed at a complete medicalization of psychoanalysis contrary to what Freud himself upheld, improved the quality of American psychoanalysis, or harmed it?

Since the 1980s, psychoanalytic institutes here become interested in training more than just psychiatrists. In the United States, strong institutes inspired and directed by clinical psychologists developed their own psychoanalytic education and thinking, institutes which had been excluded from the IPA because of the 1938 agreement between the IPA and the APA, which gave the APA exclusive training rights in the United States, and exclusive rights for membership in the IPA. These important and creative institutes, having successfully challenged this infamous legal process, opened up membership in the IPA and the APA institutes to psychologists. This was a very positive development. I had personally felt critical of the exclusion of clinical psychologists from psychoanalytic training, the reason being that the level of training of clinical psychologists in this country is excellent, probably the best training in clinical psychology in the world, not only for clinical skills, but also for research methodology, which is not as intensively taught in medical schools. Residents in psychiatry once again became interested in psychoanalysis to complement their training, and this has contributed to balancing out and renewing interest in psychoanalytic training, at least in some of the leading psychiatric centers, as we can see in New York very clearly.

American psychoanalysts feared that opening up to psychology would demedicalize psychoanalysis. But other fields of medicine, where psychologists are doing crucial research work, such as physiology, pharmacology, biology, and the basic sciences in general, have not become demedicalized. The relationship between psychoanalysis and medicine will depend on the scientific value of psychoanalysis, on its capacity to explain normal and abnormal psychic functioning and development. If psychoanalysis has something fundamental to contribute to the understanding of these areas of normality and abnormality, it will continue to have a strong bridge to medicine and to psychiatry. Psychoanalysis needs to expand its relationship both to psychiatry and psychology, and the humanities, and not to link itself exclusively to any particular specialization, because psychoanalysis has boundary functions with many other sciences; for example, the psychoanalytic theory of drives and the neurobiology of affects are intimately linked. Treating patients in psychoanalysis requires making differential diagnoses with all kinds of other psychological and psychiatric conditions, which requires an intimate relation with psychiatry. Opening up to non-psychiatrists will not demedicalize the field.

What is your opinion of the Diagnostic and Statistical Manual of Mental Disorders (DSM) on which you collaborated? Do you think that the DSM IV has assimilated or misunderstood the contributions of psychoanalysis?

DSM III and DSM IV have positively influenced the development of uniform, operationalized definitions and delimitation of major psychiatric symptoms. But it is an irregular classification, with some excellent and other not so excellent areas. Unfortunately, the poorest area in DSM III and IV is that involving personality disorders and symptomatic neuroses, the field in which psychoanalysis has the most to say.

The DSM wants to classify descriptively major syndromes in an atheoretical way, although what is called atheoretical very often reflects a non-acknowledged theory underlying a somewhat simplistic empiricism and a non-acknowledged bias against psychoanalysis. Some of its significant weaknesses derived from its effort to dismantle psychoanalytic semiology and classification: here it lacks the direct clinical relevance that the DSM classification has in other areas. The area of personality disorders is particularly weak in the DSM III; DSM IV has corrected some of the shortcomings, but has others.

It will take quite some time before the DSM system incorporates psychoanalytic knowledge. So, DSM has had both positive and negative influences. Efforts are now underway to modify and enrich DSM IV with the incorporation of psychodynamic findings, and we will see significant changes in our classification system by the time it gets to DSM V and VI.

What has been American psychoanalysis's relationship to the great intellectual figures and movements of recent decades which have in some way drawn on psychoanalysis? I'm thinking of figures like Erich Fromm, Herbert Marcuse and Christopher Lasch, or of Marxist, women's, gay and ethnic studies...

Psychoanalysis has been intimately linked with many cultural currents, and psychoanalytic methodology has been used, both here and in Europe, in an attempt to understand different cultures, including primitive societies. For example, Parin and Morgenthaler in Switzerland have studied West African tribes in a psychoanalytic way.

At the same time, there has been what I consider a more questionable tendency to use psychoanalysis as a universal remedy for social, cultural and political conflict, which I think is utopian. This is a kind of very American cultural optimism that Erich Fromm, although of German origin, represents. So while the Utopian utilization of psychoanalysis has been questioned, it still forms part of the critique of American psychoanalysis as being too adaptive and conventional.

Psychoanalysis of course did have links with existentialism and surrealism, but these have been relatively weak in the United States. Herbert Marcuse used a psychoanalytic approach to discuss the repressive nature of the capitalist system, linking a psychoanalytic perspective with a Marxist one. Of course, a very particular counter-culture approach led him to talk about a repressive de-repression of sexuality as an escape from social conflict, and he linked this with a utopian revolutionary approach to the totalitarian developments as he saw them within both capitalism and communism. He was very critical of the Russian regime as well as of Western democracy.

European Marxists had a more sophisticated approach. The Frankfurt school in particular tried to link psychoanalytic thinking with socialist thought, considering psychoanalysis a science that could be incorporated in what they called a 'critical approach' to social conflict, the influence of which has continued to this day in France, Germany and Italy. At the same time, the utopian tendency to apply psychoanalysis to the social sciences has been a strong temptation for social psychologists. Important psychoanalytic theoreticians have warned against the adaptive aspect of psychoanalysis, stressing that one of Freud's fundamental contributions was his insistence on the pervasiveness, the unavoidability, and the profound nature of aggression in the individual and in society. French theoreticians, especially André Green, have focused on the importance of aggression as a basic human reality that operates in self-destructive ways within the individual, groups and nations. This is a potentially interesting contribution of psychoanalysis to the social sciences, and runs counter to the optimistic, social-psychological, Marxist-inspired approach.

In short: psychoanalysis has made important contributions to social psychology, even if its Marxist elements have been criticized in recent years particularly in light of the disenchantment with Communist regimes. And psychoanalysis has important contributions yet to make in understanding the development of irridentist and cultist ideologies inspired by severe, aggressive tendencies: one thinks of the mass murders of Pol Pot's regime, of the Shining Path in Peru, the small religious extremists and cults in this country and the Maoist terrorist groups in Europe and the Middle East.

Psychoanalysis can tell us something about the psychology of these groups, and also about important social phenomena where intense violence prevails – as in the inner cities of this country. Psychoanalysis was also incorporated into Eurocommunist theories in France, where Althusser drew inspiration from Lacan. Lacan's sharp critique of the American adaptational psychoanalytic style, the revolutionary nature of psychoanalysis itself, and Lacan's closeness to surrealism made the Marxist left, particularly in France, become interested in psychoanalysis. And Althusser, a major theoretician of the communist party, incorporated Lacanian thinking into a psychoanalytic perspective on ideology: the capitalist ideology was part of the infantile Super-Ego. This fell apart with the downfall of Communist doctrine in Western Europe. Of course, in the Soviet Union all of this was completely forbidden; as an aside, there is now a budding interest in psychoanalysis in Russia and in Eastern Europe.

About feminism. On the one hand, more than in probably most other sciences, several major psychoanalytic theoreticians were women: Melanie Klein, Anna Freud, Edith Jacobson, Margaret Mahler, Clara Thompson, to name just a few. Freud himself, in his revolutionary questioning of bourgeois morality, contributed to the theoretical dismantling of traditional bourgeois culture with its patriarchal aspects. From this viewpoint, psychoanalysis has had a pro-feminist approach. On the other hand, Freud was undoubtedly influenced by conventional views on male and female roles, and held certain beliefs that were strongly questioned by feminist psychoanalysts: for example, that women had a less developed super-ego than men. While Freud described women's irrational feelings of inferiority in connection with the fantasy of infantile penis envy, he left an uncertainty as to what extent these were pathological fantasies or whether all sexuality really was centered around the penis. This led to a strong critique of Freud's description of female psychology by leading psychoanalysts, ranging from Melanie Klein and Edith Jacobson to all the culturalist psychoanalysts, such as Chasseguet-Smirgel, or Clara Thompson in this country – basically, the entire cadre of major contributors to the understanding of the psychodynamics of women. So within psychoanalysis, the traditional patriarchal attitude which influenced early psychoanalytic thinking was met by strong opposition on the part of later psychoanalytic theoreticians. Lacan, who strongly supported feminist ideology, developed a notion of the archaic Oedipal complex that completely reformulated some psychoanalytic ideas on early development and became the theoretical basis of a psychoanalytic feminism, particularly in France and Germany, and to some extent in the United States.

So, in general there is a growing confluence and harmony between feminist strivings and psychoanalytic theory. Of course, feminism encompasses a broad spectrum ranging from the demand for social, economic and cultural equality for women, to the declaration, by some extreme lesbian theoreticians in the United States, proclaiming a self-contained femininity, wherein all sexual intercourse is rape. But the mainstream of feminism deals with a more objective study of commonalities and differences in psychological developments in order to study the mutual relationships bewteen the sexes, without using an ideology of female superiority to respond to traditional patriarchal psychology.

In this sense, psychoanalysis has been very important in providing a theoretical and clinical basis for reviewing traditional views about the psychology of women, the nature of sexual relations and intimate relations. I myself have tried to bring together some of these psychoanalytic studies in a book titled *Love Relations* that I published in 1995.

There is currently a big controversy within psychoanalysis about the nature of homosexuality. To what extent is homosexuality a normal form of sexual development that parallels heterosexuality, or to what extent is it always a pathological development which raises the question of its causes and origins. Intense studies are going on, in both the biological and the psychodynamic fields, with opinions sharply divided. Traditionally, psychoanalysis has viewed homosexuality as always pathological. Nowadays, many psychoanalysts believe that homosexuality operates along a broad spectrum, with its causes varying from biological to psychological, in varying degrees of combination in each individual, and that in general, psychological causes are much more important than biological; I agree with this perspective.

Clinically, we now know that there does not exist only one type of homosexuality, but rather a broad spectrum ranging from patients who are very sick, to those who are practically normal, if you exclude their sexual orientation as part of the definition of abnormality. There are differences also in the homosexuality of men and women: in men, there is generally a sharper divide between homosexual and heterosexual identities, so that in men bisexuality is usually coupled with significant character pathology. By contrast, in women there are more graded transitions between homosexuality and heterosexuality, a continuum which makes it easier to see a group of women at the transitional field, with nothing abnormal except for a flexible orientation towards homosexuality or heterosexuality. What I say here is, of course, a simplification, as things are much more complex.

Why this difference between men and women? Again, we have no definite answer. It may derive from early identification. Some psychoanalytic theoreticians believe that it may derive from the infant's early, first identification with the mother, which makes female identity stronger than that of the male. Women can more freely tolerate, and not be threatened by, homosexual impulses than men, unless they are homosexuals. Another theory proposes that there are cultural reasons derived from traditional patriarchal society which strongly opposes male homosexuality to female infidelity (in contrast to matriarchal society which opposes male infidelity and incest) that make homosexuality so forbidden and suppressed that the transition between homosexuality and heterosexuality does not appear in males. Clearly, in this field, all research is influenced by ideological features.

The large majority of psychoanalysts probably still feel that there are biological and unconscious tendencies to bisexuality, and that the individual becomes oriented and fixated to either a homosexual or heterosexual direction in the first five years of life. Up to this point most analysts would agree. But opinions are sharply divided between psychoanalysts for whom a homosexual definition always indicates a psychological pathology, a non-resolution of the normal Oedipal challenges and conflicts, and a minority for whom homosexuality may in itself be as normal a solution to Oedipal issues as a heterosexual one.

The position that homosexuality is a normal variant is perhaps most importantly represented in the United States. The traditional position – all homosexuality is an illness to be treated and changed – is represented by Charles Socarides. I very much agree with Richard Friedman's intermediate position, which insists on a broad spectrum approach on biological as well as psychodynamic features, and on a willingness to leave controversial questions open until we have more information, from both clinical psychoanalytic, as well as other, areas of research.

Ethnic issues. Psychoanalysis can contribute to understanding the psychologies of ethnic minorities, of persecution and racial bias. Psychoanalytic contributions to the understanding of ideology and individual super-ego formation; and of identifications with national, social, racial, religious or political groups; and of how regressive phenomena may bring about splitting between in-group and out-group (and generate enormous paranoid tensions and aggression in conflict) are still not fully explored. But to understand does not necessarily mean to control. One can of course apply psychoanalytic thinking to the particular ideological formation that impacts certain national, social or racial groups as a consequence of their particular sociocultural circumstances. But psychoanalysis's contribution to understanding social conflicts should not be interpreted as a way to resolve conflicts, even if other sciences can use that understanding to try to find solutions. So, while I do not underestimate the potential of psychoanalytic thinking, I am concerned about overestimating this potential, and the disappointment that necessarily ensues.

Is there any relationship or dialogue between American psychoanalysis and other forms of psychotherapy influential in the United States of America today? Do American psychoanalysts always consider themselves the aristocratic elite of psychotherapy, or are they often interested in the theoretical and practical contributions from other schools?

The contemporary attitude of American psychoanalysts is that psychoanalytic psychotherapy is of great value for particularly severe personality disorders that have contra-indications for psychoanalysis proper, or for mild conditions that may be helped by a psychoanalytically inspired psychotherapy without having to undergo a long psychoanalysis. Psychoanalysis has derived psychotherapeutic techniques. I myself and my research group have over many years developed a psychoanalytic psychotherapy for borderline conditions. Using brief procedures, we have also applied these psychoanalytic psychotherapies to couple and group psychotherapy, to family therapy, and certainly these procedures have influenced systemic group psychotherapy, which has a psychoanalytic background. There are also growing contacts between psychoanalytic psychotherapy, on the one hand, and cognitive behavioral therapy on the other, in the treatment of a specific patient group. For example, research has shown that cognitive and dialectic behavior therapy – a particular method of combined cognitive and behavioral therapy – is very effective with chronically suicidal borderline patients, who also respond very well to psychoanalytic psychotherapy. The effects and methods are different; there is growing interest for comparing psychotherapeutic approaches to learn what kind of symptoms respond or don't respond to each approach, and through which mechanisms.

The relationship between schools is opening up, with less elitist thinking going on and more appreciation of the fact that modified psychoanalytic psychotherapy may be the treatment of choice for many patients. So psychoanalysis as a technique has an enormous capability for generating psychotherapeutic techniques with individuals, groups and families, and these techniques are being developed in various areas in this country, as well as in Europe.

Because we know better about indications and contraindications, we know that certain significant personality disorders are best treated by psychoanalysis. One might say, psychoanalysis represents a major surgery, to be reserved for certain cases, but for those cases able to obtain more improvement and change than any other methods of treatment. The Psychotherapy Research Project of the Menninger Foundation, directed first by Dr. Robert Wallenstein and then by myself for many years, found that where psychoanalysis is really an optimal indication, its effects are by far superior to other methods of treatment.

Why has American psychoanalysis focused especially on narcissism? Is it perhaps the most prevalent type of pathology in the United States?

It is quite prevalent, although I don't know whether more so in the United States than in other countries. It was a natural development because Ego psychology was very interested in character pathology, which means personality disorders. My work has contributed a little in this direction, but important contributions have also been made by other ego psychological authors: Andy Reich, Edith Jacobson, Helen Tartakoff, Herman Bandavals, etc. Social psychologist Christopher Lasch's use of the psychoanalytic theory of narcissism to explain aspects of American culture contributed enormously to generalize the concept. But the exact relationship between a narcissistic culture and a narcissistic individual pathology is not clear. It is tempting to describe certain cultures in terms of certain pathologies of character, but one must keep in mind that while character may be influenced by culture, these relationships are more indirect and complex than meets the eye. For example, to say that the Victorian age, with its sexual repression, produced a hysterical culture is a fine first approach, but it misses the complexity of sexuality during the Victorian era. Or to say that czarist Russia had a culture of depressive personalities may say something about Russian psychology, but again it misses the complexity. Certainly a consumer society like the American one appeals to consumers' narcissistic wishes, but from there to describe the culture as narcissistic is a big step. So there are, I'd say, more indirect and complex connections between American consumerism and narcissistic personalities.

Selected Bibliography

'A Concerned Critique of Psychoanalytic Education', *Int. J. Psychoanal.*, 2000, 81, pp. 97–120.

Ideology, Conflict and Leadership in Groups and Organizations (1998). New Haven, Yale University Press.

Love Relations: Normality and Pathology (1995). New Haven: Yale University Press.

Aggression in Personality Disorders and Perversions (1992). New Haven: Yale University Press

Severe Personality Disorders: Psychotherapeutic Strategies (1984). New Haven: Yale University Press.

Internal World and External Reality (1980). New York: Jason Aronson.

Object Relations Theory and Clinical Psychoanalysis (1976). New York: Jason Aronson.

Borderline Conditions and Pathological Narcissism (1975). New York: Jason Aronson.

THE 'IMPOSSIBLE' TRAINING OF ANALYSTS

Elvio Fachinelli

ELVIO FACHINELLI, MD (1928–1989) was a 'dissident' psychoanalyst in Milan where, in the 1970s, he founded the important counter-culture journal *L'erba Voglio*. For many years he also published a series of witty 'psychopolitical' articles in the popular Italian weekly *L'Espresso*, establishing a strong link between psychoanalysis and the emancipation movements of the time. Although he remained a member of the official IPA-affiliated Italian Psychoanalytic Society (SPI), in 1969 Fachinelli led a public protest against the psychoanalytic establishment, which he strongly criticized for its conservatism. He was also one of Italy's foremost translators of Freud, responsible for the translation of *The Interpretation of Dreams* as well as other texts in the Standard Edition. Among his most daring and important works – all untranslated into English, save for occasional excerpts appearing in the *Journal of European Psychoanalysis* – are the books *La Freccia Ferma* (1979), *Claustrofilia* (1983) and *La Mente Estatica* (1989), all published by the prestigious Adelphi Edizioni (Milan).

In this conversation dating from the 1980s, *JEP*'s Sergio Benvenuto explores with Fachinelli the state of psychoanalysis in Italy at the time, highlighting particular possibilities for crisis beyond any national borders. In a thorough critique of the training system of the Italian Psychoanalytic Society (which was/is, in fact, common to most psychoanalytic societies), Fachinelli questions the very notion of 'training analysis', reaffirming the autonomy of the analytic relationship against all professional controls and requirements for 'proper' training. In this light, he also examines the shortcomings of the alternative strategy of the *passe* put forth by Jacques Lacan, a friend of his whom he squarely confronted on such matters.

This interview with Fachinelli, titled 'The Impossible Training of Analysts', while yet to appear in the *Journal of European Psychoanalysis*, holds a special meaning for its editors. Excerpted from a slightly longer conversation included in the volume *La Bottega Dell'Anima* (S. Benvenuto and O. Nicolaus, eds. Rome: FrancoAngeli, 1990), it appears here for the first time in English translation, courtesy of FrancoAngeli Editore.

* * *

Sergio Benvenuto

You are a member of both the Italian Psychoanalytical Society (SPI), and of the International Psychoanalytic Association. In the SPI, as in other IPA societies, there is a hierarchy that ranks its affiliates, moving from candidates to associates to full members…

Elvio Fachinelli

I do belong to the SPI, but only as an associate. In fact about half of the full members are also training analysts…

You're known to be hostile to the role of training analyst…

A few years ago, at an assembly of the SPI, I proposed we abolish the role of training analyst. I did so partly because the role of training analyst is not, or at least was not, even universally instituted in all the societies adhering to the IPA. A commission was then set up to study the matter, which I presided over for two or three years – following which it was disbanded, without having accomplished anything. Since then things have worsened, and the society has become even more hierarchical! Yet even in this situation, I still did not want to leave the SPI, given my origins there: Musatti[1], you know, was my analyst, and perhaps a transferential residue, or one might say an affection, kept me there, together with the wish to avoid being ostracised. I remained resolved, however, not to climb the career ladder, but to persist in the 'lateral' position of associate. This was a provocation, if you like, something that many imbeciles who have since passed me by in the hierarchy do not even understand. But to me it seemed consistent with an attitude I have always maintained vis-a-vis the society.

How does one enter the SPI? And how does one climb that career ladder?

Every year one pays membership dues, like in any other club. If someone does not pay, after a few years he is considered to have resigned. But very

1 Cesare Musatti (1897–1989) was one of the founders of the SPI in 1936, together with Edoardo Weiss, Marco Levi-Bianchini, Emilio Servadio and Nicola Perrotti. At the time of the interview he was the most celebrated Italian psychoanalyst in Italy, also due to his frequent and successful TV appearances.

few people do indeed resign. In order to pass from one level to the next one makes a series of case presentations and in this way gradually climbs the ladder, moving from candidate to associate to full member and, ultimately, to *training analyst*. In the course of this itinerary nearly everyone – and especially those closer to the top of the ladder – is subjected to a set of arbitrary criteria of co-optation. Personally, I have never taken any of the necessary steps to move beyond the level of associate. I've continued to write and publish on my own, refusing to play such a game and involve myself in procedures where bureaucracy and infantilism are so combined.

If it is the structure that you disagree with, why propose the abolition of the role of training analyst rather than a restructuring of the whole process?

Because a differentiation between those who've worked as analysts for a year or two and those who've done so for five, seven or more years does not seem pointless to me. That which is still called a 'training analysis' out of habit should indeed be conducted by an experienced analyst – who ought not, however, need to belong to a sort of corporation of *training analysts*. Upon completing his analysis, the person wishing to enter the psychoanalytical society should make his application and the society should be free to accept or refuse him. Then, once admitted, one enters fully, without the extent of one's rights being dependent on the need to rack up more and more points along the way. All this while the analysis itself should, ideally, not be subjected to any institutional evaluation or control.

There is often, even if rarely evidenced, a desire to become part of the constituted order. But the desire for one's training analysis to function as a gateway into the psychoanalytical society should be minimal, and should itself be subject to analytic scrutiny. Instead the existence of a privileged circle of training analysts gives the analysis a sort of preliminary *imprimatur*, a sort of guarantee that carries with it a right to enter the society – which is an obstacle to the process of analysis itself. And this is so whether the training analyst is directly involved in the admission procedure, or whether he is not (as is the case in the Italian society). The training analyst himself, precisely because of his privileged status, is too often concerned that his own students or protégés be admitted. This is something that radically falsifies the analytical process. Perhaps instead of 'training analysis' we should use the term 'pseudo-analysis', for the former is but one of the several kinds of pseudo-analysis existing today.

Your proposal to eliminate the role of training analyst ends up putting the very concept of training analysis into question. For example, in one of Italy's

Jungian associations, positions prevail that are similar to yours: for example, there is no distinction made between a training analysis and an ordinary analysis. Some Jungians even go so far as saying that so-called training analyses are a fraud…

I maintain this paradox: every personal analysis is a training analysis in the sense that if the analysis proceeds, the patient inevitably assumes the position of analyst. If you learn a craft you will be able to do what you want with it, whether you become an analyst or not, with one exception: which is precisely that of the training analysis. This is because the training analysis is strongly conditioned by an external goal: namely, admission into the SPI country club, or other similar societies, which by definition can only falsify the process.

An analyst of the SPI once made the claim – citing his barber, who in turn was referring to an apprentice of his – that 'a craft has to be stolen'. In other words, it is not a mere matter of teaching: a pupil must learn what to do from one who is more experienced. Still, in the SPI it is necessary to have interviews with three training analysts before being accepted into analysis and, subsequently, into training…

In the very moment someone is interviewed by a training analyst – no matter the number of interviews – he is looking to be co-opted into the psychoanalytical society. As regards the criteria with which one is accepted or not, these are always and invariably extra-analytical, based as they are on impressions, intuitions, idiosyncrasies... or on that which the training analyst considers his personal intuition, not unlike a dog sniffing out truffles... It is evident that faced with this first passage of the psychoanalytical Aereopagus the candidate will be extremely prudent, and certain to act in a contrived way. He will do his best to find out what it is that each examiner looks for, in order to always make the best possible impression. He will be sure to put his best foot forward, or show his most seductive mask, or simply just an 'average' face, that won't reveal any dangerous peculiarities… This is one of the passages in which psychoanalysis becomes a form of comedy, which could easily lend itself to a theatrical or movie script…

After such an entrance exam, if the candidate is accepted, he will be considered *destined* to enter this society that promises him security, recognition and – *last but not least* – clients. He feels that he has been promoted to the role of analyst of the society from the very start, and from here on will be very careful not to do anything that could hinder or deter this 'destiny'…

Doesn't your own personal training also fit this pattern? On what experience do you base your claim that SPI training analyses are, paradoxically, the least formative of all?

My analysis with Cesare Musatti would probably, according to present-day criteria, be judged a 'wild' analysis, as would most analyses conducted by the first generation of psychoanalysts. And yet, in my opinion, it was a good analysis: I was often surprised, something I hold to be fundamental to every analysis. I learned a lot, and also enjoyed myself. This is certainly a merit of Musatti's, who in his best moments was an ingenious clown, a trickster who certainly did not fit the bill of the neutral or absent figure preached, but not practiced, by Freud himself. My analysis, moreover, took place at a time when the SPI had nothing of the central position it now enjoys. Back then, it was the centre of itself, not the centre of the vast psychotherapeutic nebula that has formed in recent years. The society was more similar to the first Freudian enclaves than to the bureaucratic fortress it has since become. And Musatti himself was very uncertain regarding the future of psychoanalysis, envisioning times of scarcity for his students, if not of all-out disaster.

Belonging to the SPI was much less a guarantee than it is now. In a certain sense membership was much more significant: one belonged to a work group, a research team, inhabited by different persuasions and currents of thought where each person was free to think for himself. But some very strong, and by no means diplomatic, personal skirmishes and conflicts resulted from this state of affairs. I do not wish to idealize things: the fact that belonging to the SPI of that time was different from the present situation does not mean that the society did not also contain, in its origin – albeit not in a fateful way – the seeds of the evolution that unfortunately followed. My own analysis was also negatively affected by the problem of belonging to the group. An absolutely 'pure' form of analysis does not exist. But the level of impurity reached by today's training analyses seems to me excessive, and the results, in terms of colourless mediocrity and watered-down standards, seem palpable to me.

What makes you think that today's situation is so catastrophic?

Catastrophic! What a drastic term for a situation in which the SPI exists and prospers as a strong society... and yet it seems to me that the state of things is deeply distorted and not sufficiently analyzed. Take a macroscopic piece of data: among the people that come into analysis, the idea of becoming a professional analyst is much more widespread today than it was fifteen years ago. Just consider the increasing number of psychology graduates (itself an effect of the increasing 'psychologization' of society in general), as well as the interest in psychoanalytical training not only on the part of psychiatrists, but of non-psychiatric doctors as well... All this, alongside the enormous societal demand for *professionalism* in general, has reinforced the importance of the SPI as a centre for training and belonging.

At the same time, one's *personal* relationship with analysis tends to pass into the background if compared to the prospect of a guaranteed professional training. Consequently, the SPI tends to develop as sort of association of registered professionals, like that of doctors or lawyers: an association that confers legitimacy to those who belong to it and denies or tries to deny legitimacy to those on the outside. Consider the issue of the title *psicoanalista* ('psychoanalyst') which, according to some exponents of the SPI, should be restricted to members of the society, while the rubble of therapists would only get to call themselves *psicanalisti* (without the 'o'). This is a ridiculous distinction, marking a grotesque aspiration towards legitimacy.

It nevertheless remains true that the demand for professional training is on the rise all over the world. Nowadays I myself have many more requests of this type than I did before. It is a disturbing situation: the genuine patients are disappearing while the numbers of future colleagues grow.

Many people come to you, even though you are not a training analyst. This does not seem to me the best way for them to guarantee themselves a career.

My position is one of strength and weakness at the same time. If, during a person's initial interviews with me, it becomes clear that he or she is intent on becoming an analyst, I immediately inform them that I am not a training analyst, have no intention of becoming one, and that if they want to enter the SPI they will have to go through a bureaucratic process from which I am completely extraneous. But generally the people that come to me who are thinking of becoming analysts already know this position of mine. They just want to be in analysis with me. Some of them say they have no intention of entering the SPI, while others declare that they will later on undergo a period of analysis with an official training analyst. This arrangement is a sort of double régime: *personal* analysis with me and *professional* analysis with an enabler of the society.

One might say such people turn to you to learn the art, rather than to build themselves a career...

Basically what happens is the exact opposite of what happens in a so-called training analysis. People come to me for who I am or what they imagine me to be. Others go to a training analyst for what he represents within the society. And therefore many so-called training analyses are conducted by people who are non-existent on a cultural and scientific level – at times even on a simply 'human' plane – or by outright imbeciles. But they are, nonetheless, imbeciles with a licence...

Yes, people come to me to learn the art. And herein above all is evidenced the paradoxical fact that with me one embarks on a personal analysis, in which the desire to become an analyst is explored like everything else. As is the reason they've chosen me to be their analyst – surely not the best or most favourable way to ensure a career for oneself!

What you do, in a way, is set up a workshop, in the tradition of medieval arts and trades…

It is true that the workshop, as you put it, means organizing into a group. And a group tends immediately to promote practices and ideologies which – it is no coincidence – in this context look a lot like those of the SPI. Personally, I mistrust psychoanalytical groups; indeed I mistrust most any kind of organized group, the result of negative experiences of my own. Freud wanted to set up a rigidly organized group, but he would have been better off had he explored in depth this desire of his... and he'd have been better served had he scrutinized the group itself, once he'd constituted it (rather than privately criticizing it): just as he'd done with the army, or the church. Lacan too wanted to set up a group, although on different grounds, and that outcome as well was certainly not encouraging. Basically, for me analysis is an adventure, a private journey that takes place within the bounds of a historically structured relationship, between one person who speaks as freely as possible and another who, essentially, is there to listen. Freud invented something unique, something with no historical precedent. Something that persists in the same way the Platonic dialogue persists. Psychoanalysis is a configuration within which everyone is allowed to practice, which certainly does not exhaust the range and scope of human relations and which has very little to do with those professional societies that claim to be based upon it. For them, other rules are relevant and other types of observation are necessary.

But, to come back to my own activities, I should mention that people also come to me for clinical supervision…

Does the SPI have specific rules regarding supervision as well?

No, it would be the height of absurdity if the title 'supervisor' existed... like something out of Gogol. But one cannot deny the possibility that, considering present developments, it could be created as an intermediate title somewhere between that of senior analyst and training analyst!

These people who come to ask for supervision... are they mostly people who have already been analyzed? Are they psychiatrists or doctors who work in the public sphere?

They make for a rather diversified group: doctors, psychiatrists and anti-psychiatrists too, to use the faddish terminology of some years ago. They are people who at a certain moment have asked themselves: 'What can I do to help this person in difficulty?' They consult me, together we discuss their patients, and they then proceed to work on the basis of what they can contribute within their specific contexts – and not on the basis of what they 'should' do from a strictly psychoanalytical point of view.

Do you purposely keep these supervisions brief?

I tell people from the start that it's how I work. Supervisions that drag on for years involve the same risks as training analyses: the supervisor fatally tends, whether he is aware of it or not, to impress his own stamp or style on the person being supervised. Some actually do so deliberately, and it should be said that there are many students who want to be branded in this way. With training analyses and supervisions, a relationship of a pedagogical nature, often authoritarian, easily tends to become institutionalized. And the transference as well can't help but get inflected in this sense.

It must be truly difficult for an SPI candidate or a student in training analysis to accept the fact that his analyst is also, in a way, his judge. This will provoke some distressing dilemmas, not the least of which concerns the patient's freedom to bring his or her deepest issues into the analysis: issues the analyst might consider psychotic, whether rightly or wrongly so, that will invariably conflict with the student's need to present his or her best image to the analyst-judge. That the role of analyst and the role of judge are on a collision course seems totally obvious to me...

This is also true when the figures of analyst and judge are not combined within the same person, but are 'located', so to speak, in different people. In every analysis, alongside repression and other unconscious defence mechanisms, reticence and lies get thrown into the mix. This degree of dissimulation obviously tends to be greater in institutionalized analysis.

How is it possible that the leaders of the SPI, people with a great deal of experience, do not realise things that seem so obvious to the two of us?

I think many perceive this state of affairs, but consider it to be an irresolvable problem. They recognize the existence of these distortions when they get pointed out – that is, of course, if they themselves have not already been deformed by their own identification with their role in the society. But they hold the situation to be unavoidable. They are unable to think outside of an institutional perspective. They say: 'But we have a course of study to salvage, analyses and supervisions that do manage to train people with a certain degree of proficiency'. Still, the process of training and co-optation ultimately selects dulled and smoothed-over personalities without any sharp edges: people without any obvious abnormal traits but also without any real personality. They make for a crowd of 'grey' candidates: analysts without any soul, ritualistic ghosts of analysis. This is the fundamental problem according to most lucid observers.

Are these candidates dull to start off with, or is it the training that dulls them?

In effect one asks oneself: were these 'young people', who often have grey hair and two or three children, already this way before entering analysis, or did they become this way because of analysis? It's a question to set you trembling... There are some thirty-five- or forty-year-old candidates who are always absolutely silent at meetings. I call them 'the tongueless ones'. Analysis certainly provokes situations of regression, but it should also resolve them! In these meetings (which, by the way, almost none of the training analysts attend, as if they were of no interest to them), those who present a body of work are almost always associates or senior members. Out of about fifty people present, for example, there might be thirty or thirty-five candidates and very few of them ever open their mouths.

But in Italy, even if outside the SPI, is there a vitality that counters the 'greyness' and the silence of the society?

It's hard to say. But, in Italy at least, the fact of whether one belongs or not to a 'serious' society is a mark of selectivity. This distinctive sense of belonging moves people to say: 'We may have all these hoops to jump through, all these trials and tribulations to endure, but in the end at least we'll have had the best possible training'. But this class-like system also takes its toll on those who do not directly participate in it. The former derive a sense of security from the society, while the second derive only insecurity, that goes hand-in-hand with a tendency to idealize the very society from which they are excluded. I also have the impression that, except for our Lacanian groups, which have a rather consolidated and autonomous system of references, the other psychotherapy organizations all criticize and/or imitate the SPI.

Why is the SPI so strong in Italy and why is its prestige on the increase? It seems stronger than the official societies in other countries with a long-standing psychoanalytical tradition, and yet only a few internationally recognized figures have ever come out of the SPI. Aside from Edoardo Weiss, founder of the SPI and the only Italian analyst to have enjoyed international fame (due also to the fact that he later went to the United States), no Italian analyst has ever had an international reputation: no Klein, Winnicott, Lacan, Bion, Balint or Kohut has ever come out of Italy. The most famous is perhaps Ignacio Matte Blanco who, however, is not Italian-born and otherwise writes in English.

Localism, so to speak, is a problem of Italian culture in general which, to put it succinctly, imports a lot and exports little. There are many reasons for this. In any case, it does not seem appropriate or justified to me to derive, as you seem to do, a value judgment from this. Otherwise one risks falling into the typical Italian attitude of self-denigration, which personally I far prefer to the attitude of nationalistic arrogance of the French, just to give an example, but which in the end can turn out to be harmful. We might however consider a peculiar feature of Italian psychoanalysis, which is its tendency to adopt masters from other shores. This is the case for Bion, who today is the undisputed master of psychoanalysis in Italy.

How do you explain the great popularity of Bion in Italy, which even exceeds that which he enjoys in Great Britain? There Bion is certainly considered an important analyst, but not the undisputed beacon that he is here. Some years ago the Tavistock Clinic opened a school in Rome, which is now almost more important than the original centre in London…

The status of 'undisputed beacon', as you put it, is in fact the product of an idealizing provincial insecurity, which runs the risk of not understanding the very model it adopts, and in the end diminishes and detracts from its true grandeur.

As for Kleinism, it entered Italy thanks to Franco Fornari, who introduced some themes and topics and elaborated others in original ways. One wonders if Klein's popularity in Italy might not also be connected to a generic consonance between Catholicism and the themes of guilt and depression typical of Klein. Whatever the case, in the 1950s Klein was an authentic breath of fresh air within the SPI, above all as regards the way analysis was conducted. Personally, I found the seminars of Marcelle Spira and Salomon Resnik to be very meaningful. In those years Melanie Klein had for the SPI the function of an outsider whose thought was nonetheless permitted, since all attempts to marginalize her had failed. For some years it even became fashionable to go to London to attend Kleinian courses and seminars, and even to undergo a personal analysis with an analyst of the Kleinian school. Whereas I don't think many people moved from Italy to follow Anna Freud...

Instead it was the Americans who went to find Anna Freud... But I want to come back to the people who approach you for analysis. Some elderly analysts consider the request for analytic training as a neurotic symptom to be analyzed. In fact, in order to deal with this complication Lacan proposed the formula of the 'passe'. For you is it a negative thing that an analyst may still be tackling problems that brought him to analysis in the first place?

Evidently no one has ever ended his or her analysis. To claim as much would be to admit to a sort of total transparency of an unconscious which can be tamed: a destiny for the unconscious which is certainly not to be desired! On the other hand, it must be said that a person in analysis goes only so far as his analyst can go: the impossibilities of the latter constitute the limit of the analysis that he conducts. I said: 'so far as his analyst can go', not where he actually has gone personally. I therefore admit that the analyst can transcend himself, and his own personal limitations (as indeed every human can). Otherwise I would have to accept what one often hears in analytical circles, that homosexuals or lesbians, for instance, cannot be analysts. At the same time, this problem of the limits of the analyst is a serious thing. At the moment of the passage to the position of analyst – the *passe* of Lacan – there is a personal dynamic upon which the institutional passage is superimposed, as also happens in the SPI. They are two different situations, but in practice they are assimilated – or otherwise garbled and confused with each other...

It is as if the institution arranged the 'passe' in the candidate's place, perpetuating his dependency and to some degree his lack of responsibility...

One could say so, even though the moment of *recognition* theoretically cannot be only one of self-recognition, since it always necessarily implies an Other. It is instead the modalities of this recognition that are in question. In any case, the person who does *not* wish to be an analyst has always been more interesting for me, in the first sessions at least. When a psychologist comes to me and says that he wants to be an analyst, I feel a sense of heaviness... to me he seems to be someone wanting always to remain on the same treadmill, and wanting to drag me along with him...

Nevertheless, as you've said, the percentage of people asking to undergo analysis for reasons of professional training is on the increase...

It is a widespread fact, and the numbers have increased greatly in recent years. The analyst slowly but surely becomes a machine that reproduces itself. And the people who have no intention of becoming analysts do find a way to exit this circuit, which they perceive as too long and arduous and in the end not appropriate to them. It is a process that leads to a paradoxical situation: less and less patients in the classical sense and more and more future colleagues. It is what Karl Kraus observed when he said that psychoanalysis is the symptom of the disease it proposes to cure.

But this tendency is only one side of the coin. An inverse trend also exists, one I'd call a form of 'psychoanalytical colonialism', which involves bringing the gospel of psychoanalysis out of its usual 'territory' and into the public services and national health system: marking, in this way, a passage from the patient to the consumer. I'm thinking, for example, of the genuine boom in child psychoanalysis, the therapeutic offshoot of which, in any event, is the complete opposite of the self-reproduction that characterizes institutes.

What you call psychoanalytical colonialism is also its pioneerism, or its ability to supply a *listening* – which comes before all else, and can rightly be attempted in new and different directions. I am not speaking about our theoretical baggage, which is already spread out into too many suitcases. I am speaking about an openness and willingness to receive the other, that begins historically with Freud and that represents the effective measure of the ability of an analyst, of a psychiatrist, or of anyone who operates with some degree of curiosity on this 'terrain'. This is the ambiguity of psychoanalysis, its being a sort of new passage, born in this century, that cannot be ignored even by those who operate in a completely different way. When you speak about self-reproduction and colonialism, which are certainly real phenomena, you seem to conclude that *this* is psychoanalysis. If this were so, everything would already be over and done with. But it seems to me that things are more complicated. I feel it is important that when dealing with a troubled child, rather than resorting to tranquilizers and sedatives to silence him, or to pedagogical manoeuvres, there should be someone saying: 'Wait a minute, let's allow him to *speak*, whatever his way of speaking – or not speaking – may be'. This moment of suspension and of emptiness is the wellspring of psychoanalysis as a possibility for self-awareness, and is certainly a very different model from the one in which the desire to become an analyst and enter the SPI is at issue.

Speaking about difficult children and enigmatic patients: it is well known that these most trying cases are more and more often left to the young and inexperienced analysts, while the older analysts at the top of the career ladder prefer the far easier training analyses…

That is very true. I believe that if there is no surprise in analysis, in *each of its participants*, there is no analysis at all. There is only the rediscovery of something that has already been found, and not of anything new. To solely apply technical principles does not work even in the most rigorous of settings, and it is no coincidence that in institutional analyses there is an insistence – which verges on an obsession - on the rigour of the setting and its purity, while very little emphasis is placed on the type of inner attitude every analyst ought always maintain: on the need, above all, to let oneself be taken by surprise. This is the inevitable consequence of the normative position occupied by the training analysis, conceived to be *in compliance* with certain given rules and as a *model* analysis to be replicated. And what you say about the more difficult cases corresponds exactly to the abandonment of the frontier zones by most training analysts, harassed as they are by the demands of those who want to receive the 'right' brand of training. And so they have little to say about such cases, or about the new and sometimes distressing situations that the younger analysts report to them. In these cases training analysts and supervisors issue sentences or judgments that sound like advice from old aunts.

An analyst I know, who had a Kleinian and Lacanian dual training, once pointed out that Kleinian analysts always theorize in terms of the pre-verbal, of crude and elementary feelings, but then turn out to be veritable chatterboxes in their sessions, often speaking more than their patients. This, while many Lacanians, who insist a great deal on the power of the word and exhibit a genuine logorrhoea in their conferences and seminars, often confront their analysands with thick walls of silence…

Yours is an interesting observation, and points to how systems and practitioners compensate for their respective forms of training. But here another factor also intervenes: the strength of the group, and not only of the psychoanalytical group, even though the psychoanalytical group above all others would seem to be in a position to criticize and modify the ferocious dynamics of exclusion that characterize every group. *Nulla salus extra ecclesiam...* In any case, nobody is scandalized by a citation *extra ecclesiam*, or if someone bases his work on the ideas of a reprobate. In Italy there is more tolerance, or indulgence, compared to what occurs in other societies...

In 1953 Lacan was hosted by the Italian society in Rome, when he delivered his celebrated *Discours de Rome*, precisely at the time when the war between him and the French society was raging. It is difficult to imagine an exclusion such as that practiced against Lacan taking place in Italy, even though Lacan was certainly able to seriously rattle the nerves of any society. In Italy cases of exclusion are very rare. When I organized a conference with Bertrand Rothschild in Rome in 1969 – which actually took position against the international congress being held only a few blocks away – there were lively internal debates, but colleagues never got to the point of voting for my dismissal.

What reactions do you provoke among your colleagues in the SPI, given your knack for public claims that often also end up in the press?

It depends. Some probably see me as blowing smoke, making much ado about nothing. Others, instead, are aware of the problems and situations of which I've spoken, and they respect me and are even friendly towards me. I do not feel there is any widespread hostility towards me in the SPI. Certainly there are 'institutional' differences of opinion. I do provoke the institution, and it is therefore legitimate that it should react to me. But I am not interested in the 'long journey' through the institutions in order to change them, which Rudi Dutschke spoke about in 1968; and the idea of founding a new, radically different institution has never convinced me, however stimulating or exciting it may be. Sooner or later every group generates difficult and engulfing problems. Basically I only believe in what can be achieved, over the long haul, through a person's intelligence, and with one's own limited but personal efforts – the fruits of which may then be gathered by people unexpected or even unknown! Groups, as such, are always later developments. What's important strategically is to avoid the ostracism and sectarianism of others, and to keep in check one's own tendencies towards sectarianism, closure and self-exclusion. You could say it's a matter of deploying the astuteness of Galileo, as portrayed by Brecht, when confronted by the self-assuredness of today's psychoanalytical churches…

But isn't the weakness of Lacanism in Italy due to the very fact that it has remained so diffuse? Wasn't the weakness of Lacan's École freudienne *ultimately proven by the very fact that Lacan himself closed it down?*

I do not think the *École freudienne* was a feeble institution. There is some evidence which contradicts what you say: take for example the expulsion of Luce Irigaray and the repeated internal 'purges'. But in any case it was a genuine institution, with characteristics different from orthodox ones: an institution that carried its own weight and institutional destiny.

Lacan, like Freud, wanted to found an institution of his own. I met Lacan personally in 1965, before the *Écríts* were published and before he became Lacan, so to speak, the universally famous master. For some years I kept track of what he wrote, in the magazine *La Psychanalise* and elsewhere. They were essays that one had to seek out, and for me he was a truly secret master, as he was for just a handful of others in Italy, among whom I knew Michel David, Andrea Zanzotto and Michele Ranchetti. (I still remember Fornari's disdain, when I mentioned my discovery of Lacan to him.) Well, when I personally met Lacan in Paris he immediately insisted on the necessity of setting up an *école* of his own, and of attracting disciples. I took the liberty of openly telling him that I did not see this as a necessity, and to consider my own case. I remember saying to him: 'I have come to you because of certain texts of yours, and I consider you to be a master for me, perhaps even my only one. But when you speak about an *école*, I immediately feel that I am faced with a prospect that I cannot relish or agree with. In doing this you would only repeat Freud's mistake'. But Lacan was evidently deaf to such talk.

But today, when I think of how he closed the *école* at the end, I find this gesture of his both admirable and at the same time totally futile. And I wonder if it might not have derived from the very knowledge of his mistake: the mistake of believing that his discourse, the Lacanian *text*, needed an institutional support. A support that in the end, right in the middle of a tidal wave of Lacanians, in the midst of his success, ended up isolating him and limiting his possibilities of communication. To use a definition of his, the full word became, through the Lacanian psalmody of the institution, empty.

The weakness of Lacanism in Italy can therefore also be connected, as you suggest, to the fact of not being an institution like the SPI and of being more fluid, or diffuse. But from another point of view, this weakness could have become a strength. Its articulation could have served as a radiating core, if only Lacanism had been introduced, say, as a focal and vital research centre. Instead you had the attempt to establish an institution, through Lacan's own direct initiative no less; but what resulted immediately loomed as a failure when compared to the SPI.

What do you think of his idea of the passe*?*

It was one of his best known and most controversial innovations and, at the same time, it remained quite a mysterious thing for anyone not directly involved in a Lacanian group. The strong point of this innovation consisted in its putting the moment of transition to the position of analyst – a key moment of any analysis – at the centre of everything. Lacan tried to connect this personal and autonomous moment, this moment of authentic movement, to the requirements of the institution – an institution seen, in turn, as the very guarantor of the passage's authenticity. In order to reach this objective, he invented the figure of the *passeur*, or 'witness' (a term we might also translate as *ferryman*): a witness of the *école* to whom the *passant*, or '(s)he who passes through' (who looks to be accepted into the *école*), must speak about his own analysis. The *passeur* thus finds himself in the same position as the *passant*, which is a position of *passé*; and as a result he must report to the *jury d'agrément*, or kind of admissions committee, about what he has heard, after which the jury decides whether or not to accept the *passant*.

I believe that this was Lacan's original scheme, one which immediately caused a fracture in the group and led, according to Lacan himself, to an *impasse*. Lacan basically proposed putting a distance between the institution and the candidate by means of the creation of an intermediate figure – one could call it a brother figure – who would take on the burden of testifying by proxy regarding the validity of the *passant*'s request and on whom much of the responsibility for the final decision would therefore depend, even though he would not be a member of the judging committee itself (the *jury*). The solution Lacan thought up had the admirable goal of avoiding the paternalistic and bureaucratic co-optation of the Freudian societies, but it in no way resolved the problem of the weight of the admitting society, that becomes still more intrusive and ubiquitous via the ambiguous figure of the *passeur*. The latter, in fact, incorporates all the ambiguities of figures otherwise juxtaposed: figures, to use judicial terms, like the witness to the truth, the defence witness, and the 'crown's witness' ... All this, without even citing the breach of confidentiality that takes place by speaking of one's own analysis to a stranger, or the consequences this breach has for the relationships between the various fraternal figures involved in the *passe*. It was a confused and confusing procedure, which risked creating a certain type of perverse society, in which circulating *gossip* takes on an enormous importance... a bit like the situation centuries ago in the Republic of Venice, when anonymous accusations ruled the day.

In effect Lacan realised that there was a stalemate here, and he declared as much openly. Perhaps the decision to close the *école* also derived from this knowledge. In any case I still have not heard a complete and circumstantiated report of what actually did lead up to the event. Moustapha Safouan also saw a stalemate in what amounted to a factual deficiency of the *école*, which was founded on the charisma of its leader and had, in short, become a mass movement. I do not believe this explanation in the least, intended as it was to salvage Lacan's proposal at all costs, even if at the expense of Lacan himself. I think that the stalemate was implicit in the original proposal, as the dissidents immediately pointed out.

And yet, where Italy was concerned, Lacan had originally thought of you as a privileged interlocutor, although you'd not had any analytical relationship with him. Even at the time you were known publicly for your anti-institutional stance, and you were very vocal and relentless in asking 'why should an institution even be formed?' Still Lacan came to you, asking you to become the fulcrum of a new institution! I can't help but wonder then if, in his request to you, one might not discern an ambivalence of Lacan's: on the one hand his desire to found an institution, and on the other a desire to destroy it…

The contradiction inherent in his request became apparent at the end, at the moment of the closure of his school. Perhaps it was also an enormous revelation for Lacan himself... But during his visits to Italy he certainly did not let on about any of this. He wanted very strongly to establish his school in Italy; and he definitely wanted me to be a part of it. In order to achieve this aim, he completely sidestepped my objections, which from his institutional vantage point were marginal at best; or if he did understand them, they could only pertain to other institutions, and certainly not his own... There was, clearly, a despotic aspect to Lacan, that members of the *école* experienced firsthand, and for which many still carry the scars. His contradiction consisted in the fact that, despite having spoken in an extraordinarily lucid way about the analyst as a 'subject-supposed-to-know', in the moment he directed his school and dispensed with his teachings he loomed as Knowledge itself, indeed as the only and absolute knowledge. And he himself would proudly assert as much.

Nevertheless you seem to be still very interested in the history of Lacanism, without having been an actual follower of Lacan.

Well, it was enough to read ten lines of Lacan to realise that he soared high above the majority of contemporary analysts – or to sense that his flight was taking him elsewhere! His idea of founding psychoanalysis as a science of meaning was certainly partial because, by his own admission, it cut out a significant part of what happens in analysis. But it was a new, original, and compelling idea. Lacan is an altogether complicated and baroque text... indeed, curiously enough and at a distance, he makes for a sort of fantastic poem, like Berlioz where music is concerned... a poem that takes inspiration from every aspect of culture... the effect is a strange one, for a man who tried his whole life to found a rigorous science. In any case, it is this text or poem that has kept me interested in Lacan, much more so than his societies and schools. His invention of the *passe* seemed to me, looking in from the outside, to be a provocation aimed at the Freudian societies and, if you like, at Freud himself. But at the same time it revealed, on an enormous (and therefore funny) scale, a Sade-like aspect of his personality: '*Psychanalistes, encore un effort pour être vraiment...*'[2] What? Just one more trick Lacan ended up playing on us…

Translated from the Italian by Tristram Bruce and Anthony Molino

[2] A paraphrase of de Sade's invocation, 'Francais, encore un effort pour etre vraiment républicains': 'Psychoanalysts, yet one more effort to truly be…'

INTO FICTION, THROUGH CATASTROPHE

Christopher Bollas

A MEMBER OF the British Psycho-Analytic Society and one of the most stimulating authors in contemporary psychoanalysis, Christopher Bollas divides his time and practice among North Dakota, Los Angeles and London. Over the years, he has held a number of distinguished positions worldwide, including honorary non-medical consultant at the London Clinic of Psychoanalysis, director of education at Austen Riggs Center in Massachusetts, and visiting professor at Rome University's Institute of Child Neuropsychiatry. One of the editors of D.W. Winnicott's writings, he has also served as book review editor for the *International Journal of Psychoanalysis*.

In this conversation, Anthony Molino engages Bollas in an exploration of the radical turn in his recent literary output. Focusing primarily on his novels *Dark at the End of the Tunnel* and *I Have Heard the Mermaid Singing*, Bollas here discusses in detail his move away from the traditional psychoanalytic essay into the realms of fiction (and theatre). Finding the former suitable to 'a much more radical form of theorizing', Bollas explores both the internal pressures to which he responded in resorting to the genre, as well as contemporary societal pressures and themes which the genre more readily accommodates. Among these are analyses of modern-day Islam's rise and revolt against the West, and of what Bollas sees as the loss of character in our globalised consumer culture: expressions both of the 'catastrophe' that engulfs and pervades our culture, the determinants of which remain, for the most part, 'unconscious'.

The following interview with Christopher Bollas, originally titled 'Into Fiction, through Catastrophe', was first published in the *Journal of European Psychoanalysis* n. 22 (2006).

* * *

Anthony Molino

Since the publication of The Mystery of Things *(1999) and* Hysteria *(2000), you have turned out three novels and a collection of plays. The novels*

– *Dark at the End of the Tunnel, I Have Heard the Mermaids Singing and Mayhem – seem to want to pursue a new way not only of writing about psychoanalysis, but literally of writing psychoanalysis. Can you explain this most recent and, indeed, prolific turn?*

Christopher Bollas

I now give only one or two public presentations a year that require me to write an essay. I prefer small working groups to the larger public event. That means that I am booked up to three years ahead of time and usually around fifteen months before the engagement I am asked to give a title of my talk. So I come up with something. And some years ago I came up with 'Object and Other' and didn't think about it any further. Ordinarily about a year before I write an essay for presentation I ask myself, 'so what's up?', and hope for some internal feedback. But that did not happen in this case. I deferred the question and asked it about ten months before the event: still no reply. Then eight months: same thing. By then ordinarily I would have assembled whatever thoughts I had about a topic and at least unconsciously I would be working on it, adding bits here and there, on a daily basis. Bits to my notebook. I usually write the essay three months before the engagement, but when that time rolled around I was nowhere near to writing the essay and the institution sponsoring the event was now asking for a translation of the draft. It was the first writing block in my life and although I would haul myself to my desk and sit before the computer admonishing myself to get going, no luck. But one Saturday morning I sat at my desk, spontaneously decided to write about this topic from a fictional point of view and I wrote it in one sitting. In a sense I booted the problem over to an imaginary psychoanalyst who was thinking about it, but who had no answer to the question. That struck me as about right, so the character and I were on the same page so to speak.

Your reply speaks to the genesis, if you will, of this turn in your work. But beyond its origins, it is a turn in which you have persisted – for approximately five years and three novels now. This leads me to presume that you've come to elect the form of the novel, again, as a way of writing psychoanalysis and grappling with its status in our world today...

After I discovered how liberating this form was then I certainly elected to follow that path. I do think for me it is the right thing to do now because I have come to find the traditional psychoanalytical essay oppressive and not such a creative form. I also enjoy the greater freedom fiction allows to my own unconscious to have its say in representation.

Is it your impression, or indeed intention, that fiction of your kind can be deployed in the service of theorizing? A recent review of your novels identifies therein a number of concepts you've contributed over the years to the language of psychoanalysis (fate, destiny, transformational objects, genera, idiom, *and many others), and has me wondering if the freedom the genre allows also makes for a space for the further elaboration and dissemination of these concepts. Or, perhaps, for the germination of new theoretical constructs?*

I do think fiction allows for a much more radical form of theorizing than can take place in an essay. For example, I found that by using the conceit of different characters reporting on books they have read – a book on the oppression of black men or a book on Middle East conflict – that I could put forward diverse psychoanalytical perspectives in a very short space. Also, by using circumstance – such as a conversation between two characters ending because they have come to the end of their walk – I can throw forward quite radical ideas without the burden of proof weighing down the writing. I have been able to 'say' more in these three novels than I have in any comparable number of essays that touch on the same topics. Of course, we all know that novelists intentionally used this form for the exploration of the human mind and the nature of human relations. The history of the novel is, in many respects, a history of theory-making. The downside is that because this is just fiction an astonishing number of people, and I mean well-educated people, think that it is therefore not real! So the problem to some extent is with the readership as people still think, much the way they did in the eighteenth century, that fiction is not reality. When I proposed to the editor of *International Journal of Psychoanalysis* that they consider reviewing my novellas, pointing out that to me this was another way of thinking about psychoanalysis, I was summarily dismissed: 'We do not review fiction'. Astonishing really. But fortunately other journals, such as *Psychoanalytic Review*, the *Australian Journal of Psychotherapy*, the *Journal of the British Association of Psychotherapists*, *JEP* and *Psyche* (the German analytical journal) are more up to this kind of thing.

Psychoanalytic theories and theory-making are often referred to – especially by critics of psychoanalysis – as a form of fiction. In a way, Freud, Klein, Bion Winnicott, Lacan – even Bollas! – have all conjured up fictional accounts of the human mind and life, developing what you yourself have referred to as differing 'modes of perception'. Assuming you agree with this premise, are your own novels, in some way, paradoxically part of an established tradition in psychoanalytic writing, or at least an expression of what we might call a shared aesthetic that looks for ever-new ways of thinking and representing itself?

I think making fiction and writing an essay are different mental phenomena. If they were the same then the difference between the two would not only be meaningless, but difference itself would succumb to the hegemony of sameness. I think when commentators argue that Freud or Winnicott's writings are poetic, or that their cases read like fiction, they are trying to find some way to identify something unique about the psychoanalytical essay or the writing of a case. I do not think these are fictions. They are psychoanalytical writings. The fact that I could no longer write like this is not a repudiation of that form of thinking or writing – and it is unique – but a comment on my own unconscious block at the time. On reflection I think I had simply tired of that venue for thinking. I was also fatigued by my own voice as a writer of that kind of prose. For me writing fiction was liberating, but for a full time novelist the personal account of the self 's relation to that form of thinking and writing could be quite different.

In Dark at the End of the Tunnel *you deal squarely, and what I found to be honestly and compassionately, with a topic psychoanalysis often eschews: namely, the darkness of death. In the recent literature, I know only of Franco De Masi's* Making Death Thinkable *tackling the theme, which you vivify in the touching relationship between the psychoanalyst and his dying female patient, Selina Tano. Can you comment on this preoccupation?*

Dark at the End of the Tunnel followed the death of two friends, one whom I was just really getting to know – and liked him the more I knew him – and one whom I had known for twenty-five years and who was a remarkable and profound man. My father had died two years before and had given, much to his own pleasure, a death-bed speech to my brothers and myself. He had not prepared it, but he certainly was 'up' to death. I also had my own brush with death round about this time, so it was in the background. But I had no idea that I was going to write about it. It showed up. As it did, one thing led to another and I was able to write about some aspects of my work with a patient who was dying. I have for a long time been struck by the phrase 'loss of life', which seems to me more apt than 'one dies'. I think the tragedy for the dying person – if he or she has time to think about it – is that one is losing one's life and contact with the living. I believe the mourning over this loss of life that occupies the dying person has been overlooked and submerged in the too familiar notions of the stages of dying: i.e., I can't believe it is happening to me, I am furious and whatnot. I do not think death as such is so shocking. It is the loss of life. And that continues to interest me.

You mention the work of mourning. In a review of your novels, the Anglo-Italian psychoanalyst Pina Antinucci cites Jean Clair, former director of the Picasso Museum in Paris and of the Biennale in Venice, who not too long ago organized an exhibit titled 'Melancholia' at Paris' Grand Palais. By tracing the history and vicissitudes of the concept of depression, the reviewer writes that 'Clair speaks directly to our world's inability to mourn. And in so doing, he puts forth the scandalous proposition that we consider the work of mourning as the paradoxical 'utopia' of our post-historical times. A utopia for the post-historical subject who can no longer distinguish between past, present and future...' Do you see your own work, concerns and characters reflected in such a 'utopia'? and can we speak of mourning as a contemporary quest of sorts? I recall Adam Phillips years ago being quite critical of just how indiscriminately analysts celebrate the concept...

I don't believe it is only mourning that our culture refuses. It is thinking. So if we do not think about who we are, where we are, where we have come from, where we are going, and what effect we have on our world, then we are not aware of our identity, we are not aware of what we 'have', so we will not know what is loss, and without such self-awareness of course there can be no mourning. We thought Freud's discovery of psychoanalysis was the beginning of a new era, and, at least through to the middle of the twentieth century that seemed to be the case. Freud infused Western culture and it looked as if this would be generative and generational. But I now think Freud and psychoanalysis marked the end of an era, not the beginning. I think the existentialist movement – the time of our last great thinkers – was the end of the search for meaning. I believe we now live in a time that was foreseen by Eliot in 'The Wasteland'. In *Theraplay & Other Plays* I attempt to 'stage' our time, not equationally. I hope I have found future figures that nonetheless are our ghosts: ghosts living purely as functional beings, without meaning. And in two of the plays in the collection, 'Theraplay' and 'Apply Within', I try to explore the loss of character endemic now to our time and the self – asset stripped – living in the so-called globalised world.

We'll come back to your plays later. It's your reference to existentialism that I find intriguing, having already noted elsewhere that your novels evoke for me the work of Albert Camus. Your character of the psychoanalyst seems to descend, in a peculiar sort of way, from the line of protagonist/anti-heroes of works like The Stranger *and* The Fall*; and the Catastrophe – on which I'd like you to elaborate – readily echoes Oran's plague...*

I think fiction captures the atmosphere of an era far more so than non-fiction. I was certainly influenced by the writings of Camus because he established a mood – one of reflective remove from the march of horror – and I was also transformed by the surrealist brilliance of Ionesco. I realise you want to discuss the plays later, but my novellas are part drama. The crowd scenes, for example, are meant to be like the Greek chorus, reflecting the psychotic element of the social order. Ionesco also used the crowd, the herd, to echo the mass movements of fascism and communism, but for me his plays capture the impossibility of the individual life amidst the mass. I think the existential anti-hero may be the last personification of self before it succumbs to mass commodification. The characters in the novellas are just on the cusp of discovering that they are living in a world where the unconscious has departed and where there is no longer a memory of the search for individual meaning. The plays extend this realisation, so that the characters in a play like 'Apply Within' are simply functional beings. Still I find there is some possibility of redemption in all of this. People remain people. Their failings and vulnerabilities become ironic portals to a different world than the one proposed by the commodifiers. In human failure one finds a comedic talent – symptom as joke so to speak – that could put a wrench in the production of false selves. The novellas intend to find that redemptive dimension and to illustrate how in human imperfection one finds strength that inevitably collides with mass movements. We are a long way down the road from the era of Camus. His generation were just coming out of the trenches of war and resistance and their literary works were like an après coup that generated fierce debate around them. They benefited from the fact that in fighting Nazism they had fought evil. But we – and by 'we' I mean the Western World – cannot occupy this innocent place precisely because we are now the Nazis and we choose not to know it. Our occupation and oppression of the rest of the non-industrialised world in which millions are dying every year of starvation and death by ordinary diseases is calling up our opponents: the anti-Nazi. But that figure is horrifying. Made ill by us. Mad. An ignorant army of millions of dispossessed people who will try to destroy us and may manage it. And we still refuse to discover who we have become.

Your answer suggests an acute awareness of this troubled historical moment of ours, and indeed both your novels published to date unfold in the diffuse, eery ooze of an otherwise unnamed Catastrophe. In I Have Heard the Mermaids Singing, *published shortly before the London bombings of 2005, you imagined a terrorist bomber seeking the help of the psychoanalyst so as to carry out his deadly mission, and thus make one of your few explicit references to the threat posed, say, by today's Islamic fundamentalisms. In recent times, we have seen angry, mindless hordes driven to violence across the globe by the supposed sacrilege of a Danish newspaper's publication of cartoons representing the Prophet. Isn't it also a bit simplistic to say that we are our era's Nazis, when so much of the world, arguably, inhabits the kind of 'primitive', or un/self reflective, medieval mindset that Freud fathomed in works like* The Future of an Illusion *and* Group Psychology and the Analysis of the Ego? *Your analysis of our occupation and oppression of the Rest almost seems predicated on a Marxist analysis that shies away from considerations other than the socio-economic...*

If we look specifically at the world of Islam most historians agree that after the Ottoman Empire this civilisation declined as it withdrew into itself. It regarded Western developments – especially science and armaments – with disdain and elected to live on its past accomplishments. It would be folly to blame the West for this. But Western policies toward the Third World – in the middle East, Africa, South and Central America and elsewhere – have been to exploit vast populations, turning a blind eye to continued colonial activities. The United States and other governments have again and again supported dictators who have oppressed and terrorised their own people. We knew this. We continued with our policies. To this extent I liken us to the Nazi occupation of Europe. The United States and Western governments are hated by most of the rest of the world population and I think hated for good reason. My point is that we have destroyed people. The destroyed, driven mad by us – and their own leaders who are our puppets – now embody the return of the oppressed. We are now to pay a huge price for more than fifty years of such oppression. Camus, Sartre, Fanon and others were deeply disturbed by this oppression, and theirs was a time, also, when psychoanalysts were taking up literary arms against Western oppression. But now I think the West has cut its ties to thinking about this issue. Links have been broken. We have forgotten who we propped up and what they did. Even as we do it now – through the outsourcing of torture and Guantanamo – we are still oblivious to our own criminal activities. When the cartoons stirred up Islam they did indeed rouse the insane. If we are not responsible for the entire history of their descent into madness, we discovered them in this condition and we have exploited them, which is a very grave crime against tens of millions of people.

Are your plays and novels, then, to be understood as the equivalent of what literary arms can be taken up today by psychoanalysts? Or do you intend, at the least, to disturb the slumber of fellow analysts and waken us/them – in your words – 'to what we have become'?

I do not have an agenda for my novels and the plays. I write them because I enjoy doing it and because it allows me a range of thought-possibilities denied to me by the more limited form of the essay. I do not, for example, know what will happen in the novels or the plays. I just begin and something shows up. But if we stand back and have a look it does seem to be the case that sometimes the psychoanalyst, a flawed hero, is disturbed by his profession. Unsurprisingly it seems to me, he finds within the analytical movement what we can think of as the ordinary fascism of everyday life. To be sure, there are points where I quite agree with his views, especially on the here-and-now transference, but there are other points he makes that I consider silly or evidence of different forms of prejudice. He is impulsive and careless at times. I realise that most of the analytical readership thinks the psychoanalyst is myself and although that is certainly true at times the aspects of him that I most like are the not-me dimensions. It was becoming tedious to represent my own views in prose. So I am glad this character has shown up, and the not-me is a relief.

I'd like to pursue this line of thought with you. Is not Christopher Bollas also disturbed by aspects of his profession, and does he not suffer – and therefore knowingly choose to denounce in his work – the 'ordinary fascism of everyday life'? The dehumanization of depression, say, and the Orwellian politics of today's pharmaceutical industry, themes you do take up in I Have Heard the Mermaids Singing? *Your novels, like it or not, do mark a break within the world of psychoanalysis – so much so that the IJPA, in refusing to review them, evinces its own (our own?) narrow-mindedness and parochialism...*

I should clarify that the *International Journal of Psychoanalysis*'s refusal was, to my knowledge, simply categorical. They do not review fiction. I have no reason to believe that they did not wish to review my work because of my views. I do of course understand the point you are making, that certainly I personally must have views that are placed with some of my characters. But if I were to embark upon a commentary in which I agreed to point out where I was in these works, then I think I would defeat them. In turn, I think I would limit the possibilities of my own within this realm which I find liberating. Looked at another way, have I suffered from and do I oppose the ordinary fascism in psychoanalysis? – the answer is yes. Do I wish to discuss this from a personal point of view? The answer is no. We all suffer in life and I am no exception.

Perhaps I should clarify. By no means is the emphasis of my question on what you, personally, suffer or may have suffered. But where psychoanalysis is concerned, in an interview we did a decade ago, already then you claimed that psychoanalysis had to survive the psychoanalytic movement. In your own words: 'If it survives psychoanalysts and their schools, then it will grow and develop. But this remains to be seen...' Already then you perceived what I might call normalizing or conformist tendencies (in training, thinking, the transmission of psychoanalytic knowledge and the power relations that inhere therein) that troubled you, which your novels and plays seem to acknowledge....

I suppose it should not be a surprise that psychoanalysts in groups behave no differently than other groups. For a long time I think I was under the sway of a wish that as psychoanalysts had been analyzed they would have a better understanding of, amongst other things, human destructiveness. I think I believed that they would therefore behave differently. I now know this is not so. I often tell myself to get over this disappointment, but obviously – even in the fiction – I continue to protest this fact. A few analysts over the decades have tried to address this issue but it is surprising how quiet we all are about the distressing reality that psychoanalysis really has no effect on the behaviour of psychoanalysts. We are, therefore, our own worst advertisement.

Earlier in our conversation you mentioned your writing for the theatre, recently collected in Theraplay & Other Plays. *Is it just an impression of mine, or is the vision you bring to the stage generally a starker one than inhabits your novels? Redemption, as you put it – the reclamation, today, of a life of meaning and the possibility that the individual unconscious can indeed be recognized and engaged – seems more within the reach of your fictional creations than your stage characters, whom I've had occasion to describe as a Giacometti-like, 'alexithymic army of post-human beings'. Can you discuss the differences?*

I think a novel demands that the author create some kind of world. Even if the characters are more like vehicles for ideas – which is true of my fictional characters – one must still attend to them to make them credible as imaginary others. Also, my fiction is clearly comic and that genre means that every so often something is quite amusing, thus breaking up whatever is transpiring. The plays are different. One does not have to create a world. Indeed the plays, which some see as Beckett-like, may only be two people talking in such abstract terms so that for a long time the audience may have little idea of what is going on. Reference points may be barely visible, reality suspended, connections absent. Theatre of this kind can approximate the workings of the unconscious in a way that the novel never could, not even the novels of Joyce, Robbe-Grillet, Faulkner or Saramago. At the moment I am writing what, for lack of a better term, one might call dramatic fragments or poetic dramas. They are written like poems and have stanzaic structure. But they are simply conversations between two anonymous characters about highly abstract anxieties or interests. They are even more open to this kind of thinking than the plays proper.

Both genres, in any case – and perhaps this new form with which you are experimenting as well – are vehicles for you to evoke or represent our contemporary Catastrophe. What do you see as the fate of the unconscious in this era of diffuse, worming, stratified yet all-engulfing crises? Again, your stage characters especially seem alien to its workings – and seem, tragically, all the more realistic for it...

I think it is quite challenging to represent the departure of the unconscious as participant in contemporary culture and yet keep it on stage in the act of representation. So the characters in the plays are rather empty beings, asset-stripped by decades of soul-mining by social structures with vested interests only in profit margins. I think the unconscious as a figure – as something the audience feels is present even if absent from the individual character – occurs as the form the plays take, the kinds of dialogues between characters. The unconscious has receded if you will into the medium of representation itself, retreating into language-in-itself...

In preparing for our interview, I found myself reflecting – thanks to your work – on the implications for unconscious life in this confounding time of ours. One need only consider the recent waves of Freud-bashing, the DSM'ing of our human condition, the lobbying to patent human genes, or our global denial of the Other (unless or until forcefully democratized and commodified, and made unto our likeness)... In sum, I began to wonder what this turn in your work must reflect of your own personal and professional life. Now in your sixties, you've about reached the age when Jung, for example, became disillusioned by what he saw as modern man's break from the psychic richness and connectedness of African and New Mexican tribes, or when Freud looked with pained disenchantment, between the two world wars, at man's monstrous, murderous capacity for evil and destruction... Might I invite some closing reflections along these lines?

My turn to theatre in some ways is a return to the 1960s as it was then that I wrote plays for a brief spell. Along with all my childhood objects they were burned in a fire set by an arsonist who torched a block of storage lockers. Several of the plays were produced in 2005 at the Berkeley Repertory Theatre, so this was an evocative moment as that is the city where my first lot of plays got written. In other respects, however, I have had occasion to reflect on that period of time. I was involved in the Free Speech Movement at Berkeley. I had been active in the civil rights movement in the south and later became an ally of the Black Panther Party in California…

But looking back it is interesting to contrast the American left with, say, the French left. The American left was almost completely without psychological insight into themselves and were not interested in psychoanalysis, while this was certainly not to be so in France, where 1968 launched Lacan. Even though American writers looked deep into the soul of man, American letters – when compared to Europe – have had very little impact on American consciousness (or indeed the American unconscious). Every European country I know of has valued its great writers, but this is not so in America and has never been the case. American writers rarely even attend to their society but reflect this life – as outsiders – by concentrating on the individual as a kind of isolate, even when surrounded by social forces. For several decades now, however, we have witnessed the rise of globalisation, part of which means the export of American culture across the globe. I believe we can see the mind-numbing effect of this form of trade. Indeed we are now at the point where I think there is little difference between European and American culture. Visit Paris and you might just as well be in an American theme park. And Florence might just as well apply for American citizenship. The transformation of value, from an individual who lives in a culture and who means something to himself and others, into a commodity asset strips the human soul of its worth. We live in an age where there is no longer meaningful contact with unconscious life; in fact, where the idea of the unconscious is often held in absolute contempt. This stretches into the realms of psychoanalysis as well, where analysts have for the most part lost touch with what Freud proposed as the unconscious. There is little use for a theory of free association, although lip service is paid to it. But analysts come to the clinical hour with an agenda – i.e., finding the transference, finding the drive derivative, finding the castration complex, finding the intersubjective or whatnot – that not only canalises psychoanalysis, but is part of the social simplification of mental life. Regrettably, psychoanalysis is now part of the problem and no longer part of the solution. A few writers seem to know this and I believe they are trying to address it, but they are up against the 'movements' in psychoanalysis that are only interested in promoting their own limited brand of psychoanalysis – at the expense, moreover, of all other theories and forms of practise. Psychoanalysis, then, has become a commodity, marketed by middlemen who work within an intellectual-corporate structure. If I am not optimistic about the short term – and I see no evidence of a big shift in Western thought, much less within psychoanalysis – then I am not pessimistic about the long-term future. Psychoanalytic theory was an important revelation within the history of Western consciousness. If it has been repressed, as looks to be the case, I believe it will certainly return some day.

Selected Bibliography

The Freudian Moment (2007). London: Karnac.
Mayhem (2006). London: FAB.
Theraplay & Other Plays (2006). London: FAB.
I Have Heard the Mermaids Singing (2005). London: FAB.
Dark at the End of the Tunnel (2004). London: FAB.
Free Association (2002). London: Icon Books.
Hysteria (2000). London: Routledge.
The Mystery of Things (1999). London: Routledge.

II

PSYCHOANALYSIS, PHILOSOPHY AND POLITICS

THE EMERGENCE OF THE UNCONSCIOUS IN WESTERN THOUGHT

Michel Henry

MICHEL HENRY (1922–2002) was one of the most famous phenomenological philosophers in France. Born in Haiphong, Vietnam (formerly French Indochina), as a young man already impassioned with philosophy he was active in the French Resistance under the code name of 'Kant'. He later studied with Jean Hyppolite and Paul Ricoeur before becoming himself professor of philosophy at the University of Montpellier in 1960. The driving force behind Henry's philosophy was his absolute concern with subjectivity, which is to say the real life of living individuals. This concern marks his entire lifework, yielding what has been acknowledged as probably the most profound theory of subjectivity produced in the twentieth century.

In this 2001 conversation with Sergio Benvenuto, Prof. Henry shows how the Freudian theory of the unconscious is actually the point of arrival of a long process of European thinking that began with Cartesian doubt and Descartes' idea that one's sense of the 'I' is the only human certainty. This process then basically continues in Schopenhauer, Kierkegaard and Nietzsche and into phenomenology. Starting out from an analysis of Freud's *Project for a Scientific Psychology* – which Henry views as a theory of subjectivity – the French philosopher goes on to examine the role of the life drives in Freud, arguing that the foundations of the subject lie not in psychic representations, as Freud would have it, but in affects. Henry then concludes by examining the common ground between Marx and Freud, insofar as both insist on individuality and on the subjectivity of human life.

Originally published in Italian in the *Enciclopedia Multimediale delle Scienze Filosofiche*, the following conversation with Michel Henry appeared in the *Journal of European Psychoanalysis* n. 12–13 (2001) under the title 'The Emergence of the Unconscious in Western Thought'. It is here reprinted courtesy of RAI – Radiotelevisione Italiana.

Sergio Benvenuto

Prof. Henry, you have written a book, The Genealogy of Psychoanalysis, *which is in fact a book about the emergence of the unconscious in Western thought.*

Michel Henry

The idea of the emergence of the unconscious in the West had its origins in my phenomenological work, since phenomenology does not reflect on different phenomena but on what makes each one of them a phenomenon; that is on phenomenality, on that which at a certain moment in classical philosophy became called 'consciousness'. Now this is a fundamental problem because, whether one thinks of it explicitly or one lets it intervene without paying attention to it, it is phenomenality that acts as a support for phenomena and ensures that something shows itself to us in such a way that we can talk about it. In relation to the unconscious, phenomenality is a paradoxical theme or affirmation. In fact if one takes as a criterion the classical definition of phenomenality in terms of consciousness, this criterion seems to purely and simply deny this phenomenality, this appearing, without which there is nothing: there is, for us, no experience. And so what is left? What can we talk about if nothing remains, if there is no giving left? For phenomenologists, who think that every philosophical discourse should be based on some piece of giving, the very affirmation of an unconscious leads to a sort of *aporia*. What does it mean to speak, to think, if nothing reveals itself? That is why I wanted to clarify the paradox of the unconscious starting from the phenomenological presuppositions of my philosophical thought.

You start your analysis from the cogito *of Descartes, which you consider as a source of this thought of the unconscious.*

The Cartesian *cogito* seems far removed in relation to psychoanalysis and twentieth-century thought. But it is a source that cannot be neglected, for reason that not only the unconscious of psychoanalysis, but every form of thought in the twentieth century has questioned the *cogito* of Descartes. And with this calling into question of the *cogito*, phenomenality was called into question. In this way one wanted to say not that phenomenality does not exist – because that would be impossible – but that it is an appearance, that it is deceptive. That is why, instead of considering it as a sound and safe basis for our thought and for our intellectual practice, it is necessary to cast doubt on phenomenality. It was the famous 'age of suspicion', as Ricoeur expressed it: that is, the contestation of a moment in which, on the contrary, philosophy would have liked to be grounded on an indubitable phenomenality. Because fundamentally the *cogito* is this: it is the affirmation of a phenomenality, of an absolutely incontestable appearance, upon which one can rely.

This appearance is not just any sort of appearance, but is an appearing to myself and above all my own appearing to myself. 'I think' means: I appear to myself and this appearing to myself is absolutely indisputable. On this certainty rests all the knowledge that I can acquire about myself and the world. According to Descartes, in as much as I have a certain knowledge of myself and all the instruments of knowledge, everything that I know benefits from this invincible certainty that I carry within me. As a consequence, if the thought of the twentieth century, all taken and considered together, calls into question the *cogito* of Descartes, it calls into question that which was considered by classical modern philosophy, but not by contemporary philosophy, as a certain foundation. Thus everything is called in question: it is the age of suspicion.

Thus the *cogito* of Descartes is called into question, which acted as the foundation not only of our thought, but of the truth of all our experience. And so one has to ask oneself why this truth is called into question by all of modern thought, and one has to ask oneself first of all if one has understood what Descartes meant by affirming the *cogito*. This was one of the themes of my reflection, to which I have dedicated three chapters of *The Genealogy of Psychoanalysis*. There has been a very serious misunderstanding of the *cogito* of Descartes: it was believed that the *cogito* meant 'I think' – and in fact this is the meaning of the Latin word – in the sense 'I represent [something] to myself', and in the sense that 'I have some evidence' and [in the first place] I have the evidence of my existence. Now evidence is something that one sees and it is something that one sees in such a way that one cannot doubt it. Thus the sensible experience seems indubitable for common sense. I can see very well that I am here in a room, that I am talking to you, that near me there is a lamp, etc. And there is further evidence, rational evidence. I see that in a circle the radii are all equal. I see that '2+3=5' and I also see that, if I think then I am, because if I didn't exist I could not think. That is what the *cogito* is for the readers of Descartes and for modern thought.

Unfortunately, with his *cogito* Descartes says exactly the opposite. Descartes says: I doubt everything I see. I doubt not only everything I see with my physical eyes, with my senses – and the doubt regarding the judgment of the senses had been known ever since antiquity – but I doubt also the rational truths. It is here that Descartes says: 'Let us suppose the existence of a god who is a malignant spirit who wanted to deceive me when I believe that 2+3=5; well then I would be deceived; I would be wrong and my thought, my intelligible seeing would not be worth anything'.

At this point Descartes re-formulates the *cogito* in a strange way, to which sufficient attention has not been paid. Let's see how. In the very moment when any seeing is cast in doubt, Descartes must find the indestructible foundation he is looking for. This foundation appears in *The Passions of the Soul*, article 24, in which Descartes makes the hypothesis of the dream and says: when I see or imagine one or another thing in a dream it is all false. Now the dream has an important role in psychoanalysis. The dream is a sort of hallucination. I see myself running on the pavement after a train which is leaving, but in reality there is neither a pavement nor the train. At this point Descartes says: 'I doubt everything I see'. And so what remains? And immediately afterwards there is a fantastic phrase, which invalidates all the criticisms that modern thought has launched. Descartes says: if in a dream I feel sadness or any other passion, anguish for example, even though it is a dream, that passion exists. It exists in as much as I feel it. If I feel fear, in the moment in which nothing is left in the world because I have doubted everything, everything about which one can doubt, here is something that I cannot doubt: the fact that every sentiment – if I limit myself not to what I relate about it, but to that which I feel – is indubitable. Here we find the genuine *cogito* of Descartes: the 'I think' is an 'I feel'. Sensation testifies to itself in such an incontestable way that if I feel pain I can find for myself all the explanations in this world, but for all the period that the pain lasts I will continue to suffer. Nobody can deceive me about this, pain does not lie. This kind of revelation has remained hidden.

And so when the French existentialist philospoher René Le Senne proposed his 'I suffer, therefore I am', he was not really so far from Descartes. But Freud in The Interpretation of Dreams *says the same thing: that the sentiment in a dream is never interpretable; the latent and the manifest coincide. The images in the dream can be interpreted: that which is seen, but not the feeling – which is always authentic. If in a dream a beautiful scene provokes anguish in me, the scene should be interpreted in such a way as to make my anguish comprehensible.*

This is a thesis which I maintain in *The Genealogy of Psychoanalysis.* The problems raised by Descartes, which have not really been understood, open the modern age, as much as they are valid, just as much as they are false. What does Descartes doubt? He doubts representation, which is that which one sees. And that which we see is always that which is put before us, that which is in front of us, such that we can see it, thanks to its distance, both with the eyes of the body and with the eyes of the spirit, with the intellect; as when we see that the radii of a circle are all equal, which is a rational truth. Here we are dealing with representation. Western thought believed only in representation, while Descartes was basically the first to call representation in question. This means that the Heideggerian interpretation of Descartes is completely false: 'I think' actually means everything except 'I represent to myself'. And from the moment in which Descartes casts doubt on representation, then phenomenality, falsely identified with representation, becomes the unconscious.

In his article 'The Unconscious' of 1914, and in other texts of the period, Freud can introduce the concept of the unconscious precisely because representation disappears. One of his most relevant arguments is memory. I believe that if one looks at the world of representation, with its structure, one sees clearly that in the world of representation, before my gaze, there is only room for one thing [at a time]. Thus the clearing [*clairière*] in which I can see limits my horizons, such that the thing I see rapidly leaves this zone of light, to relinquish its place to another – so that then I see this other object. But there is a price to pay. In the world of representation, when I see a thing I do not see all the others which are then called unconscious representations. At this point, initially Freud demonstrates the unconscious by saying: there are some representations I think about, but from the moment that I cease to think about them they leave the circle of light of representation, which identifies them with the conscious mind. They become unconscious representations, or memories, and they go to fill that container, that is my unconscious. Thus is born the unsustainable aporetic concept of an unconscious representation, that is of something that is there in front of me, that I see and I do not see: it is the case of all the representations that I see only for an instant and that in the next instant disappear. This is the first period of psychoanalysis: the moment in which the unconscious affirms itself as regards the representation.

Representation as a finished mode of appearing gives origin to the idea that true reality is unconscious. But what is true reality? It is important to recognize precisely that it is a reality of a different kind from that of representation, which can be found in the depths of myself and that Freud will call 'unconscious'. It is invisible, but not in the sense of something that is temporarily visible before passing into an equally temporary invisibility, in a field of unconscious representations, from which it can return to the condition of visibility, as when I perform a reminiscence or an analysis which permits me to rediscover repressed memories. Thus we find ourselves in a world which is that of the passage from the represented to the non-represented, in such a way that the non-represented can always return into the represented. And this is the world of representation; it is the world as such. But our reality is of a different kind. It is a very particular reality, which subsists in a condition of invisibility – Freud would speak of the unconscious – which does not have the power of passing into the visible, and which does not even have the power of disappearing, in the sense of an invisible void, of a represented thing which has always been there within me, invisible. And so is it necessary to call it 'unconscious' or give it another name instead?

Its true name is life. It is life, if life is what I feel, just as Descartes felt it in his dream, and as Freud also found it at the bottom of the unconscious. It is life as it is lived, but invisible, something that I feel without it ever being able to appear before my eyes. All my experiences are of this kind. I feel anguish, but I don't see it. Perhaps it is destined to modify my vision, and in fact it certainly will do so: it will completely modify the world of representation – it is one of the great themes of Freud, but it had already been a theme of Schopenhauer and Nietzsche. But anguish in itself is of another nature, it is not in the nature of representation, and it is however me myself: it is my life.

And so we should return to the emergence in Western thought of this essential theme of life and the world-of-life. We should go back to what was behind Freud – to Kant and Schopenhauer – to see how this growing centrality of the theme of life and thus of sensation develops in the thought of the twentieth century.

Your question is essential, because this theme has a history. The unconscious did not suddenly break upon the scene in the moment when the *cogito* was not understood. It is a historical fact that, at the moment of its formulation, the great Cartesians did not understand the *cogito:* neither Malebranche, nor Leibniz nor Spinoza understood the *cogito.* Precisely because it was very difficult for them to understand it, they believed that the *cogito* was evidence and was thus a representation. And again Heidegger criticizes this way of understanding it, when he says: '*I think* means *I represent to myself*', 'I present myself to myself', 'I present myself in front of myself', exactly as I represent the things of the world. Here there is a massive contradiction.

Schopenhauer too thinks along the same lines as Kant. Kant created, with transcendental aesthetics, a theory of representation – of the world as representation. The forms of intuition are in fact forms of representation: the space in which things are arranged in front of me, as in this room, and the time in which things are arranged in my spirit, one after the other. And then the categories of the intellect allow me to link up everything which is arranged in front of me by means of syntheses that are of the nature of thought. Forms of the intuition and concepts of the intellect together constitute the universe of representation. Schopenhauer, who is fuelled with Kantism, has an overwhelming intuition: *the world is representation, but there is something else*. What else is there? There is within me the desire to live, which is totally different from a representation: it is a sort of force that passes through me, against which I can do nothing and which is reality. The reality, for example, of the sexual impulse, which leads me towards its own objects? The reality of desire. The reality in addition which dwells within sentiments to the degree in which they all have a dynamic value: for example love, which leads me towards its object, or hatred, which makes me feel repugnance. This is our reality.

Here the destiny of Western thought before Freud is being played out. Schopenhauer affirms that there is something totally different from representation, from the world, and that this something is within me. But since he continues to identify phenomenality, appearance, with representation, he is forced to say that this force in me is blind, it is unconscious and anonymous. Not by chance does Freud speak of Schopenhauer as a great thinker. He says: that which Schopenhauer called 'the will to live', I call 'drive' (*trieb*). We are dealing with a reality which from this moment – they are texts of 1818 – is understood as man's deep reality; while everything else, the world of representation, is an unreal, phantasmagorical world, basically analogous to that of the dream. And this is the reason why Schopenhauer so easily accepts the thought of India, because the world is the veil of Maya, it is appearance, illusion. Thus on one side there is the world of representation, which is the world of unreality: that which I see which continually deceives me and deludes me; and on the other side there is a reality which passes through me without my feeling it.

If we had the time to enter into the details, we would see some contradictions in the texts of Schopenhauer. He said first of all that the will is felt by itself and that the will is the same thing as the body – but here the subjective body is intended; the body as I live, it and that is unrepresentable. And on the other side there is representation, the only center of light. At this point the antinomy of the modern world is already proposed: either the light of representation, of thought of the world, or the unconscious. Schopenhauer therefore affirms the reality of the unconscious in a contradictory form. At first he attaches meaning to the evidence of the will to live in me, saying that basically the will to live, Will – which here is nothing to do with the intellectual will of classical thought – is something like a way of appearing. There is an extraordinary phrase of his which seems to me to be a timeless truth: our body appears to itself in two ways. On one side it appears to itself as an object in the world of representation – and in effect I see my body, my hand, I can touch them. But on the other side it appears to myself without being seen, from within, in the desires, the sentiments, in suffering, anguish, in the will to live.

Can one say that representation, according to Schopenhauer – and according to those of us who read him – is the subject as studied by science, the subject as studied by scientific psychology, or that which calls itself such?

One can say so. And in fact in the further evolution of Schopenhauer's thought there is a moment in which he says so. But the important thing for the formation of modern thought is this extraordinary chiasmus: on one side the unreal which is the light and the visible, and on the other side the real which is immersed in the unconscious. This great chiasmus is taken up by Nietzsche, who should be seen as an intermediate reference point, between Schopenhauer and Freud, although Freud is much closer to Schopenhauer than to Nietzsche. So in Nietzsche there is an effort, which we see as pathetic and movingly passionate, to save *life*. To simplify things a little, Nietzsche basically accepts the thesis of Schopenhauer regarding representation. There is a world of representation, which in his mythological universe he adopts and corresponds to the figure of Apollo. Apollo is the realm of visible forms, the realm of beauty, and he is also the realm of everything that is revealed before us and that can have a cheering or placating function. Placating because there is another realm, that of the will, which for Nietzsche becomes the will to power. But one should note that Nietzsche more often defines this other realm in terms of pathos: it is the realm of Dionysus, and Dionysus is essentially our life seen as suffering...

And pleasure too!

... as suffering that also makes for pleasure at the same time. And here we encounter one of the greatest intuitions of Nietzsche. You are right to underscore it: it is the ambivalence of the sentiments in our own depths, an ambivalence that can be understood. In *The Essence of Manifestation* I have tried to propose an explanation which is able to make this ambivalence fully intelligible. Nietzsche is content, one might say, with giving some particularly pertinent historical examples: cruelty, for example. What is cruelty? It is the pleasure of inflicting suffering. Nietzsche insists on showing how, as much in primitive Greece as in the Middle Ages, there were ceremonies whose purpose was to offer the pleasure that the suffering of others gives us. In the Middle Ages public executions were great festive events. People went there not only to see someone being hanged, but also to see him tortured. The masses went to see spectacles that for us in the modern world, sensitive to pity, would be intolerable. Now for Nietzsche the strength and the greatness of man consist in the fact that in him can be found the pleasure of suffering. And so, in Nietzsche the connection between suffering and pleasure is extraordinarily interiorized, which prefigures Freudian themes. Not only can I obtain an extraordinary pleasure from the suffering of others, but I can also in a certain sense be the sculptor of myself and, to make myself suffer, cut and engrave my own flesh. From this derive the great phenomena of the bad conscience, of self-disgust, in which I am pleased with myself despite everything, because they contain their own joy. But in the end the problem that Nietzsche did not deal with, and which we need not address here, is that of the internal comprehension of suffering and joy. Why does this connection exist originally within life? This is one of the great problems that we have inherited from the moment in which Schopenhauer formulated the antinomy between unreal representation and this dark world which is ours.

When you say that Nietzsche 'saved life', just what do you mean?

The great merit of Nietzsche was that of having given back to life its phenomenological dimension. Because basically the affirmation that life is unconscious has no meaning. Living is above all having the sensation of oneself [*s'éprouver*], feeling oneself. This is true even for the most simple modality of life. If one considers an impression of pleasure, what meaning could a pleasure have that one does not feel? The armchair, which does not have the sensation of itself [*ne s'éprouve*], does not feel either pleasure or pain, even if we give it an axe-blow. That is why pushing the affirmation that life is unconscious to its limit is nonsensical. Therefore the merit of Nietzsche is immense, in as much as he did not give a phenomenological definition of life in terms of representation – that is of putting things at a distance thanks to which the *gaze of observation* becomes possible – but rather he gave a definition of phenomenality in terms of *feeling*, of pathos. A figure such as that of Dionysus, who suffers and enjoys at the same time, is essentially that of a living being, because pleasure and pain are in my opinion the primary modalities of life. Life is above all pleasure or pain, it is need, but need is painful; it exists only on the affective level. If need were not felt, it would not be anything.

Thus there is in Nietzsche a deep desire to make of life something splendid, and to understand that this splendor comes from the fact that it is a revelation; in fact a self-revelation, because every affect reveals itself alone, it feels itself. We have a proof of this phenomenological character of life, utterly opposed to the abandonment to the unconscious, the dark, and anonymity, such as we find in Schopenhauer and partially also in Freud. The proof of this value of revelation of life is that Nietzsche made of life the source of values. While in Schopenhauer it was a source of absurdity, and while in Freud it will often be a source of delirium, madness and phantasms of every kind, in Nietzsche life is the *initial principle* of values. Life creates values: for Nietzsche there are not values in nature, in objects, but it is life which gives them a value, and so life is the initial principle of evaluations. That is why the fundamental question that one should ask is: why does that initial principle of evaluation, which is life, have a value itself ? Why does life have a value and why in the end does life have a value for Nietzsche? Because he is happy to be alive, because having the sensation of oneself [*s'éprouver soi-même*], which is peculiar to living beings and which will be taken away from us when we die, is an extraordinary thing.

In Nietzsche life is analyzed through a certain number of figures. One of the principal figures through which Nietzsche analyses life are the nobles. Nietzsche has the nobles say: 'We nobles, the good the happy...' That which justifies life is thus happiness. That is why we have to defend it against all the processes which attack it, the most terrible of which, according to Nietzsche, is the process by which life turns against itself. This is one of the most inspired discoveries of Nietzsche: to have recognized in human experience the processes of self-destruction. And in the moment in which he discerns these processes of self-destruction, among which suicide is only an extreme form, Nietzsche draws back in horror saying: what a strange beast is man, who destroys himself! Now these processes of self-destruction are in the service of bad conscience, feelings of guilt, all that which generates disgust towards ourselves, ennui and malaise. For Nietzsche an illness of life exists, but the most terrible thing is that this sickness of life is also the awareness of suffering: only it is no longer a suffering in the service of life, but a will towards self-destruction. Thus in Nietzsche suffering has a double role: the movement towards life to put oneself to the test [*s'éprouver soi-même*], as well as the start of the terrible process of self-destruction, which we have before our eyes in the modern world as well.

And so Freud arrives. Does Freud also want, like Nietzsche, to save life?

Freud's attitude is equally ambiguous. But a precise reply to this question can only be found if one consults the famous *Project for a Scientific Psychology* of 1895. It is an extremely interesting project, because in it Freud proposes a scientific explanation of psychic activity, which in reality is a description of the neuronal system. In this sense it is truly modern, and can be connected with certain modern trends in neuroscience. Here Freud says that the neuronal system is divided in two: a *Psy* system and a *Phi* system. What characterizes the neurons is that they are of two types. One type experiences external stimuli which determine a series of behavior patterns intended to favor flight from external danger – because one can flee from it one can escape from its action, and there are many ways of doing so. But the real danger for Freud, as for Schopenhauer and Nietzsche, is an inner one. Unfortunately there are other neurons whose characteristic is self-excitement, in the sense that they undergo an excitement which is no longer exogenous, but endogenous. And this interior excitement is terrible – there is nothing to be done. And this determines entropy for Freud. For him there is an excitement of the neuronal system which itself tends only to liquidate excitements. Since excitement is troublesome the neuronal system tends towards a quantity of energy $Q = 0$, that is towards a state of inertia or of death. As a consequence the whole theory of psychic activity built on the neuronal model is centered on the flight from excitement, because, according to Freud, excitement produces a suffering in the neuronal system, and thus in psychic activity: 'the malaise of need' as Schopenhauer would have called it, the malaise of desire; the libido, which gradually becomes unbearable as the quantity of excitement increases. What should be done then? Extinguish excitement, and in order to do this it is necessary to try to bring the neuronal system – and thus the psychic system which is its reflection – towards the state $Q = 0$. Basically it is necessary to extinguish the excitement which provokes malaise in us – this is Schopenhauer again – and to extinguish the malaise it is necessary to suppress the excitement. But basically to not feel malaise it is necessary to be an armchair or pair of shoes – it is a system of death. That is why I believe that in the end the apparition of the death drive in metapsychology is not a chance event, and it is exactly this aspect of Freud's thought that I do not accept. Confronted with this Freud, I have the same reaction – if you will allow the comparison – of Nietzsche confronted with Schopenhauer. I believe that life is good and therefore that it is not a case of liquidating our affects. The opposite is the case, as it was for Kandinsky: that of making life become more intense, such that it ever increasingly has the sensation of itself [*s'éprouve elle-même*]. I believe that all great works of art have the effect not of permitting life to liquidate its libido, but on the contrary of increasing by degrees its happiness and joy, which tend towards a sort of absolute beatitude.

One could however object that this liquidation of the libido corresponds for Freud to its satisfaction; it corresponds to an enjoyment. For Freud the fact of liquidating the libido is pleasurable.

You are right. There are two moments in Freud's reply, since he himself gave a reply to his own question. There is the moment in which enjoyment is the attenuation of excitement, and thus it does not suppress it – Freud in fact says that excitement is impossible to suppress altogether. Enjoyment makes it return to a stable state, according to the principle of constancy, not that of death, and as a consequence it has to satisfy, as far as possible, both drive and needs. At this point a sort of equilibrium is found, preferable to desire. This is a first reply. Then there is another very different one, upon which especially Paul Ricoeur reflected in his fine book, *Freud and Philosophy*: Eros suddenly arrives. In this world in which the death drive reigns, in which its dominion expands, suddenly Eros arrives – we know neither where from nor why – to re-activate life and to re-animate the scene. Eros is love in all the meanings of the word, which gives back to life that character of activity which, despite everything, is inherent within it. Here Freud is correct, no doubt; but it is also true, as Ricoeur noted, that here there is an error or fault [*faille*] in the Freudian discourse, in that the principle of Eros falls in a certain sense from heaven.

Nevertheless, in your opinion, does Freud truly constitute an overcoming or superseding of the classical philosophy of representation, or is he rather a compromise between the rediscovery of life as a positive fact and the classical vision? Perhaps Freud is halfway between classicism and world of Dionysus?

Freud is very close to Schopenhauer. In him there is the decisive affirmation, which I fully agree with, that the basis of our being is not of the order of representation, that representation is a non-reality, and that our reality is to be found in the depths of the unconscious. But at the bottom of the unconscious there are two things in conflict. On one side there is the affect which, Freud said – in a marginal note which to me seems magnificent – is never unconscious, in the sense that the affect feels itself [*s'éprouve*]. But on the other hand there is in Freud a theory of the unconscious which remains on the side of representation. Since basically, in the texts of 1912 and 1914, it is through unconscious representation that the unconscious regains its right of citizenship. While as regards deeper reality, there is also in Freud a contradiction: on one side there is an unconscious that, at its limit, is absolute; and on the other there is an affect that is for him, as it is for me, the basis of life. In the last formulation of analytic therapy, a history of affects is in question. In this context Freud had some intuitions of admirable profundity, for example in his theory of anguish. He puts anguish on the same plane as all affects. Every affect, before becoming realized, in the moment in which it still has not found its fulfillment, when it is in some way abandoned to the simple weight it exercises on itself, turns into anguish. And the anguish is not overcome until love finds a new incarnation. Here Freud, in relation to classical philosophy, has explored an essential dominion.

Philosophically speaking, what is in your opinion the essential difference between Freud's anguish and that of Heidegger?

The anguish of Freud seems to me much closer to reality. It is much closer to the anguish of Kierkegaard than to that of Heidegger – or, if you prefer, I feel much closer to the Kierkegaardian description of anguish than to that of Heidegger, because for Heidegger anguish puts us into the presence of the world, while for Freud, as for Kierkegaard, anguish arises from the relation of self [*du soi*] with itself. More precisely, it arises from pure suffering, in which life gives itself up to itself and in which the suffering of malaise gives itself to itself. The weight of need, when it becomes intolerable, leads to the rise of anguish. Thus in Freud anguish is born from the relationship of the ego with itself. In some phrases Freud says it explicitly: the ego cannot bear itself – while in Heidegger anguish puts me in relationship with the world. But I do not believe that this relationship with the world truly provokes anguish in people, such that this phrase of Heidegger – 'anguish puts me in front of the void' – is taken up by Kierkegaard, in whom it however has a completely different sense. I said 'the void', because Heidegger, like Hegel, identifies the world with the void. The world is this horizon of visibility in which there is still nothing and in which things reveal themselves. And so here there is a complete shifting away from the anguish of life, which is that of Kierkegaard and of Freud, towards an anguish of the world, which to me seems less pertinent.

But one could object that also for Freud anguish is relation with an object. Especially when he speaks of phobic anguish: there is a phobic object, an external object is a source of anguish.

Yes, but in Freud anguish, in order to become relieved, *searches* for an object. The phobic object, which has nothing to do with the real situation, is simply a way to project outside oneself the unbearable weight of anguish. Thus the phobic object is a sort of deceit into which anguish leads itself in order to flee from itself. But it is not the phobic object which allows anguish to free itself from itself. Only an authentic transformation of the affect allows anguish to become free from itself. It is a self-transformation of life which can unblock the situation – for example being able to love again, without deceitful projections. In these projections consists the illness. This illness that tries to flee anguish within the world of representation is indeed a curious one, as it ends up trapped in a dead-end street where it will remain trapped: unless, that is, it finds the one true way out which Freud indicates, via the *abreaction* of the affective traumatic event in treatment. It is necessary to start again from this traumatic event in order to find the solution in the context of life and reality, accepting the plane of reality, rediscovering on the plane of reality a reason to live, that is an actualization of our affective power.

You have also worked for a long time on Marx. In closing, can you tell us something about the affinities and differences between Marx and Freud?

The same contradictions are expressed regarding Marx as those for Freud. Marx has been assigned to the 'age of suspicion', as Ricoeur said. Like Freud, Marx is a thinker who leads us to treat our discourses as suspect. The solution, for Marx as for Freud, is to be found on the plane of reality. For ten years I did nothing other than read Marx. And what I found remarkable in Marx, and what I discovered by chance, is that at the root of reality he places a subjective body. He says so not only in his youthful writings, but also in his last manuscripts, which are admirable, and which went to make up Book III of *Das Kapital*. For Marx all explanations start from work, which is a mode of bodily activity: here we re-encounter Schopenhauer. But this work is understood as subjective and not unconscious work; because after all if work in the nineteenth century – which demanded much of the body – was painful, then it was not unconscious. Computers and machines do not work. One can make them 'work' as much as one wants, but in another sense.

Human work is subjective, individual, living. It is subjective in as much as it is suffered, but it can also be joyful. Human work is individual – while an anonymous force is not individual. And to say that human work is living means that it has the sensation of itself [*s'éprouve*]. If I had here the late manuscripts of Marx I could show you that every time he defines man he always speaks of the 'subjective force of living work'. And when this theme comes up in the manuscripts, Marx always writes it in italics. In order to construct the economy, it has been necessary to quantify – an impossible thing – and to qualify – an equally impossible thing – this subjective and living work. It is impossible, because one cannot quantify and qualify an existence, a suffering, love – unless we are dealing with prostitution, and perhaps not even in this case. And so human reality is basically always the same, even though we study it in such different fields as psycho-pathology and economic life.

Translated from the French by Tristram Bruce

Selected Bibliography

I am the Truth. Toward a Philosophy of Christianity (2002). Stanford: Stanford University Press.

The Genealogy of Psychoanalysis (1998). Stanford: Stanford University Press.

Marx. A Philosophy of Human Being (1983). Bloomington: Indiana University Press.

Philosophy and Phenomenology of the Body (1975). The Hague: Nijhoff.

The Essence of Manifestation (1973). The Hague: Nijhoff.

FREUDIAN MODELS OF LANGUAGE

Julia Kristeva

JULIA KRISTEVA was born in Sophia (Bulgaria) in 1941. Since arriving in Paris in 1966 as a doctoral fellow, she has become a dominant figure in contemporary theory, as well as one of the world's most respected and rigorous intellectuals. A member of the faculty at the University of Paris VII, for nearly two decades she has also been a regular visiting professor at New York's Columbia University, sharing the chair of literary semiology with Umberto Eco and Tzvetan Todorov. A practicing psychoanalyst and member of the French Psychoanalytic Association, Kristeva has continually sought – through the merging of disciplines as diverse as philosophy, linguistics, semiotics, feminist and literary theory, and psychoanalysis – to formulate new modes of critical discourse in order to reflect logic and reality differently.

In this conversation with Sergio Benvenuto, Prof. Kristeva starts from what she calls today's 'new maladies of the soul' (autism, psychosomatic disorders, borderline and 'as-if ' personalities) to question the essential link of psychoanalysis with language. In doing so, she isolates three Freudian theories of language which dominated three distinct periods of Freud's career: 1) what Kristeva terms a 'layered' or *stratified* conception of language, which acts as intermediary between feelings and logic (corresponding to Freud's intuition that drives and libido are incommensurate with language); 2) a later 'structural' model (which Lacan would take up), wherein Freud assimilates the unconscious to a sort of primitive, hieroglyphic language (an 'optimistic' model insofar as it is based on the idea that free associations can directly affect drives and traumas); 3) beginning in 1912, a third, more 'skeptical' model, whereby language holds no guarantee of truth but may, indeed, even prove illusory.

The following interview with Julia Kristeva took place in Paris, in May 1994, at the Italian Cultural Institute, and was originally published in Italian in the *Enciclopedia Multimediale delle Scienze Filosofiche*. It first appeared in the *Journal of European Psychoanalysis* n. 3–4 (1997) under the title 'Freudian Models of Language', and is here reprinted courtesy of RAI – Radiotelevisione Italiana.

Sergio Benvenuto

What were Freud's conceptions of language?

Julia Kristeva

Freud can be read today in light of the current analytic experience, which is connected to two recent developments. One is what I have called, in a recent book, 'the new maladies of the soul' ranging from autism to psychosomatic affections and borderline cases, 'false Selves', 'as-if personalities' and other narcissistic disturbances. In these cases the analyst is confronted by something lying beyond language which cannot be represented. The second development refers to a cognitivist push in the human sciences today, where there is a trend to approach psychic experience by shortcircuiting the materiality of language and imposing on this materiality logical strategies, with or without a subject. It is from these two vantage points that we can attempt another look at Freudian conceptions of language. Because a single schematic idea was so often made out of them, there is believed to be a single Freudian conception language, but I maintain there are at least three.

The first language model formulated by Freud is found in his early writings, particularly in the 1891 monograph *On Aphasia*, in the *Project for a Scientific Psychology* (1895), and some other texts from the same period. All these take as their starting point the incommensurability between the sexual and the verbal. Freud does not believe that sexual desire can be grasped by language: not only is it difficult for desire to enter language and be interpreted, but intelligence and language on the one hand, and sexual desire on the other, are even asymptotic (which means there is no point of convergence, no symbiosis, no commensurability). This asymptote is probably attributable to neurosis but, going back in time, perhaps also to our initial immaturity: language comes *après coup*, afterwards. Thus, there is a gap between our body and the possibility to speak, an idea which Freud develops, for example, in the *Case of Little Hans*. Starting from this incommensurability between body and language, between sexual desire and intelligence, Freud establishes an absent (or inadequate) translation between the unconscious representation and words, which leads him to prepare a model that I will call a 'heterogeneous model of language'. This first Freudian model of language is heterogeneous because of the gap between the representation of words and the representation of things.

This distinction can be found in Appendix C of his 1915 study, 'The Unconscious' (although it had already been elaborated in his aphasia monograph), where Freud speaks of 'word representations' as a set of representations which essentially involve the sound images of speech. I pronounce a word, and the psyche records a sound image of the word's essence (although it is not the only one, because the representation of a word comprises also an image of reading, writing and movement). Speech is a complex, but closed, whole. Still, the representation of words is tied to the representation of objects or things, that other component which can be called *an open whole* and which comprises the visual image of the word. When I say *television*, for example, I see the visual image of the television, but there are also tactile (I can touch it) and acoustic (it has sound and volume) images. Thus, according to Freud, the psychic apparatus, centered on the representation of things and words, proceeds towards a heterogeneous representation in the psyche because of these two essential components.

In his *Project for a Scientific Psychology*, Freud conceived of two systems: an external one, 'phi', that sets the human being in contact with the external world, and an internal one, 'psi'. He postulates a quantitative charge, a biological energy which can be hormonal, humoral or electrical which, passing from the one system to the other, can go from quantitative to qualitative or psychic. (I should also say that due to great strides in neurobiology today, Freud's proposals have become substantial, and his text now draws much attention.)

Language, because it is situated between two systems, that of energy charges and perception on the one hand, and that of logical activity on the other, favors knowledge and consciousness. In Freud, language suddenly occupies a crucial intermediary space between perception and logic, without being reduced to either of them. Thus, this first Freudian model contains a dualism which I call a 'layered conception' (*conception feuilletée*) of language, because here language is not reduced to our present-day models based on the signifier/signified opposition. Instead, it reaches towards the external world through sensation, and towards the world of intelligence via the transmission of memory on up to the complicated system of logical and, even further, metaphysical, connections. The heterogeneity of this model is very interesting because it heads off in the opposite direction of a certain linguistic trend which seeks to recover the early Freud within the Saussurean model. The Lacanian trend, in particular, applies the Saussurean model to Freud because this trend is more in keeping with the second Freudian model, as we shall see. Yet this first model is very interesting, even if the Lacanian trend does not mention it explicitly, because it emerges from Freud the biologist and medical doctor, and takes into account sensation, perception and energy charges. For this reason I call it a 'stratified' model of language.

Some analysts today are very mindful of this model, and, whether consciously or not, have made efforts to take it into account. Take Bion's work: in *Attention and Interpretation* (1970), he establishes some differences between a symbolizing 'alpha function' and a non-symbolized 'beta element'; one thus already sees a heterogeneity of the psychic, mental (and, in a more restricted sense, linguistic) operation.

Do you think, then, that Bion's later thinking was directly inspired by Freud's first neurological theorization?

I don't know if Bion was directly inspired by Freud, I am simply remarking on a similarity. Bion, blazing his own path, succeeded in finding that heterogeneity of the function of language (*langagier*), which corresponds to the thesis of the early Freud. There is an isomorphism, or parallelism, between Freud and Bion.

In the wake of this, certain books like my own *The Revolution of Poetic Language* were produced, where I distinguish between the semiotic and the symbolic. By 'semiotic' I mean that which inheres in language, a certain disposition of the senses, but also of the drives dating back to early infancy, to echolalia, to everything pre-linguistic: a dimension which poetic language recaptures and updates, if you will. This level which manifests itself yet once again through rhythm, alliterations and other intralinguistic phenomena is linked to the level of drives and perhaps, from there, more to the bodily and biological levels of the signifying function. Another level I call 'symbolic', that is, the *stricto sensu* field of language: the field of signs, feelings, synthesis and logic. One recent trend is developing in France precisely in this direction, and includes the works of Piera Aulagnier whose book, *Violence and Interpretation*, proposes a pre-linguistic *(pré-langagier)* state of feeling which she calls *pictogram*, found in certain traumatic and regressive states, but also in psychosis. These examples show that modern clinical practice, confronted with a difficult psychopathology (particularly the cure of psychosis), needs to give some thought to an infra-linguistic, psychic operation which, in fact, was put forth by the first Freudian model.

But one might object that Freud's initial theorizations were inspired by the neurology of his time, which today has been surpassed.

This is true; Freud did not have a sufficient neurobiological knowledge to refine his theories on the functioning of brain cells and synapses. Today our concepts on this, as well as on the nervous system as a whole, are far more advanced. Roughly put, there are two theories: an electrical theory,

Changeux's, which proposes a sort of neuronal map, and a humoral theory, which holds that beyond this electrical map of the brain there lies a logical one, likely to be more dynamic and fluid. Yet in all these current trends, which are far more modern and clear-cut than what Freud left us, one hiatus stands out from everything that can be said on the level of neurons on the one hand, and of language on the other. We do not succeed in filling the gap between the biological substratum and the linguistic (*langagière*) manifestation, and, thus, we find ourselves confronted with this double determination in the face of psychological manifestations, and in particular of psychiatric or psychoanalytic symptoms.

Take depression. A certain number of depressive symptoms can be eliminated thanks to neurolectics or even electroshock. This means that a certain mental functioning can be corrected and treated on the biological level; but this does not exclude an intervention on the level of language. Psychoanalytic work can have an effect even on a biological cell. For example, certain interpretations can bring on an accelerated functioning of the brain, a greater conductibility of synapses, and even a change in the rate of production of serotonin. In other words, in present models, insofar as they can be refined, there is always something that recalls the early Freud: we are always faced with a double, stratified model. I always try to rethink this Freudian dualism: not to be satisfied with it, but to stratify it, multiply it, and render it more contemporary, without losing sight of that double determination, without which the mental functioning is made to level out: one either reduces it to pure and simple biology by eliminating the signifying factor, or one is satisfied solely by the signifying factor and dismisses the biological base. The actuality of psychoanalysis can take place only through the recognition of this double determination.

But did not Freud, when he wrote The Interpretation of Dreams, *completely abandon this neurological reference? Is not Lacan's analysis of this work correct, especially when he says that the unconscious is structured like a language?*

Your question leads me to what I call the second Freudian model of language, one which lies close to the structural model which Lacan will later develop. Freud comes to this optimistic model slowly when he abandons neurology while preparing his plan for the psychoanalytic cure – which will be based on the fundamental rule of free association. Between 1892 and 1900, Freud became convinced that associative recounting is capable of translating a traumatic content. He said to his patients: 'Tell me what comes into your mind; associate freely and give me a narrative'. Thus, he will base his plans for his cure on narration, whence he will produce another model centered on language.

This second model is characterized by two particularities: on the one hand, language is constituted by preconscious intermediary terms (thus language is preconscious) which allow the unconscious to be dominated by consciousness. Thus language is intermediary and intermediate. For Freud, language remains in the sphere of the preconscious. Nevertheless, language possesses the power to go beyond consciousness because it is situated between consciousness and the unconscious. How does language possess this extraordinary power to render things conscious? Let us recall the first model: given that language is a heterogeneous construction, fed by sensations and perceptions, it anchors itself even in the body, starting from sensations and perceptions, on up to biology. It thus remains an intermediate model between the unconscious, on the one hand, and consciousness, on the other; for this reason, it is the preferred and advantageous standard on which to build the cure.

Furthermore, in order for consciousness to be dominated by the unconscious, the model of the unconscious itself will be ever more influenced by linguistic consciousness. So Freud, in *The Interpretation of Dreams*, develops a definition of language constructed, in fact, from certain notions he gleans from theories with which he is familiar, ranging from certain assimilations of the unconscious to grammar, to certain reminiscences regarding writing. For example, he compares language to hieroglyphics. Other esoteric references will also come into play. In this context, Freud also read certain linguists, above all Karl Abel, whose studies he used in his essay 'The Antithetical Meaning of Primal Words'.

There are two significant aspects to the Freudian interest in primitive words. Firstly, he wanted to establish a logic which was not coincidental with consciousness; this logic of the unconscious ignores specifically the 'no', and does not know contradiction. Secondly, at the same time Freud does not consider this logic to be a simple theoretical construction of the analyst, or something simply tied to the analytic experience, or to a neurotic or psychotic pathology, but rather a part of the human inheritance as such. Thus Freud attempts to base himself on linguistic works, sometimes erroneous ones (as were Karl Abel's), which permit him to say: 'What I tell you today is realized in the cure, but this is part of man's heredity, and can be rediscovered in the past'. In short, Freud seeks to rationalize his discovery and to extend the reach of what might be thought, not just to pathology, but to the whole of human experience. In *The Interpretation of Dreams*, he seeks to understand the logic of the unconscious by assimilating it to a primitive language.

Lacan's contribution, particularly his statement that 'the unconscious is structured like a language', is a careful and faithful reading of this second Freud, whose essential objective he makes explicit. Many analysts today feel that the Lacanian reading is an extreme one, which pushes that second Freud too much towards a *linguisteria* (the term Lacan used to poke fun at his own approach); similarly, many believe that 1960s structural linguistics had overly extended its sway on Freudian thought through Lacan. At that time structural linguistics, practiced particularly by Jakobson, was being developed by Lévi-Strauss into the basis of structuralist thought, via his own studies on phonology, kinship systems and myths. Making the unconscious mathematical as Lacanians tried to do and, in a certain way, as cognitivism attempts today, can be joined to this second Freudian attempt to think about language as one finds it in *The Interpretation of Dreams*. Because even Freud seeks a model in the linguistics of his time, on the basis of his understanding of that knowledge – in order to put the unconscious under the control of consciousness. Lacan and the cognitivists seek other models, but they think that it is possible to capture language, and the unconscious assimilated to it, through certain specific models taken from the sciences of their time.

I call this second model of language 'optimist' because Freud thought at that time that free association could permit us to gather all symptoms, and that we would be able to make traumas, drives, and all sexual and psychic disturbances appear in language. However, this optimism leaves space for another Freudian model which continues to be stratified and heterogeneous. More precisely, he speaks of drives which are not a language and of primary and secondary processes susceptible to various logics.

The primary processes involve *displacements* and *condensations*. For example, instead of dreaming about something extremely disturbing or difficult to accept because of sexual reasons such as a traumatic encounter with a woman a subject will dream about a botanical paper. I am alluding to Freud's own famous dream about the botanical monograph, a very scientific book; the final interpretation of this dream will reveal it to be a *displacement* from a traumatic sexual experience which bears some relationship to a flower and to femininity.

Condensation has been assimilated to metaphor. One takes a feature: for example, the feature 'man', along with another, say 'a bending reed'. When Pascal says 'the man is a thinking reed', he constructs a metaphor. But through condensations, in many dreams, one element of the dream is in fact overloaded with multiple oneiric thoughts, and becomes a point where many dream-thoughts meet. Freud's dream of the botanical monograph is an example of both displacement and condensation, because here the dreamer explores his relations with femininity, science, publications, culture, etc. Contrary to the primary process is the secondary process, or what Freud called 'reasoning processes', by which he means syntax, logic, argumentation. Drives operate according to a primary process of displacement and condensation, but are later subsumed by the secondary processes.

May we nevertheless say that in the primary process there are linguistic phenomena at work?

Freud himself suggested this when he said that there is a rhetoric and a grammar of dreams. This allowed Lacan to speak explicitly of metaphor and metonymy, projecting a certain number of Jakobson's categories onto Freudian notions. Thus, Lacan greatly developed this second Freudian model. And although Lacan pushes his interpretation further, he remains faithful to this specific Freud.

So does Lacan remain faithful to a more clinical Freud? In effect, the first Freud is a neurological Freud, quite distant from the concrete, real, clinical experience of neurotics. Can one then say that the second Freud is closer to his own practice?

I don't think so. All the various Freuds are part of the corpus transmitted to us. When we ask ourselves if psychoanalysis is still relevant, it is important to see its archaeology and articulation, whence it comes, which elements it gave birth to and abandoned along the way, while still remaining subject to them. For example, the neurological Freud is not just neurological, because in his book on aphasia he largely disassociated himself from Meynert's and Wernicke's neurological theories.

Freud, starting from these various neurological studies, constructed a model of language derived not from a system but from what he called *a language area*, a sort of mutation, characterized by fluidity. In this area, the various centers hypothesized by neurologists of that time would not function as fixed centers, but rather as thresholds, through which energies would pass without being fixed in traceable or identifiable areas of the brain. Thus, a sort of neurological structure is constituted which will underlie the operations of the linguistic (*langagière*) structure itself. Furthermore, this linguistic structure will be influenced by the relationship of he who speaks with the other to whom he speaks. Thus, from this moment on, we take part in the elaboration of what I have just called 'a layered representation of language'. This representation also comprises the neurological determination – considered, nevertheless, as a 'language area' – with energy transitions and passages across thresholds. It is then, in this sense, a very fluid and dynamic structure.

Secondly, it is a level of representation on which we find a representation of both the word and the thing. And, thirdly, there is already a subject, which (if necessary) possesses this function, but is not explicitly postulated by Freud as such. In fact, the theory of subjectivity and the relationship with the other are missing in this first elaboration (this lack will be filled by the second Freud), but otherwise, the stratification of the model is already there. Only later will the notion of subjectivity, so linked to the linguistic conception in *The Interpretation of Dreams*, come together; and, similarly, only later will the theory of free association develop. The Freudian theory will never reflect on *transference*, something which is quite extraordinary, considering that Freud himself established the analytic cure, that is, the fact that one subject speaks to an other.

Thus, the scene is played out by two: the analytic subject is in relation to another. Thus did Freud come to postulate the transference relationship, and lest we forget, even spoke about countertransference: by which he meant that the analyst can understand his patient only if he puts himself in the position of transferring on to the patient his own, more or less traumatic past, experiences, and memories. Yet, transference and counter-transference relations were neither rendered explicit nor thoroughly developed by Freud. On this point more recent theories, both prior to and with Lacan, have made an essential contribution.

Nevertheless, this second model should not be treated as the only Freudian model. Language as the lever of the cure, and the unconscious assimilated to language, are all elements of *The Interpretation of Dreams*, but there are also others levers, vestiges of the first and even of the third Freudian models.

In 1912, Freud seems to abandon his main interest in language for phylogeny, that is, human biological and psychological heredity. How can one understand his phylogenetic tale, which has troubled so many analysts after Freud?

The period between 1912 and 1914 marked a turn in Freud's thought, a turn that became more radical and intense with the war. In his 1912 *Totem and Taboo*, Freud imagines a primitive horde, a gathering of brothers; given that women are always and only objects of exchange these brothers desire to share the women, but without success, because their father keeps them all to himself. At first, to get at the women, the brothers kill the father whence the desire to kill, and the repetition of this killing. We are thus in a *compulsion to repeat* (a particularly Freudian term), linked to the death drive which agitates the brothers of the primitive horde. And then, during the course of this compulsion to repeat, something new appears: the totemic meal. The father will be eaten, interiorized, and thus a symbolic pact will be orally set up. Thus the paternal tyranny will cease to be a tyranny, and will become authority. And the brothers come to recognize that there is law.

Here we pass from the drive as something unrepresentable – the death drive and its violence – to the constitution of a symbolic pact which, in the history of humanity, coincides with the emergence of *homo sapiens*. Freud recounts this tale of the primitive horde to show how the social animal begins to identify himself no longer with the tyranny, but rather with the authority, of the father, and thus, to enter culture.

From 1912 on, Freud will continually refine the psychic representations proposed by his tale. The totemic meal brings us from the acting-out of the killing to symbolization (we represent to ourselves someone with whom we identify), whereby we become capable of thought, speech, and logic; in short, we become capable of culture. At this point, we are in the realm of the psyche. In some later works, Freud seeks to vary this psychic representation, this inner life which installs itself from the moment of the totemic act. It is here that he turns his attention to narcissism, which he defines as a new psychic feature distinct from autoeroticism, even predating the Oedipus.

In 1915, the term 'subject', as opposed to 'object', is penned by Freud in regard to drives. Today, the subject of the unconscious and of psychoanalysis is often discussed. Freud does not use this term at the time; he speaks of 'I' (*Ich*), 'It' (*Es*) and 'Over-I' (*Ueber-Ich*), but in 1915 he first uses the term 'subject' – albeit with regard to drives, distinguishing a subject and an object of the drive. Take for example the oral drive: I am the subject of the oral drive, and my object will be this fruit or that vegetable, that I will assimilate. It is solely from this point of view, then – in something of an instinctual opening (*frayage*) that pushes me to assimilate an object, to satisfy a need that Freud first articulates a subject/object relation: something he does not take up again. Instead, he goes on to develop a second topography.

In the so-called first topography, already outlined in *The Interpretation of Dreams,* he speaks of the unconscious, preconscious and conscious. In the second topography he will speak of Ego, Id, and Super-Ego. But the notion of subject will appear in relation to the drive: there is a subject-object polarity to the drive, but also a pleasure-unpleasure polarity, and an active-passive one. The latter, of course, prefigures the sado-masochistic relation between a dominant person and one who is dominated. These ideas are then further developed in Freud's papers on metapsychology, which mark a truly essential moment in the history of Freudian thought.

In 1917, Freud published 'Mourning and Melancholia', a fundamental text for anyone who, like me, is interested in depression. Here he goes deeper into the logic of the ambivalence between subject and object. Without speaking explicitly of a theory of the subject (which will be taken up instead by contemporary psychoanalysis), he speaks of the ambivalence of the melancholic object, of the fact that the object that provokes melancholy is itself an ambivalent object: 'I love someone yet I hate him'. In doing so I do not succeed in ridding myself of this someone; I cannot manage to lose him when he wounds me, I place him within me, but, precisely because he is ambivalent, in doing so I too become ambivalent. Thus, instead of simply loving myself, I hate, I underestimate and depress myself, and can even kill myself. Thus, Freud goes deeply into this problematic of subjectivity, finding ambivalence everywhere: but he does so without ever elaborating an epistemology of the subject, something which remains troubling even today.

In 1920, in *Beyond the Pleasure Principle*, we have Freud's extraordinary postulation of the death drive, as the carrying wave of the life drive. The human being is inhabited by this death drive, which contrary to what is commonly held, is not to be confused with aggression. In fact, aggressivity is already found in eroticism; when I attack someone, this attack is also part of Eros, of desire.

So do you disagree with certain analytic trends – the Kleinian one, for example – which interpret the death drive almost exclusively in terms of aggression?

This reading is a limitation of the concept of the death drive. The death drive is rather a loosening, a break, of the relation with the other, a return to a state of isolation, close to an inorganic state, even to nothingness. I view it, as does André Green, for example, or Bion: as a loosening which recalls psychopathologies closer to psychosis, melancholia and, perhaps, autism, that is, cases in which we are not on the same carrying wave as Eros. Eros absorbs or rejects, loves or hates, but it does not sever ties. When instead we sever ties, we are in a much more serious, more radical, psychic symptomatology linked to the evacuation of the other and of all ties to language and the senses.

Even if it is true that language can allow us access to the whole panoply of psychic life through narcissism, the ambivalence of the subject and object, the death drive, etc., nevertheless, the third Freud insinuates a very interesting thought for analysts today. In one sense, his thought becomes skeptical: he finds resistances, analysis does not always work, the results are not very interesting, the analytic cure cannot go very far, in short, the cure has clear limits. But, from another angle (and here there is a deeper doubt), it is not just language, the vector in the prior optimistic model, which gives us access to the unconscious. As resistances develop little by little, as one goes deeper into the ambivalences of psychic life, into the exploration of melancholia, psychosis, the death drive, etc., one becomes aware that language can also bear hallucinations and errors. I might say one word, but its sound-resonance might lead me to think not about the object to which it refers, but about something completely different; whence this hallucination might lead me to lose my relation with reality, go astray, become delirious. Thus, language is not an anchor in truth, whether the latter be perceived as such or linked to an unconscious trauma. Language can be a source of error, and yet, we are constrained, despite everything, to pass through language.

Thus Freud discovers that with language one is walking on quicksand. Lacan later develops, in a certain way, the consequences of this when he speaks of *semblant*, appearance. But he too leaves everything suspended. Language places us in an area of *appearanc*e which is not necessarily an obstacle for analysis, yet analysis must understand this appearance. But for the time being we are still in the phylogenetic fable. Thus, when Freud encounters the difficulties posed by language, he begins to speak less of them, as we see in *The Ego and the Id*. Here, instead of examining more closely the ambivalences, ambiguities, and difficulties of language, he puts them aside, and returns to the phylogenetic fable of the primitive man. In taking this up once more, Freud will, yet again, speak of the Ice Age, of how language appeared, of how every time difficulties emerge, one should not concern oneself solely with individual resistances but to see the living being as an end result in a process that runs from amoeba to human. Elsewhere Freud even alludes to the entirety of human history, seeking to link the various symptomatologies to its different periods. For example, he sought to link obsessional neuroses to a given period of hominization, hysteric neuroses to another, psychosis to yet another, and so on. Even in *Moses and Monotheism* we see his desire to rethink history by opening himself up to phylogeny.

Is the importance which Freud, at a certain point, attributes to phylogeny, to be understood as a recognition of Jung's collective unconscious?

I don't think so. Faced with Freud's openness towards phylogeny, many analysts have commented: 'Here we have a Freudian fiction. Incapable, in the state in which he found himself, of assuming the ambiguous relation to language and the difficulties of transference/countertransference, he throws himself into a fiction, telling us his personal fantasies as though wanting to show that even the analyst works with his own fantasies'. In effect, at that time many put the Freudian discovery on guard against an excessive subjectivism, as if Freud were confiding his own fantasies. Through this tale of the killing of the father Freud would only confess his own Oedipal desires. Perhaps there is some truth in all this; and if it were just this, I would nevertheless applaud Freud for having had the audacity to reveal his own unconscious tale, and to have proposed it as a means of investigation. Because one can question what it is the analyst analyzes with, what his analytic organ is. Is it simply his theory? His rhetorical baggage? Or perhaps his culture? Some have said that the analyst mobilizes his erogenous zones in the cure. Instead, I think that the analyst analyzes his own unconscious; but his unconscious must be available to him as a story. Thus, the analyst analyzes with his given capacity, giving a narrative form to his own fantasies. And here Freud provided an example, by attempting to construct the story of man, on which he projects his own desires. This is a possible interpretation of why phylogeny replaced language theories.

But I hold to another interpretation, in which Freud confronts the external psyche. He has shown that it is not necessary to close oneself in a pan-psychism, and that we can open the cure to another dimension, for which he found the word 'phylogeny'. It's a concept that had a certain currency during his time, by which he was fascinated, just as he was fascinated by Abel's linguistics. But what he aimed at could perhaps be understood today in terms of Nietzsche's notion of 'monumental history', or Heidegger's 'Being' (*Das Sein*). Freud wanted to escape from a narrow pan-psychism, from one-generational history; he wanted to lead the analyst to think about 'being', about all that constitutes the extra-psychic. Unfortunately, this advancement was abandoned by many analysts, even if Lacan took it up, in a dazzling way – albeit without many developments – when he called the speaking being a *parlêtre*, a speak-being. Here Lacan follows Heidegger's path. But we should go further, and introduce the extra-psychic into our investigations. It's a path we nowadays need to follow, especially if we want to tackle the symptomatologies that challenge us today. Because while our patients confront us, inevitably, with language, they also confront us with something biological, or that reaches from even beyond biology. It is here that a 'monumental history', the *Historiale* in the Heideggerian sense, may prove clinically fruitful.

Let me now try to give an example of how I try to keep in mind these three models. Recapitulating, they are: 1) the biological model; 2) the structural model of language, as developed by Lacan; and 3) the model of the extra-psyche (understanding how, in an ever-awkward but symptomatic way, the idea of Being and Freud's phylogenetic fable invite us to think about what is external to the psyche). So let me recount a clinical experience. One of my patients, a bulimic subject to vomiting attacks, is in a life-threatening state. After a number of sessions, the symptom subsides, and she begins a more classical analysis that allows her to reconstruct her history more calmly, and to work with free association. (These associations are the ground upon which Freud was able to base his conception of language as the essential lived experience of the cure: what I called his second model, the 'optimism of language'.) Now, in that phase of analysis, which I link precisely to that model, the patient told me a dream, which was actually more akin to a screen memory. She can't recall the entire dream, but remembers something like a seaside trip with her parents; she finds herself in their bedroom, as they all shared the same room on the trip, where her parents are having intercourse. But my patient considers this primal scene unliveable, because it places her before her a double identification, as both man and woman. She has enormous difficulties in becoming independent, in differentiating herself sexually, and in that scene she is summoned to a sexual catastrophe. She is at once both her parents, and cannot choose one or the other. And the memory of this dream or the screen memory which she retells through language during a session, places her in a state of impossibility and disappearance. Add to this the fact that, having found a more normal sexual life, and (thanks to analysis) a sexual partner, she has now become aware that her sexual partner very much resembles her mother. Even here she is faced with a conflict: to have a sexual relation with a man who is her mother makes for something unbearable. Essentially, it makes her bisexual.

Thus language has brought to light a trauma which, in the psychic scheme of this bulimic patient, has led to a decompensation. She is incapable of associating. Long sessions follow, without any possible verbalization, sessions resembling a stupor, as though an infraverbal level had been touched, a level of drives, close to the biological state of energy charges discussed in the first Freudian model; a level unable to pass over into symbolization.

I will spare you the details of this long therapy. However, I called on two remedies that are in resonance with the three models which we have previously discussed. The first remedy consisted of speaking to her of sensations, using in some way a sensory transplant in the cure. I spoke of the only psychic things she succeeded in experiencing: incapable of speaking, she ate and vomited; for her it was filling herself and emptying herself, something absolutely archaic and driven, without any glimmer of language. So, I tried to tell her how I imagined her eating, and her sensations: sugary, salty, pleasurable, distasteful. We unfurled a whole gamut of sensations, in which she gradually took part. Thus, through this transplant of sensory nominations, I sought to touch first an infralinguistic level of sensory experience, and from there, a suffering, black, unnameable body. The second remedy draws on a second type of interpretation: those vomiting scenes which overcame her while recalling the trip with her parents made me think of something which is part of this patient's history. She had done university research on Céline's novel, *Death on the Instalment Plan*, in which the author is travelling with his mother, and there is a terrible vomiting scene, which I described in my book *Powers of Horror*. It is a dizzying account of the horror that maternal rejection can provoke: the narrator vomits on his mother, because vomiting is violence. Here we rediscover the drive which we were speaking of before: is it simply erotic and aggressive? Or does it go much further, and annul the one and the other? I said to her: 'When you speak to me of these vomiting states, I think of your research on Céline'. This evocation, which was not sensory, not simply language, drove her instead back to history, to the extrapsychic, to something that happened outside of the analytic dyad, and outside of her own history, evoking cultural history, and even, through Céline, the problematic dimension of History, with a capital '*H*'. Céline was an essential figure in popular literature, but he was also involved in French fascism and wrote some extremely violent, anti-Semitic pamphlets. Thus, an entire historical conflict condensed, morphed around the name *Céline*, so that the evocation of the name gave her a certain relief from her psychic prison. She began to write extremely dense, elliptical poetry, which hampered her a bit in connecting thoughts, and prevented any easy, flexible rendering of her unconscious. Later, she abandoned poetry and took up stories, which were more in keeping with a somewhat bound and structured development of her psychic life. Starting from this, we touched on some dimensions of psychic life which may not go back to Ice-Age man but do bring us to an historical experience and, perhaps, beyond it, not only towards history but towards the *Historiale*. Nevertheless, it is a place of cure; because if one closes oneself solely in that space between the two subjects, one will fail to recognize the richness and great inspiration which lie at the basis of the Freudian discovery.

Translated from the French by Claudia Vaughn

Selected Bibliography

Female Genius: Life, Madness, Words: Hannah Arendt, Melanie Klein, Colette: A Trilogy. 3 vols. (2001) New York: Columbia University Press.

Crisis of the European Subject (2000). New York: Other Press.

New Maladies of the Soul (1995). New York: Columbia University Press.

Strangers to Ourselves (1991). New York: Columbia University Press.

Black Sun: Depression and Melancholia (1989). New York: Columbia University Press.

Revolution in Poetic Language (1984). New York: Columbia University Press.

Powers of Horror: An Essay on Abjection (1982). New York: Columbia University Press.

Desire in Language: A Semiotic Approach to Literature and Art (1980). New York: Columbia University Press.

PSYCHOANALYSIS AND SACRIFICE

René Girard

RENÉ GIRARD, world-renowned French historian, literary critic and philosopher of social science, was born in the southern French city of Avignon on Christmas day in 1923. Between 1943 and 1947, he studied in Paris at the École des Chartres, an institution for the training of archivists and historians, where he specialized in medieval history. In 1947 he went to Indiana University on a year's fellowship and eventually made almost his entire career in the United States – having later held chairs at Duke, Bryn Mawr, Johns Hopkins, the State University of New York and, finally, Stanford University, where he taught between 1981 and his retirement in 1995. His work belongs to the tradition of anthropological philosophy, and develops the idea – explained here in a conversation with Sergio Benvenuto and Maurizio Meloni – that human culture is based on sacrifice as the way out of mimetic, or imitative, violence between rivals. His writing covers anthropology, theology, psychology, mythology, sociology, cultural studies and literary criticism, as well as philosophy, and focuses on three main ideas: 1) mimetic desire; 2) the scapegoat mechanism; 3) the Bible's unveiling of 1 and 2.

In the interview that follows, Girard reviews where he most agrees or not with Freud, Lacan and French thinking in general over the last forty years, particularly that of Lévi-Strauss. Girard's thought, born out of comparative literature, claims yet again its distance from contemporary philosophical trends which, from his point of view, prevent us from reading the violent background from which human culture has emerged. In this sense, Girard affirms himself as the rigorous heir of the Freud of *Totem and Taboo*. Originally published in Italian in the *Enciclopedia Multimediale delle Scienze Filosofiche*, the conversation with Prof. Girard appeared in the *Journal of European Psychoanalysis* n. 14 (2002) under the title 'Psychoanalysis and Sacrifice'. It is here reprinted courtesy of RAI – Radiotelevisione Italiana.

* * *

Benvenuto/Meloni

Your interdisciplinary reflections began with your book Deceit, Desire and the Novel, *where you explore the unmasking of the Romantic hero and the phenomenon of triangular desire. Can you tell us about the genesis of your early ideas?*

René Girard

Those were youthful reflections of mine, from the time when I began teaching French literature in the United States. My training was not in literature, and I was at a loss as to just what I would say to my students. Literary criticism currently attempts for the most part to put the accent on what separates; however, my scientific inclination was towards those aspects works have in common. I perceived that simple desire connecting an object to a subject does not exist in a number of important works; there is always a third party. However, that third party is not necessarily a father or other member of the family, as Freud sustained, but a model of desire which one tends to imitate. It is often a social model, inspired by the whole of society, or by public opinion; but it can also be an individual one: a person admired, for instance, whose desire one imitates. Imitating the desire of someone else is to desire the same object as that person does, and in a universe such as ours, a democratic universe, in which men are in such proximity, it is obvious that the same object will inevitably become the object of multiple desires and create all sorts of rivalries. Rivalry is a direct consequence of what I will call *mimetic* or imitative desire, or it can also express triangular desire: a situation in which the relationship between the subject and the object is dominated by such a desire, or by a mediator model which tends to transform desire into rivalry. It was on this essential point that I wrote the book you cite, in which I study the work of five novelists.

First of all, there is Cervantes, who states openly: 'I imitate the tales of chivalry, and in particular the greatest knight-errant who ever lived and was never defeated'. And yet, Don Quixote never encountered Amadigi de Gaule as a rival, mainly because Amadigi de Gaule never existed! Another example of mimetic desire in *Don Quixote* is the desire of Sancho Panza. Sancho loves to eat and drink wine; however, he would also like to become governor of an island handed over to him, obviously, by his master, Don Quixote. Sancho has therefore a quixotic desire, and consequently he imitates Don Quixote. However, he does not imitate Don Quixote out of rivalry, for he has too much respect for him; he could never be as audacious as to consider himself his rival.

Or take the novels of the nineteenth century, Stendhal's *Julien Sorel*, for example. Julien Sorel wants success at all cost, and he is the first great nineteenth-century representation of the opportunist. He imitates Napoleon, but he is actually imitating his boss, Monsieur de Rénal; and so, as he cannot immediately become that which Monsieur de Rénal is, he courts his wife, with the desire of becoming the lover of Monsieur de Rénal's wife.

Then there is Dostoievsky, a specialist in this type of relationship. His short story, 'The Eternal Husband', tells of a man who has lost his wife, who had betrayed him constantly. He seeks out his wife's lovers and attempts to interest the latest one in the young woman he is considering marrying to take his wife's place. He has the impression that if his one-time rival fails to become interested in the woman he wants to marry, then she is not desirable. Is he mad then? Personally, I believe that in dealing with that type of illness – a combination of desire and rivalry – novelists of the Dostoevskian type achieve a depth, a knowledge, which surpasses Freud's. Within *Don Quixote*, there is another story entitled *El Curioso Impertinente*, 'The Impertinent Curious Man', that is, one who should not be so curious. The story tells of a man who married his wife thanks to the intercession of his friend. Some time after the marriage, he approaches his friend, saying: 'I would like you to court my wife, in order to test her faithfulness'. He suffers from the same illness as the eternal husband. And you can find the same story in Shakespeare as well, and in the works of many other writers.

Another example of mimetic desire, which doesn't come from a novel or a play but from a poem, is the fifth canto of Dante's *Inferno*. Maybe it's the most famous episode in Dante, that of Paolo and Francesca. It is Francesca herself who tells Dante the story of how she and Paolo fell in love. They are in-laws: Francesca is married to the brother of Paolo, and in the beginning they all live peacefully together. These in-laws are not in love at all, and they entertain each other by reading the novel of chivalry *Lancelot du Lac*. In *Lancelot* there is the queen, Genieve (Guinevere), who falls in love with the hero Lancelot, *Lancillotto* in Italian. She is moved to that by a traitor, Galot, *galeotto* in Italian. Anyway they are reading the novel, specifically the episode about the queen and her lover, and at the moment when the knight Lancillotto kisses the queen, Paolo and Francesca turn toward each other and kiss. This is the beginning of their love; there is nothing else. One of the explanations Dante gives for their love is in the line which reads '*Galeotto fu il libro e chi lo scrisse*': 'A galot [*a traitor*] was the book and he who wrote it'. In other words, books are not innocent, they have authors and try to seduce you; and then, when you are seduced, you imitate them.

The mediator, a model I derive from Paolo and Francesca and their love, is precisely this scene in the novel, just as Don Quixote imitates novels of chivalry. Don Quixote says 'the greatest knight errant is Amadigi of Gaule, and I imitate him because that's what a knight errant should do'. So the amazing thing is that, especially in Romantic times, the Paolo and Francesca episode in the *Divine Comedy* was regarded as a model of Romantic love, and therefore as a perfectly spontaneous love, by people like George Sand, who went to Venice with Alfred De Musset and Chopin, two of her lovers. But these Romantics were using Paolo and Francesca as models of themselves, because in order to be spontaneous they needed a model – which exactly is the opposite of spontaneity! And, additionally, they never mention the fact that when Paolo and Francesca fall in love, rather than paying attention to each other, they are paying attention to a book, and will do the same thing as two characters in a book. But Romantics would never see that it's a story of the book as seducer, and not the other man or woman. We are all so brainwashed by Romanticism that we don't see the book!

Don't you think that what you are saying about Paolo and Francesca and mimetic desire fits certain psychoanalytic theories? It seems in tune with Lacan's idea, when he says that desire for humans is just the desire of the Other.

Yes, no doubt. But at the same time Lacan will never point you to mimetic desire. In Lacan these formulas remain like a kind of secret. He never gives a real example of it. Why doesn't he go to Dante? Because Lacan ultimately would tell you that such desire is imaginary, or something like that. He would use that term because the imaginary is not the real.

Lacan makes the distinction between the symbolic, which involves difference – we all have to think of ourselves as different – and the imaginary, which involves a mirror effect. It is there, in the imaginary, that one can get lost, trapped by identity. But for Lacan this identity is not real, it remains imaginary. For me it's the opposite. To me what Lacan calls the symbolic is really culture, in so far as we live through its differential categories. And what Lacan doesn't see is what I call the *sacrificial crisis*. There is no history in Lacan: symbolicity is there, once and for all, it's like a fact, and the imaginary is but another aspect of life. And you either reconcile the two or you don't reconcile the two, and then you have neurosis and so forth. But this is not true at all. What I call the sacrificial crisis in Lacanian terms is the dissolution of symbolicity into pure identity. Lacan is basically a deconstructionist: he doesn't want any real identity, any reciprocity in human relations. He wants only difference. Anything which is reciprocal becomes only imaginary.

I don't agree with him. I think the reality of human relations always presumes reciprocity. Whether or not we have good relations with each other, we still exchange signs of friendship, courtesy or gifts, and it will always be reciprocal. Even if we become enemies, things will still be reciprocal because we will then exchange signs of conflict, enmity or blows or atom bombs. The entire French theoretical school – Lévi-Strauss is really the originator of it all – wants to do away with identity: they cannot have a real. They don't see anything real. There is something very profound in their refusal of real identity, because it's what culture would like to refuse. Culture tries to deny the existence of the sacrificial crisis and the dissolution of symbolism.

I don't understand precisely what you mean by identity in relation to reciprocity, because reciprocity implies identity. And in which sense is your approach better than French thought that denies identity?

The word 'identity' is really the crux of the matter because it means both identical and its opposite. When you say, 'He has an identity problem', you mean he doesn't feel different enough from other people; he gets confused. His identity is not certain, but we really mean that he is different. So when I say that psychiatrists will never solve our problems of identity, I mean that they are wrong from the very beginning: they use a word that means both things at the same time, and they haven't yet cleared up the problem of these two meanings. Why do they mean the same thing? Precisely because identity and the sense of difference always tend to collapse into identity, into a sense of complete reciprocity, which is then symbolized.

I see culture as so afraid of identity that, indeed, it never talks about it at all. And our sign system cannot express identity, or else we have to use paintings like the twelve cans of Campbell's soup by Warhol to do so: cans that are all rather identical, whether or not people like to admit so.

In general, do you think that American culture and maybe even American psychoanalysis are more interested in identity than are the French and continental European cultures?

French thinkers are interested in how far they can manage to push the notion of difference and deny the notions of reciprocity and identity, which makes it possible for someone like me, reacting against them, to say 'Hey, you forget about violence. You forget about real life. You are telling us there is no conflict'. Conflict and identity today are re-entering the picture massively, so that's why we are nearing the end of that period of denial. In a way it was a kind of attitude of luxury toward life: there is nothing but difference and therefore nothing is serious. There is no reckoning because we move from difference to difference and so on, and there is nothing but difference.

To return to Freud. Don't you think that someone could say that the Oedipal conflict, understood as a child's desire for the mother and wish to kill the father, could be interpreted, in your terms, as a mimetic triangle? That the son loves the mother incestually only because she is the love object of his father?

In my opinion, Freud tried initially to develop the Oedipus complex from the basis of desire that is mimetic, but moved towards the desirability of objects (his *Besetzung* or cathexis). Anyway, mimetic desire never did assume a dominant role in Freud's analysis.

There is something really perverse about Freud in saying that the origin and main locus of mimetic rivalry is the relationship between father, mother and son. But if you start thinking about healthy fatherhood, things appear different. I realized that in rearing my own sons. When you have sons who are growing up, and if you have one who is really successful, you find that he cannot talk to his peers about his successes because his peers have the same goals as he. If he brags about his success to his friends, there will be trouble; he will lose his friends. So then he will go to his father, who belongs to another generation, and his father will only and invariably be proud of this son.

Freud has fatherhood all wrong. When growing up, one should have normal conflicts with his father. But to say that it's a structure of fatherhood to be in conflict, that's a reversal of the truth. With my son, for example, I suddenly discovered that one's children come to their father to brag because they know you are not their rival and will be happy for them, because we all are in the same camp, the same family.

Winnicott says that during adolescence both males and females unconsciously want to kill their parents because it's the only way for them to grow up.

I don't believe it. And today I have history on my side, because fatherhood is becoming so weak that Jean-Michel Oughourlian[1], who as a psychoanalyst and psychiatrist has an eye for such issues, says that now all psychoanalysts talk in a language that Freud wouldn't recognize. They are all saying,

---

[1] Co-author with Girard of *Things Hidden Since the Foundation of the World.*

'we have to inject more Oedipus into our patients', which really is amazing! They often find today's patients spineless, and attribute this to the lack of an Oedipus!

What about Freud's theory of religious rituals and his idea that religion is essentially an obsessive ritual?

There is something true about the obsessional because ritual, in my view, is an effort to avoid violence. But the whole idea in Freud, that culture is neurotic and so on, is meaningless, because words like neurosis are essentially negative and are opposed to an idea of health; if it were true that rituals are neurotic, there would be no standard of health. Therefore the word is fairly meaningless. Rituals may be a little obsessive, but Freud doesn't admit that there is something objectively justified in them, and almost everything in religion has some justification.

What is ritual for you?

Ritual is the original human experience, a religious experience of killing a victim not out of violence but to reestablish peace. Look at the great African rituals, the ones that Glaxman, an anthropologist, named 'rituals of rebellion'. He called rebellion the original disorder. But the disorder is really just a sacrificial crisis, when society breaks down and everybody is against everyone else.

Freud doesn't explain this phenomenon. Nor do the people who claim: 'Well, people just like disorder, they like to have fun, and so they just want to do away with prohibitions'. This is really trying to put a modern spin onto things. If primitive peoples go into crisis, it's because they trust that the crisis will resolve itself, and not just for the sake of having a crisis. It's not because they enjoy disorder that they enter a crisis, but to restore order as quickly as possible. But they do think that in order to trigger the scapegoat, they first need disorder, because you can only really unite against the scapegoat if you are first in trouble, only if everything is disintegrating and the community is threatened. And that's when the transfer of emotions comes into play, because fundamentally the idea of scapegoating is an idea of collective transference.

Is there an essential difference between the sacrifice of the goat – an animal – and that of a human victim? What determines the object to be sacrificed?

The original scapegoat must almost always be – and I cannot prove this – a human component of the community, someone who participates in the violence and disorder and, suddenly, finds everyone turned against him, which then resolves the problem of the disorder. What then is the ritual sacrifice? In the human community there is mimetic desire, and therefore contagion; there then follow such crises and the subsequent phenomenon of the scapegoat who resolves the crises. We can suppose, then, that there was a crisis of the type I've described, resolved by a scapegoat whose killing healed society. However, at a certain point, the phenomenon of mimetic rivalry appears. And then, the fear arises of falling back into that state of crisis which was the cause of so much damage. So someone will ask: 'How can we avoid falling once more into that state of crisis?' And the obvious answer will be: 'Repeat the resolution of that state of crisis; choose the sacrificial victims ourselves and relive the crisis. Disorder will purposefully be created, and ended via the collective destruction of those victims, in the hope that this will produce the same results as before'. If you accept this definition of the sacrifice, you will see how it helped resolve problems, and in turn helps us understand why men are convinced that such sacrifices bring about peace. Instead, if you were to ask why sacrifice exists, the answer you're likely to get is: 'God taught us to sacrifice by his own death, or through the killing of a victim'.

Can we apply this notion to pagan sacrifice as well, conceived essentially as a gift to the god?

Certainly! Even gifts to a god can be explained by the wish to avoid the dissension and disorder menacing all communities. In archaic societies, such sacrifices are widespread. But why have the gods taught us to sacrifice? God loves sacrifice, since his acceptance of the sacrificial offering spared us his punishment and brought reconciliation. It is not a matter, then, of our wanting to create victims, but the god's own desire for them. And so it follows that we offer up victims. The gift, then, is that which covers the truth of sacrifice.

There follows, then, a kind of essential affinity between the sacred, the religious and the sacrifice?

Of course! Sacrifice implies a sacred matter.

How does your idea that the religious is at the heart of human culture derive then from your idea of sacrifice?

How far back must we trace the sacrifice I describe? The mimetic thesis has the advantage that it can be traced as far back as the animal. To begin with, there are the problems of *hominization*, which are complex enough, as biologists do not yet understand how, for example, the female of the human species, *homo sapiens*, was able to give birth to an infant which had to be protected for years, and which did not die; for, in order for that to occur, it was necessary that the males spared children of tender age so that they could be protected by their mothers, something which did not exist among animals (among predators, for example). Therefore, in the final stage of the development of human culture, what was necessary was a mix of culture and Darwinian evolution, which up to a certain point was incomprehensible. However, as regards the ethological descriptions of two animals which attack each other, Konrad Lorenz says that animals who do not know each other inevitably attack in their uncertainty; they offer combat to the adversary. If the adversary responds in a non-combative manner, then both turn on a third target which, in my opinion, is already the origin of the mechanism of the scapegoat phenomenon. Thus, one could deduce that the increasingly complex and increasingly violent forms of this mechanism became diffuse during the final stages of the evolution of primates to *homo sapiens sapiens*. Therefore, human culture has its origins in the religious; the rite is the invention of human culture. We kill this victim regularly to avoid imminent crisis.

For example, as male children in particular grow older, they become dangerous for the community, as they have not been initiated into the system of the community. So they get submitted to the ordeal of the crisis, to the ritual test of the rites of initiation: sacrifices are made, and the whole event is called a rite of passage. Rites of passage are no more than the sacrificial technique applied to the young who, in the end, will not all die (generally none die); however, there are many rites of passage in which if adolescents do die, it is considered beneficial for the others in the group. In other words, we have here a strong sacrificial characteristic: the more violence there is, the more it appears to protect against future violence.

Do you think that in our modern, Western and Christian societies there still are rites of passage?

We have done our best to render education as dissimilar as possible to rites of passage and sacrifice; we have developed an exclusively positive notion of education which – and this is to the credit of our society – has eliminated sacrifice. However, despite all this, our very notions of education remain indebted to the concept of rites of passage: school examinations, for example, are comparable to ritual ordeals.

Generally you reject all theory of the unconscious, saying that you would prefer to talk about méconnaissance *(misrecognition). It's the same word that the French phenomenologists, especially Sartre, use. Do you prefer this word because you are closer to the phenomenological trend in French thought?*

There are certainly aspects of phenomenology in my handling of these matters that are non-Freudian. And I do tend to prefer the phenomenological vocabularies. I'm not a positivist, in spite of what some deconstructionists say. The way I reintroduce identity into the picture is very different from positivism, because identity for a positivist is very innocuous and good: it is the identity of concepts and objects. What I talk about instead is the identity of conflict, and I'm not sure even I can see all the consequences of such a discourse, because ultimately this discourse involves a choice between hatred and Christian love, and it's difficult to implement in terms of a complete phenomenology. I agree with your observation, but I cannot add much more to it.

You have an original idea of identity, and write of an identity of violence. But apparently you also oppose Christian love as a new essential event, in the sense that Christian love is against identity…

No. I think that the mystery is that nothing is closer *or* more distant from the identity of hatred than the identity of love. That's why the conversion phenomenon can take place so suddenly. Think about the words of Christ, for example: 'I came to save the sinners and not the righteous, because the righteous are indifferent'. Sinners are seen to exist in hatred, and are therefore more susceptible to suddenly shift to its very opposite; they are more unstable. But the identity of hatred and love, the fact that there is no difference in either, is the real mystery. There is a possibility of suddenly seeing that the two worlds are at one and the same time totally unrelated *and* as close as possible to each other.

Do you conceive the Christian event as marking a real historical change? You explain the origin of religion by an event – a sacrifice, a killing – but don't explain what is arguably its counterpart, the Christian event…

I consider that behind any mythology there lay a real crisis and a real drama. *A fortiori* I consider that the same is true of the Gospels. The Gospels at the beginning insist very much on the historicity of what they are reporting. 'Now when Jesus was born in Bethlehem of Judaea in the days of Herod the king…,' or 'they led him away, and delivered him to Pontius Pilate the governor' and so on… these are historical figures and events, even if some of the accounts are not quite historically accurate. There is an insistence on historical facts, and we know for a fact that this sacrificial crisis was true. And we also know that the specific crisis of that time and place did go on to end with the destruction of Jerusalem and the Jewish kingdom.

The community which found itself in a very serious crisis was the little Kingdom of Judea, which was a Roman protectorate at the time of Christ. And we do have historical facts about that crisis: Jerusalem was destroyed in 70 AD, and we have the words of the evangelist John saying, to this effect, that 'it is better that one man die for the nation than that the whole people should perish...' (Jn 11:50) The texts therefore do tell us that the death of Christ was Pilate's effort to solve that crisis – an effort that failed, because the death of Jesus didn't reconcile the Jews with the Romans. And ultimately the kingdom was ended. Today people say, 'The Apocalyptic aspects of Christianity did not come true, and the Christians were disappointed. The first Christians were a little bit like the madmen of today who say that behind the comet there is a spaceship which is waiting for them'. This is not true at all: their apocalyptic hopes were not disappointed. There are apocalyptic fears as well as apocalyptic hopes. The destruction of Jerusalem was, for all sakes and purposes, akin to the destruction of the entire world for the early Christians. The fall of Jerusalem and the later destruction of the Jewish kingdom are very much part of the apocalyptic view of the Gospels, and were interpreted as such by the early Christians.

There you have the whole scheme of the crisis. And there you have no salvation to escape God, because Jesus is a scapegoat that fails. All mythical scapegoats succeeded, in the sense that they were all viewed as guilty; everybody assembled because of them and then a new culture was created. But the essential thing about Christianity is that the scapegoat system failed. Therefore it's an open world in which anything can happen, because it no longer has the sacrificial protections. So from here you can jump to contemporary terrorism, which shows the consequences of the lack of sacrificial protection.

Another quite important point in psychoanalysis is the theory of prohibition and the function of the super-ego as the agent of prohibition. What do you have to say about prohibition? In fact, you criticize any ideology attacking the idea that prohibition may be good, useful.

In my view prohibition is both good and useful. But very often prohibitions in primitive society are objectively wrong and absurd, because of mistakes in interpretation. For example, a great number of archaic communities in Africa kill twins when they are born. They kill twins because they confuse the physical resemblance of twins with reciprocity in conflict. Therefore, when twins are born, the community fears them like a germ which might contaminate the entire community and create a sacrificial crisis. Of course there are other archaic people who realize that the physical resemblance of twins has nothing to do with the cultural expressions of violence.

But there are many cultures – and the Greek is one of them – which have tragic twins. The thing about twins that is superior to all Freudian symbolicity is that in the case of twins reality and symbolicity are as one. Twins are objectively rivals, because no one knows which one was born first. Sometimes at birth they'd put a little red thread around the ankles of the firstborn, which then disappeared – as happened in the case of Romulus and Remus. Livy says that the thread was lost. Therefore it's impossible to make a distinction between the two. In this case, no one knows who is the heir of the father, if you believe in *primo-genitur*, the right of the eldest son. Therefore, reality and symbolicity merge completely in a powerful way, because only mimetic theory sees that the main symbols partake of reality. Take the symbol of the plague: a plague often is the real destruction of an entire community, but it's also the symbol of that destruction.

What do you mean when you say that some prohibitions are good? Or when you say that the Tenth Commandment is particularly important because it prohibits desire?

The Tenth Commandment says, 'Do not desire what your brother desires' – your brother or your neighbor, depending on the translation. In English you say, 'Do not covet…' – which makes for some sneakiness in the translation. In Italian you don't have that ambiguity: you say *non desiderare*. In French there is *convoiter*, like English, so you have the feeling that maybe it's not merely desire that's at issue. But the Italian translation is more honest: that the basic desire is to desire what your brother desires; and if you desire what your brother desires, you cannot have any culture because you are soon going to have everybody fighting.

It follows that something like the 1968 slogan, 'Forbidding is forbidden', is nonsense. As soon as you get away from the bourgeois comedy of the supposed revolution, you realize that prohibitions do make sense: that they are indispensable to the life of the community and are the first line of defense against the mimetic crisis. When things become violent, the mimetic crisis ensues, and so you shift to sacrifice.

But Freud might object that the Tenth Commandment is a failure, because you can't completely forbid desire. What he calls the unconscious is just that, 'forbidden' desire. In conscious life you may not covet, but from an unconscious point of view you continue to desire, say, your neighbors' property. Freud could say, 'I agree that prohibitions are essential, but at the same time there is an unconscious order in which for mimetic reasons you always desire what your neighbor has or desires', because, as you have explained, the object of desire is always the other's object. What's your answer to such a Freudian objection?

These desires can be very concrete. When the Bible first instructs you, 'Don't desire your neighbor's wife', that's essential. Two-thirds of world literature is about sexual rivalries. And then, do not desire the donkey of your brother: in other words do not desire the Mercedes Benz of your brother. And that Mercedes is much more important than anything Freud talked about!

But a car may be a symbol for a woman…

It may be, but you desire the car far more often than you do the woman. It can, of course, be something else: for example, you may desire your neighbor's servants. But you don't need any unconscious there, to desire whatever it is that is deemed good. And on this score the Bible goes straight to the point. The Bible expresses in clear and rational terms what the prohibitions are.

There is never a 'Do not covet your mother' rule. The best answer to the Oedipus complex comes from Joyce. About one-third of the way through *Ulysses* there is a lecture of Stephen Daedalus, one of the heroes of the book, on Shakespeare. It's the greatest thing on Shakespeare ever written, because it's a mimetic interpretation of Shakespeare. In that interpretation there is an attack on a certain Viennese school that tells us that the seventy-five-year old mother of Hamlet is more desirable to him than Ophelia!

Suddenly the whole scholastic aspect of our world is shattered by Joyce's humor. Now it is not enough to take on the Oedipus complex. I grant you that tensions between parents and children are very complex and that Freud did capture some of them. But he probably arrived at a moment in history when the role of fatherhood was already being questioned. It's at the beginning of the twentieth century that the father disappears for the first time, and Freud comes onto the scene just before this disappearance becomes real. In the history of culture it often happens that important factors are most clearly defined, and seem to be as powerful as ever, right at the time of their demise. It's then that they come into focus.

Do you see even the fading of fatherhood as an effect of Christianity?

Oh yes, because it does involve a destruction of the family. It's amazing that while Christianity obviously doesn't say to turn against one's family, it does significantly de-emphasize the family. Christ says, 'My real mother and brothers and sisters are those who follow the rules of the kingdom of God'. In Mark and Matthew, when people come and say, 'your mother and your brothers are there, and are mad at you', Christ says, 'I don't want to talk to them, because my real mother and brother are these people I'm talking to'. This de-emphasis is unique. It's absurd to say that the Gospels are 'against the family'. But Christ does say, 'The family is not everything, the family should not get in the way of one's spiritual life'. In the Gospel there is also a man who because of his family doesn't follow Jesus. So the family should be put in its place, and seen as but one cultural institution among many.

Is the family also not central to the Gospels because of the words of Jesus, 'I bring you the sword, and come to pit father against son…'? This famous phrase rings strangely for many Christians. What does it mean?

It doesn't mean that Christ wants to do away with the family. He says, 'I'm bringing you the peace that surpasses the peace of this world, that is incomprehensible in the terms of this world'. And the peace of the world is always the peace of the scapegoats. And in a way there are scapegoat aspects within the unity of the family. When you meet with your closest family, you usually spend time making fun of people from the wider family circle, those who are relative outsiders, and who make perfect scapegoats. This scapegoating is not necessarily bad, but you unite around almost any mythical story, in which there is some kind of scapegoat, even if only a funny one, because a funny scapegoat is also an important one. In trickster myths there are funny scapegoats. And the family very often has its own mythology, usually constituted around some form of scapegoating, in order to save a weak unity of the family.

What is your interpretation of the fact that apparently through these words Christ is promising a kind of conflict? He says, 'I am bringing a sword'... Is this in order to inject conflict into the family?

Since Christ is doing away with sacrificial protection, since all institutions, which includes the family, will weaken, they will weaken in a sacrificial crisis type of way. Jesus is announcing a situation in which there will be trouble in the family, as there will be trouble between nations, more trouble maybe than in ancient times, because sacrificial protections will be weakened or disappear completely.

Could you tell us something about your idea of scandal, skandalon, *which basically means obstacle? Maybe you won't agree that this idea has psychoanalytic implications, but even Lacan talks about obstacles...*

The word *skandalon* is the Greek translation of a Hebrew term which, in Greek, comes from a verb which signifies 'to limp': *skazo* is to stumble over an obstacle. And the literal translation of *skandalon* is the obstacle. In the Hebrew bible, very often the word *skandalon* is translated with the Hebrew equivalent of 'obstacle'. However, it is a very particular obstacle; and when one is considering an obstacle for the first time, it is normal that one circles around it. But *skandalon* is the obstacle which one cannot avoid; the more one collides with it, the more one has the desire to collide. It is a situation not unlike that of suffering from a toothache; one is always touching it with one's tongue, in order to feel the pain more intensely.

The principle of the *skandalon* can really be defined as the principle of repetition in Freud, something which keeps repeating itself and assumes the form of a symptom. The obstacle up against which you run is also the object of your desire. Why? Because it is mimetic desire: you desire the object of your model, or you yourself provide the first model. It doesn't matter if you are the first model or the imitator. You are still in the imitation-imitated mode, or in the passive-active mode, with someone else who is both obstacle and model. So you keep running into them because you keep trying to get the object, even though they resist and may be stronger than you, in which case your desire increases. Therefore you will run up against them even more, entering into a vicious circle of repetition of the symptom.

Let's consider Christ's famous words in the Gospels, when he talks about the scandal: 'If your leg or hand offend (scandalize) you, it is better to cut them off…' What is the real meaning of this obscure prescription?

In mimetic theory it means that you are getting into a vicious circle, which is very easy to get into and very hard to exit. Because as you get into it, this desire will increase because the obstacle always resists your desire; and if it resists successfully, you'll desire more and more, and will run up against it more and more. Freud doesn't talk about the fact that obtaining the object is the death of desire. If you can win over your model, if you get hold of the object, desire is extinguished. It won't be transfigured by any transcendental light that exudes from the model. That's why we live in a world of total disenchantment. One thing Freud forgot was that one of the worst phenomena in our world is the death of desire. For Freud, desire was eternal, because you have only one mother and you always desire her.

But desire can change its object, according to Freud…

It can *only* change its object. But the death of desire – one of the worst experiences of the modern world, that only a novelist can fully describe

– plays no role in psychology or psychoanalysis. This is because you can have only one patient at a time on the couch. So psychiatry, psychology, psychoanalysis always focus on the individual, and not on the relationship. If you focus on the relationship, like a novelist, you know that human affairs are such that desire is usually a one-way street. If it goes one way, it doesn't go the other way, and vice versa. As you desire more and more, and more and more in vain, it is very important to conceal your desire.

But why is it so important? Desire is humiliating because in desire you confess your own weakness: you need the outside world, and desire is always a desire for narcissism, in my view. Freud sees certain aspects of that. Therefore the other must prove himself more narcissistic than you, and the game of seduction means always trying to seem more indifferent than the other. Psychoanalysis doesn't quite get it when it comes to indifference. But every great classical playwright does: Goldoni does, for example, in *The Two Venetian Twins*, in a way that is very close to Molière and Marivaux…

Molière also has a twin play, *Amphytrion*, and Shakespeare has *The Comedy of Errors*. In these plays there's always a game of misunderstandings, where you expect something from the other which you do not get. These documents are tremendously important for our psychic life, because these twins talk about this reciprocity, and this reciprocity from the other is what we never expect. Shakespeare's is an early play of his, but it has the structure of all his comedies: whether the heroes are twins or not, everyone is always trying to be more narcissistic than the other and failing, and ultimately being fascinated by the twin who is not really different.

For both Lévi-Strauss and psychoanalysts, the taboo of incest is essential. For Lévi-Strauss it is the basis of all societies, even if the prohibited relative differs in every society, because it is the condition for the generalized exchange of women. What do you think about this?

In fact, in the *Elementary Structures of Kinship*, Lévi-Strauss talks about this quite at length. This book about kinship was his first book, and made him famous, but it's a very dry book. At the beginning he says precisely that he is going to interpret the incest taboo not on its own terms, but in terms of the law of exchange. He says that people decide to exchange women just as they decide to exchange words or gifts.

There are some totemic societies in which corpses get exchanged, and to me it is tremendously suggestive of what exchange is really all about. Someone dies in your community, but you don't want to bury him since it might be dangerous, because everybody is going to accuse everybody else of having killed the man. So you always want a nearby tribe to bury your dead, and in exchange you bury theirs because that tribe is less likely to cause you trouble. You are like an undertaker doing business, except that you don't bury your own dead. Burying one's own dead may lead to fights over the past, we may accuse each other of having caused their death, and so on. It's the same thing for women. The local women are the women you may fight over, because they are going to be the objects – in particular if they are sisters – of mimetic rivalry.

So, the law of exchange is the result of many sacrificial crises, many scapegoat systems, in which ultimately man does what no animal does. Instead of helping himself when he wants food, women, or territory, instead of taking the easiest route – which is to go for what's nearest at hand, which is what all animals do – man sets up rules for exchange. Of course animals have dominance systems, whereby one animal goes first and the others will be served only if the dominant animal allows. But men enter into an entirely different system, into the system of exchange, and the main purpose of this system is to avoid internal conflict.

Ultimately, your interest is to get rid of your own women, who are intolerably conflictual, by giving them to a nearby tribe, which is also trying to get rid of its women. And you turn these women into gifts. The word for *gift* in many languages, in German, for instance, means poison: all traditional gifts are poison. That means that we want to give to other people and rid ourselves of whatever it is that causes so much trouble between us. But in exchange we get their women. We give one to this man, one to another and so on, and hopefully we all will then get along together. But if we try to divide and share our own women, we may all end up fighting until the community is destroyed.

So over hundreds of thousands of years, men developed this system of outward movement, of moving abroad: something no animal does, but which marks our way of opening up to the world in order to obtain from far away what animals get nearby. Fundamental to man is his exploration of the outside world, and his capacity for exchange; this is the beginning of culture. But I think, contrary to Lévi-Strauss, that all this stems from a fear of violence. We can suppose that to get one particular race to reject, at times even with horror, the closest object at hand and shift to a more distant one, took a great amount of effort. That's why all stories about exchange are also stories about conflict, within and without, because initially the people with whom you want to exchange resist the overture. Or they agree only with great difficulty, and very often with rituals connected to it, and a lot of fighting.

Is there any resemblance between Lévi-Strauss's stress on primal exchange function and your idea of reciprocity?

No, because Lévi-Strauss will tell you that he basically sees the human race as a race of human structuralist scholars. He says: one fine day people wanted to classify things, to make things orderly, so they started to exchange goods, and name them, making them separate. But it's almost akin to a scholarly urge to classify things.

Lévi-Strauss' theory escapes the real tragedy of violence…

It escapes tragedy completely, it's even laughable. And if it's not entirely laughable, it's only because there is something very positive about being able to think in terms of difference. But it does so without a concept of identity, without a sense of that fear which I think is the motor of culture. So I wouldn't say I'm anti–Lévi-Strauss, I'm against certain structuralist exclusions that Lévi-Strauss makes: the exclusion, for instance, of the violence that the scapegoat system ultimately channels into something positive. Namely, the fear of violence.

Culture originates in the mastering of violence through the scapegoat business; what structuralists say about culture does not satisfy me. I feel closer to the pre-Socratics, to Anaximander first. That famous saying of Anaximander, which Heidegger labels the most ancient saying in Western culture, is: 'From the place where all things originate, there they will return. And this place from where all things originate from other things, we know by the word *apeiron*'. In Greek *apeiron* can be translated as *kaos*, which can be translated as *undifferentiation*. 'From the place where all things originate, there they will return, punishing each other for their meanness and hostility according to the order of time'. This punishing of each other constitutes, for me, the sacrificial crisis. And it is therefore a cyclical view of society which issues from chaos. Heraclitus says something to this effect, apropos violence, or *polemos*, when he claims: 'Conflict or fighting is the father and king of everything'. Such is the origin of culture. If you take the sayings of Anaximander and Heraclitus, you have my whole system, which you can view as my own take on the pre-Socratics.

This is why, you see, I'm very interested in Heidegger, who was returning to these ideas and interpreting them, within a context of Nazism, as a resurgence of violence. It's all both very powerful and very disturbing, if you consider that in the *Introduction to Metaphysics* Heidegger so favors violence. The worst Heidegger is the most interesting, because he's the one who says we have to go back to the pre-Socratic philosophers; while I say we have to move even further back, to mythology and religion. So, even though my conclusions are totally different than Heidegger's, there are aspects of twentieth-century intellectual life that are both very far and very close to me. It's the case, you see, with both Freud and Heidegger.

Selected Bibliography

A Theater of Envy: William Shakespeare (1991). New York: Oxford University Press.

Things Hidden since the Foundation of the World (1987, with J-M. Oughourlian). Stanford: Stanford University Press.

The Scapegoat (1986). Baltimore: Johns Hopkins University Press.

Violence and the Sacred (1977). Baltimore: Johns Hopkins University Press.

Deceit, Desire and the Novel (1965). Baltimore: Johns Hopkins University Press.

THE PSYCHOANALYST'S NARCISSISTIC WOUND

Isabelle Stengers

ISABELLE STENGERS teaches philosophy at the Universitè Libre De Bruxelles in Belgium. Known mainly for her studies in thermodynamics with Nobel Prize winner Ilya Prigogine, Dr. Stengers' interests centre around both the constructivist adventure of modern science and the problems that inhere in how this adventure relates to power and claims to rational authority. She is also working on the crucial challenge, both political and cultural, of an active ecology that might make room for diverging scientific practices in a democratic and demanding environment: that is to say, for an ecology that opposes both the ideal of the sovereign autonomy of the sciences as well as any prejudicial subjugation of the same to social demands.

In this conversation with Sergio Benvenuto, the Belgian philosopher criticizes psychoanalysts' rejection of hypnosis as a taboo inherited from Freud – a symptom, she claims, of a 'purity myth' shared by many in the psychoanalytical community. Yet Stengers also criticizes what she calls the 'sad sciences' (*sciences tristes*) – experimental psychology, sociology, and economics in particular – where method reigns supreme, and does so at the expense of any genuine form of *jouissance*. While affirming that psychoanalysis is itself not a 'sad science', Stengers nonetheless denounces the risk of dogmatism among psychoanalysts, especially when they come together in institutions – a consequence, she claims, of their peculiar fear of a threatened communal 'purity' and of the discipline's original adoption of physics as a model for the kind of science it wanted to be.

The following interview with Isabelle Stengers is a slightly revised version of the original text titled 'The Psychoanalyst's Narcissistic Wound', first published in the *Journal of European Psychoanalysis* n. 1 (1995).

* * *

Sergio Benvenuto

Professor Stengers, for some time now you have been dealing with the sciences humaines *[social sciences and psychology] in general and with psychoanalysis in particular. Would you care to summarize the results of this interest of yours?*

Isabelle Stengers

I have now published two books on the subject with Léon Chertok, one of which, *A Critique of Psychoanalytical Reason*, has come out in English. Chertok, who was psychoanalytically trained, has been for some time trying out hypno-analysis, an application of hypnosis to the psychoanalytical field. On those two books – the other, as yet untranslated, is titled *L'Hypnose: Blessure Narcissique* (Hypnosis: A Narcissistic Wound) – I collaborated with him not because hypnosis particularly interests me, but because it gives me access to some interesting aspects of psychoanalysis. I do not wish to intervene in the clinical problem, that is to say in the efficacy of the techniques, but to deal with the consequences of the way psychoanalysts inherit and ratify Freud's condemnation of hypnosis, often redoubling it via rather dubious moral arguments. Freud's judgment was part of his own technical struggle, and we know now that the story is much more complex and ambiguous than the one he told. But the kind of rigid and horrified reaction you get when speaking about hypnosis with psychoanalysts – at least French ones – tells another story. It is as if psychoanalysts, who are expected to fear nothing, were dealing with something taboo, using stereotyped reasons that go back to a vision of hypnosis which already Joseph Delboeuf, for instance, proved false more than a century ago. It is as if they were themselves fearful of something, of having to defend themselves from something. Chertok was convinced that they were defending themselves for fear of admitting that they too were hypnotists of a sort…

Are you implying that this contempt for hypnosis – probably signaling fear – would be a neurotic symptom of psychoanalysis itself?

Yes, it is a symptom, but I would resist interpreting it in psychoanalytical terms. The point is not the psychoanalytical unconscious but the psychoanalysts' reasons for their claim that their technique has broken with a past that is always threatening to come back. Again, I do not situate myself on clinical ground and do not mean, for instance, to imply that analysts should practice hypnosis. My point would rather be that if psychoanalysts adopted a less defensive attitude, that very change could produce more creative results, especially in relations among colleagues. I also wonder if a less defensive attitude would change the relationship between analysts and their patients.

It is possible that psychoanalysts, especially Freudians, are reluctant to have their respectability placed in question, given the conviction many hold of being scientists in the practice of a profession that, like medicine, has a solid scientific basis. Freud's theory is a guarantee of sorts for their practice much in the same way that modern biology is a guarantee of a doctor's respectability in his. The contempt which analysts show for other psychotherapists and counselors is usually not due to their failure to produce therapeutic effects but because their effects cannot be justified within a grand theoretical and scientific framework such as Freud's.

> Even those convinced they have avoided falling prey to this myth – who no longer claim that psychoanalysis is a science – often fall prey to another, even more ancient one: the myth that their technique is not an influential one. It is, again, the *purity myth*: the myth of pure science, or of the pure freedom of the patient. This is the ground of the opposition against hypnosis, that is correlatively defined in terms of suggestion. My conviction is that this opposition is lethal for our understanding of a cure: whatever the technique, it is always a production. In fact, those who strive to avoid influencing others end up doing so in a way which is even more worrisome. Because the will to be pure, the will not to influence, is in itself a mighty but uncontrolled source of influence. More generally the claim of purity (to be distinguished from rites of purification) must be understood as a polemical one: it is both the denunciation of others as impure, and the claim to define those very others in terms of a lack, from the 'pure' standpoint which is one's own.
>
> In my opinion, the 'will to purity' can lead us back to the origins of psychoanalysis, to Freud's desire to do experimental science: a practice which indeed needs a purified and well-controlled frame. This wish of Freud's, still present today, is a symptom I want to challenge.

Some of the more hardened critics of psychoanalysis accuse it of a lack of purity, for being less plausible than modern physics. Grünbaum's book against psychoanalysis, The Foundations of Psychoanalysis, *has received much attention. Employing all the classical criticism that positivist methodology made against psychoanalysis, Grünbaum launches a long attack on the difference between natural sciences and sciences of the spirit, as upheld by Habermas and other hermeneutic philosophers. In other words, there are today two conflicting epistemological conceptions: one which runs from Dilthey to Habermas, according to which there are two forms of science, one concerned with physical nature, the other with human beings; and the positivist conception that there is only one kind of scientific rationality which can be applied to everything from neutrons to sexual fantasies.*

As regards the debate between Grünbaum and Habermas, I do not agree with either of them. Both, in their peculiar way, give too much importance to the model set up by the experimental sciences. In different ways both think that those sciences have succeeded in conquering nature, and they disagree about the possibility for the same methodology to conquer the so-called sciences of the spirit. I would claim that experimental achievement may well define physics and chemistry, and also molecular biology, but already in biology it is a partial, often debatable achievement. When you deal with natural beings gifted with the capacity to entertain a standpoint and to learn, experimentation becomes mutilation. The present-day brain sciences may well produce interesting insights, but the brain is utterly not an object for experimental science.

To summarize, would you say that each scientific object, each realm of nature, needs its own particular epistemology?

Yes, if one sees epistemology as dealing with the positions and questions that are relevant to a given inquiry, as that which makes learning from such an inquiry possible. A whole series of sciences have followed a generalized epistemology and have attempted to create an object on the model of this generalized epistemology. But they appear to me extremely sad, depressing – what I call *sciences tristes*. They exist because science departments in universities exist. They do not create their own passion, their own intensity. If you take experimental psychologists, for instance, you get the impression that their questions are at the same time limited and determined by the ambition of *making* science. They will not wonder how to learn but how to address a situation in a way that produces science. Science, for them, demands renouncing interesting questions. If I ask a physician or a chemist what science is, she will not have a ready answer. Science is just what they do and they are not worried that, should they get carried away by a strong interest in their particular object, or allow passion into their work, they would cease to be scientists. Science for them means obtaining results that will 'hold'. It will hold, thanks to other people's *criticism* and *interest*, and from these things that hold it, it will be possible to make a shared history. Therefore, it is for them a passion, and for the sake of this passion, of arousing the interest of their colleagues, the feeling that something new and maybe important has been learned is essential. In experimental psychology nobody is really interested in the results, only in the recognition that they are scientific. This is why a history of experimental psychology hardly exists. When I ask experimental psychologists, 'What do you know now that you didn't know twenty years ago?', they usually take on an air of sadness and answer, 'Experimental psychology, you know, is a very complicated science'. But is not ethology also a complicated science?! Yet it has attempted to investigate animals as interesting subjects, and not because they must be scientific objects at all costs.

Do psychoanalysts create their own passion?

In their own way. I would never say that psychoanalysis is *triste*. Rather, I think its practitioners are passionate, but may well be poisoned by its claims.

I have always been struck by the ways that practices, be they scientific or not, provide for their own particular *jouissances* [pleasures]. The *sciences tristes* – and here I might include current economics, psychology and sociology – are the sciences in which method reigns supreme and where anxiety, and not *jouissance*, rules. Their practitioners are so fearful of not doing science that the methods they have adopted have handicapped them, forbidding them to think and invent. One of the reasons for my work and interest is to try and weaken these self-mutilating models so as to emulate, instead, the adventurous and inventive character of the experimental sciences.

Some might object that you see this fear only in the 'social sciences' – to use the Anglo-American term – sciences that are considered soft, not altogether exact or rigorous. Could it be that the 'methodologism' you challenge is legitimate in the context of the current softness, or weakness, of these sciences – without intending to give the term 'weak' any negative connotations?

Not all human sciences are *tristes*. Human ethology, as practiced by Daniel Stern for instance, is not. His book *The Interpersonal World of the Infant* is extraordinarily interesting and should be read by all philosophers, because it puts the issues brilliantly, and proposes new perspectives. It can be part of an history because whatever its criticisms and modifications, these will attest to the fact that Stern's colleagues have learned to produce still more interesting questions. I do not think that social sciences in themselves cannot avoid being *tristes*.

Not all human sciences are 'sad', but you are saying that all the sciences which are sad happen to be social sciences. Why is this?

The social sciences, including psychology, were the earliest and preferred victims of the idea that the methodology of physics – or a more general 'scientific model' really just derived from physics – was to be adopted and replicated. A methodology, that is, that identified scientific understanding with 'laws' the object would obey...

Why did the 'human sciences' surrender to this idea more so than chemistry or biology?

Paradoxically some social sciences are closer to physics than chemistry or evolutionary biology are, because those sciences produce their own questions with no need for an external model. However, present-day evolutionary theory – as heralded by Richard Dawkins for instance – is dangerous precisely from that point of view, since it has become a colonizing doctrine, the first aim of which is to submit the social sciences themselves to the rule of selection. Again, in the name of Darwin – who does not deserve such a fate! – human beings must be shown to obey, must be turned into witnesses of the 'law' of selection.

Speaking of the biological theory of evolution, what do you think of genetic psychology, and in particular of the theories of Piaget or Wallon? It would appear that genetic psychology, when concerned with stages of development, is inspired more by evolutionary theory than by physics.

Piaget was not investigating evolution but indeed a genetic development, leading to an adult rational capacity he understood to be normal. This is exactly the kind of understanding evolutionary theory has to avoid, and that leads to the idea of 'stages' you can experimentally identify since you know in advance the relevant questions (i.e., 'Is the child already able to...?'). Several psychologists have clearly demonstrated that all Piaget's experiments with children are artifacts: phenomena not representative of children as they learn and interact together, but rather the result of the situation created by Piaget's investigation dealing with isolated children. These psychologists have proved that if you allow children to talk among themselves and discuss your questions, you will find that children two years younger than those Piaget believed capable of doing the set task become perfectly capable of it. Consequently, we could say that, for the sake of experimentation and reproducibility, Piaget had excluded an entire dimension of intelligence which actually belongs to the child. He created laboratory children who do not exist in real life. His generalizations have interested educators because pedagogy is a normative practice. They are not reflective of children, but of the ways to get children to learn how to perform in the required way...

On the subject of history and time, you are familiar, of course, with the development in France, through Lacan, of Freud's concept of the après coup:

the idea that history is somehow constructed in a retroactive way. What is your opinion of the après coup*?*

Phenomenologically speaking, not as a theory, but as a way of understanding a set of experiences (our own experience, or that of others), I think that the notion of *après coup* is extremely productive. But it was not invented by psychoanalysts. Henri Bergson approached it when he spoke of the *le mouvement rétrograde du vrai*, or the backward movement of truth. When an event occurs, you cannot but understand history as leading to it. It then seems that we deal with a causal history that is able to explain what happens. This does not coincide altogether with the psychoanalytic interpretation of *après coup*, as it is not linked with an elucidation, rather with the power of the present to retro-direct the interpretation of its pasts, transforming invention and multiplicity into a well-ordered narrative. Bergson would therefore have been suspicious of psychoanalytical *après coup*, but we may see it as part of the specific power of the psychoanalytical technique.

Voltaire wondered how two priests avoided laughing whenever they met. One thing is certain: although neither priests nor psychoanalysts burst out laughing when they meet, the latter are more likely to have this Voltairian fear of being impostors. Lacan warned analysts that they should take seriously fantasies and suspicions of fraud. Is not being a fraud or being a hypnotist more or less the same thing for analysts?

Yes, this is where the fear of hypnosis originates. It is also the origin of a strange experience of mine. Psychoanalysts, individually, are often extremely intelligent and lucid. However, when psychoanalysts come together the contrast is striking. I even experienced a feeling of collective terror, in France at least, as if everybody was fearing the accusation of not being a 'true' analyst, of being a fraud. This may have something to do with the threatened 'purity' of the profession which I discussed earlier.

What about Lacanians?

Even among Lacanians you find different personalities. But the Lacanian doctrine is a very powerful one, as it conjugates the power of analysis with more ancient powers. For instance, Lacanian analysts are very proud of saying that they know psychoanalysis is not a science. But the way they define a 'true' analyst is even more demanding. It recalls the old question of 'grace' in Christian theology: just as a Christian is not allowed to affirm he 'has' grace, a Lacanian analyst is not allowed to say 'I am an analyst'. She is rather the one 'who knows there are analytic acts'. What's even more frightening is the Lacanian susceptibility to fraudulence. Theirs is an extremely difficult position, a fascinating one obviously but also quite a dangerous one. Because, if they behave in a 'terrorized/terrorizing' way with their colleagues, some of this terror may well also be passed on to their analysands.

Some schools of psychoanalysis are more dogmatic than others. Lacanians and Bionian Kleinians in Europe, for example, are in constant danger of becoming dogmatic, even haughty, contemptuous. Analysts of other schools find it hard to justify such contempt.

Some schools are more tolerant than others. Unfortunately, the most interesting schools are also the most dogmatic. Tolerance as such is not a very interesting virtue, it is nice but rather easy to come by...

That could also be an objection to your own theses. If interest and dogmatism go hand in hand, then this combination is necessary. We could say that the illusion of method – a requirement for being scientific – could be a vital and necessary illusion. Jungism is, perhaps, more authentic, more sincere than Freudianism because it seems to follow the line you suggest. However, the price is a loss of epistemological interest. Might not the imitation of physics be for social sciences what a character in Ibsen's The Wild Duck *called a 'vital lie': a lie essential to survival?*

No, I don't agree. The idea that you need to believe what may well be a lie, in order to be able to perform, is a reason given most everywhere. I have to believe, for instance, that the brain can be understood in terms of 'states' of a nervous system, that it can answer the same kind of questions as any material system, if I have to survive as a creative researcher. Or I need to believe there are laws... I would say that an analyst does not even need to 'believe' there is an unconscious: this unconscious is part of her technique. Here Lacan was right, it seems to me, when he emphasized, against anthropological realist generalizations, that psychoanalytical concepts are relevant in the vicinity of the 'couch' and not in general. It is too bad that this was basically forgotten by all those Lacanian analysts who speak about the 'subject of the unconscious' on TV and everywhere else. Psychoanalysts need nothing else, or should claim to need nothing else, but the experience of analysis; as for the imitation of the physical model, it may well be a matter of social survival in our academic world. But then we have to enter the question of academic survival. I would just say that the academic world is not a very healthy world.

You criticize the dogmatism of many psychoanalysts. What about the dogmatism of a number of your fellow philosophers of science?

The task of a philosopher of science is not as difficult as that of a psychoanalyst. Therefore philosophers of science have less justification for their dogmatism. I have devoted the past few years to a reflection on psychoanalysis, but I would certainly not devote the same amount of time to a search of arguments to convince epistemologists. What academic epistemologists do today is of no great interest to me…

Translated from the French by Gianmaria Senia and Joan Tambureno Mosconi

Selected Bibliography

The Invention of Modern Science. Minneapolis: University of Minnesota Press, 2000.

Power and Invention: Situating Science. Minneapolis: University of Minnesota Press, 1997.

A Critique of Psychoanalytic Reason: Hypnosis as a Scientific Problem from Lavoisier to Lacan (with Léon Chertok). Stanford: Stanford University Press, 1992.

Order out of Chaos: Man's New Dialogue with Nature (with I. Prigogine). London: Flamingo Press, 1984.

OF AUTONOMY, INDIVIDUALISM AND PSYCHOANALYSIS

Cornelius Castoriadis

CORNELIUS CASTORIADIS (Constantinople 1922–Paris 1997) was a political activist, revolutionary philosopher, psychoanalyst, and for some time a professional economist at the Organization for Economic Cooperation and Development. Philosopher of the social imagination and co-founder of the legendary group and journal *Socialisme ou Barbarie*, he was credited with inspiring the May 1968 events in France. At the time, Castoriadis also challenged the reigning Lacanianism in French psychoanalytic circles, instigating a break with Lacan's 'Third Group'. He opposed the group's conception of ethics as an ideology of desire with the idea that psychoanalysis – like pedagogy and politics, albeit in different ways – seeks to privilege human autonomy.

In this conversation with Sergio Benvenuto, Castoriadis explains precisely how, in his view, the common aim of both political action and psychoanalysis is human autonomy and freedom, and not necessarily happiness. The truly autonomous individual, Castoriadis argues, is one who has transformed his relationship with his unconscious so as to distinguish between selfish individualism and rightful autonomy. Whereas individualism claims, 'I do what I wish', autonomy proposes: 'I do what I believe is right; I do not deprive myself of doing what pleases me, but I do not do something simply because it pleases me'. It is on the basis of this distinction, then, that Castoriadis takes issue with Lacan's ethic of desire.

This conversation, which took place in Paris on May 7, 1994, was originally published in Italian in the *Enciclopedia Multimediale delle Scienze Filosofiche* It first appeared in English in the *Journal of European Psychoanalysis* n. 6 (1998) as part of a 'Homage' to Castoriadis following his death in December 1997, and is here reprinted courtesy of RAI – Radiotelevisione Italiana.

* * *

Sergio Benvenuto

You are a philosopher of politics, but you are also a practicing psychoanalyst. Does your profession of analysis influence your philosophical concepts?

Cornelius Castoriadis

There is a very strong bond between my concept of psychoanalysis and my concept of politics. The aim of both is human autonomy, albeit via different processes. Politics aims at freeing the human being, making it possible for him to accede to his own autonomy through collective action. The prevailing concept during the eighteenth and nineteenth centuries (including that of Marx), according to which the object of politics was happiness, is a mistaken, even catastrophic, one. The object of politics is freedom. And politics is collective conscious and considered action, aimed at transforming institutions into institutions of freedom and autonomy.

The American Declaration of Independence does not proclaim that the aim of the state is happiness, but it ensures everyone has the freedom to pursue happiness. That individual quest for happiness has gradually been identified in America with the criteria of 'problem solving'. However, does every man's quest for happiness not imply also the autonomy of every man? The idea that society must permit everyone to search for his own happiness implies a certain liberal concept of autonomy. Is it in that American sense that you intend 'autonomy'?

No, not in the American sense. The American Declaration states, 'We believe that all men are created free and equal for the pursuit of happiness'. But I do not believe that God created all human beings free and equal. In the first place, God created nothing at all because he does not exist. Secondly, since human beings came into existence, they have practically never been free and equal. Therefore, *it is necessary that they act* in order to become free and equal. And once they have become free and equal, there will doubtlessly be demands regarding the common good, which will, however, contrast with the liberal concept according to which each and everyone must pursue his or her own individual happiness (which in turn would imply the maximum happiness for all). There are certain kinds of social services which are not exclusively directed to the interests of individual happiness but are the object of political action: for example, museums, or roads. And all the same it is in the interest of my own autonomy that others are autonomous.

However, if society interferes with my happiness, the result is totalitarianism. In that case, society will tell me: 'It is the opinion of the majority that you should not buy records of Bach's music, but those of Madonna. That is the will of the majority, and so much for your happiness!' I believe that happiness can and must be pursued by each individual on his own. It is up to each individual either to know or not know what constitutes his own happiness.

The very notion of happiness is a fairly complex one, both psychologically and philosophically. However, the object of politics is freedom and autonomy, and that will only be possible within an institutional, collective framework which permits freedom and autonomy. The object of psychoanalysis is the same. And there is the response to the question as to the *fin* of psychoanalysis (to which Freud returned often), in the two senses of the word *fin* (aim/end): the termination in time and the objective of the analysis. It is the aim of analysis that the individual become as autonomous as possible. This does not mean autonomous in the Kantian sense, that is to say complying with moral dictates, established in the same way, once and for all. The truly autonomous individual is one who has transformed his relationship with his unconscious to such a point that he can, to the extent that it is possible in the human universe, know his own desires and at the same time succeed in mastering the acting out of those desires. Being autonomous does not imply, for example, that I am moral because I do not covet my neighbor's wife. That desire is basic, since each one of us began life desiring his own mother, the wife of a fellow human being. If one has not begun life thus, one is not a human being but a monster. However, it is quite another thing to put that desire into action. Individuals of fifty or sixty can still have incestuous dreams, which proves that that desire persists. An individual who at least once a year has not wished the death of someone who has in some way wronged him is a seriously pathological individual. This does not mean that he *must* kill that person, but it is necessary to realize that 'in that moment I was so furious that if I could have made that person disappear from the face of the earth, I would have. But then again, I wouldn't have, even if I could'. That is what I call autonomy.

You speak of autonomy. Other analysts who, like you, tend towards the Left prefer to speak of psychoanalysis as an instrument for emancipation. Is this the same thing?

It is; however, autonomy is more precise. Psychoanalysis cannot be an instrument for *social* emancipation, it cannot free us from our money-dominated society or the immense power wielded by the state. Psychoanalysis does not have the capacity to make revolutionaries of patients, but it can help them to overcome their inhibitions, rendering them more lucid, more active citizens.

However, the problem of psychoanalysis is the relationship of the patient to himself. There is Freud's famous comment in the *New Lectures on Psychoanalysis*: '*Wo es war, soll ich werden*', 'where it has been, I must become'. That is to say, the *I* must take or occupy the place of the *It* (or *Id*). The phrase, however, is more than ambiguous, even if its ambiguity is lessened by what follows: namely, that what we're dealing with is an effort at drying something out, similar to efforts at draining the Zuyderzee Sea in Holland. The intent of psychoanalysis is not to drain the unconscious; that would be an absurd, as well as impossible, undertaking. What it does look to do is to transform the relationship of the agency of the *I* – of the more-or-less conscious, more-or-less reflective subject – with his drives and his unconscious. The definition of autonomy on the individual plane is: knowing what one desires, knowing what one would really like to do and why, and distinguishing between what one knows and does not know.

Today a sort of official ideology of autonomy prevails. Isn't your ideal of autonomy close to the ideas that dominate today's advertising campaigns, where happiness is everywhere on sale? You wrote that Marx was anti-capitalist, but that in reality he shared the same prejudices and the same assumptions of capitalist society. You could be accused of the same thing, because you propose as an alternative an ideal which is today altogether dominant, even banal.

There is clearly, on the part of contemporary society, an extraordinary capacity to assimilate and recycle most anything. However, I began speaking of creativity, the imaginary and autonomy approximately thirty years ago. At that time, it was anything but an advertisement slogan. Gradually, the ad-men appropriated my words because they became the ideas of May 1968. However, the mystification of these ad-men becomes apparent when they speak of creativity. 'If you really want to be creative, come and work for IBM': that is a publicity slogan. But at IBM, you are neither more or less creative than you are elsewhere. The creativity I speak of is of human beings who must be freed, which is quite a different thing. In France, one does not speak so much of autonomy as of individualism. Now, individualism, as it is referred to in advertising, in official ideologies, or in politics, has nothing to do with what I call the autonomy of the individual. In the first place, individualism amounts to 'I do what I wish', while autonomy is of a different order: 'I do what I believe it is right to do, after reflecting on a given matter; I do not deprive myself of doing what pleases me, but I do not do something simply because it pleases me'. In a society in which each one does what he pleases, there will be murder and rape. Moreover, advertising and ideology are deceptive, because their brand of individualism, the narcissism with which we are inundated, is a pseudo-individualism. The current form of individualism is that at 8:30 every evening, in every French household, the same dials are tuned to receive the same television programs, which all propagate the same rubbish. Forty million individuals, as though obeying a military command, all doing the same thing: and that is called individualism! By 'individual' I mean someone who attempts to become autonomous, who is conscious of the fact that, as a human being, he is absolutely unique and attempts to develop his singularity through reflective consciousness. Consequently, there is no relationship between the ideology of ad agencies and what I've said.

Apparently, your idea of the aim (fin) *of psychoanalysis is virtually opposite to the one proposed by Lacan. He strongly criticized the idea that that aim was to create an autonomous ego, calling that theory an 'American ideology'. Do you consider Lacan's criticism to be fair?*

Partially so. For in it there were two potential, perhaps even real, deviations. The first was the absolute over-estimation of the Ego and consciousness. Freud's expression, 'where It was, I must become', should be completed by the symmetrical: 'there where *I* am, the *It* must be able to appear'. We must succeed in making our desires speak. Letting them pass into reality, allowing them to be translated into action, is obviously quite another thing. Therefore, it is necessary to let drives emerge; it is necessary to know even the most bizarre, monstrous, and abject drives which could appear in our everyday, conscious life. On the other hand, the autonomous Ego referred to by certain Americans was, in fact, the *socially constructed individual*: the Ego as constructed by society, which made for an individual who knew that he had to work to live and that if he opposed his boss it was because he had not resolved his Oedipus complex. There have been job application questionnaires in American companies in which, if the candidate responds to the question 'When you where a child, did you love your mother or father more?', by 'I loved my mother more', he scores negatively. Because, clearly, if he opposed his father, he could be a potential troublemaker in the company. That is an ideological utilization of psychoanalysis for the purpose of adaptation. In 1940, when there were fifteen million unemployed in the United States, an article appeared in the *International Journal of Psychoanalysis* by American psychoanalysts interpreting the psychoanalytical roots of unemployment: one is unemployed because of an unconscious desire to be unemployed. This is an aberration, as well as an idiotic position, since unemployment is clearly an economy-related phenomenon.

However, Lacan's criticism of that tendency was somewhat in bad faith. In the first place, because he chose an easy target; in the second place because he wished to propose an ideology of desire. The Lacanian ideology of desire is monstrous, because desire as such is murder, incest, rape. For Lacan, there is the Law, but that Law – which he fails to situate in a social and historical context – could be any law. There was law at Auschwitz; there was law in the gulag; and there is law in Iran today.

But Lacan spoke of symbolic law, constituted by language, and with a universal structure. It is not a question of just any law, imposed by any regime...

Of course, with language we can say anything we please. But what exactly does he mean by symbolic law? The word 'symbolic' for Lacan is a skeleton key, a word to conceal the fact that one is speaking of the institution and the instituted. However, in saying that it is symbolic, what he wants is to endow the institution and the instituted with a pseudo-transcendental dimension, as Kant would say. But the symbolic is quite another thing. Language belongs to the symbolic, in the sense that all signs are symbols of a referent, or that there are symbols of another order. But we must put an end to that Lacanian mystification of the symbolic. There is no 'symbolic' as independent domain; there is a symbolic as part and function of the imaginary. Otherwise, there are institutions, and there is a question of the validity of the institutions. However, the question is not symbolic. Is then the institution valid by right? It will always be valid *de facto*, as long as it is sanctioned. But it was valid *de facto* at Auschwitz and is so also in Iran today. Is it valid by right? Now, there is nothing in the concept of Lacan to lead us to make a distinction between the law of Auschwitz and the law of ancient Athens, or the present laws in the United States. Thus the famous expression of Lacan, to the effect that the master relinquishes nothing of his desire. Now, it is the master who knows what his desire is, and if his desire is like the desire of Lacan, i.e., to transform his followers into slaves, then his desire is realized. But that is fundamentally alien to the psychoanalytic project, which does not seek to realize the desire of the master, nor of anyone else, when such a desire is by definition incompatible with real, social life. So, Lacan ultimately returns to the most utopian aspects of the ideologies of both the young Marx and the anarchists, although he would have laughed sarcastically at such a suggestion. The young Marx and the anarchists, you know, conceived of society as a place in which there'd be neither law nor institutions.

To hear Lacan accused of being an anarchist surprises me. His left-wing critics usually accused him of being repressive, due to his insistence on Law and castration. For Lacan, remaining faithful to one's desire means castration, i.e., renouncing to put into action one's fantasies…

Not so, because the assumption of castration in Lacan is extremely ambiguous. It is the renunciation of desire directed at the mother, but that is the condition of realizing desire. For Lacan, there is neurosis because the individual has not succeeded in assuming his castration, and if he does assume it, then his desire is liberated, with the exception that he obviously no longer directs it towards the mother but towards other women.

But for Lacan, assuming one's own desire does not imply enjoying that which one demands in reality. He makes a distinction between desire, demand and jouissance, *or the reality of pleasure...*

All this is very ambiguous. Lacan is, theoretically, all that which is most banal and suspect, similar to one of those Parisian fads which appear and then disappear after five, ten, or twenty years…

But coming back to the history of psychoanalysis, the particular problem of the human being is to succeed in creating a relationship with the unconscious which is not simply a repression of the unconscious, or its suppression according to a given social dictate and, in particular, the social heteronomy. Here we have once more a point at which psychoanalysis and politics meet. To what extent might I call the social law also *my* law, and not simply a law which has been imposed on me in a heteronomous fashion? It is *my law* only if I have been concretely active in the formation of the law. Only in these conditions can I be truly autonomous, given the fact that I am obliged to live in a society which has laws. Thus, we have a second point of conjunction between the sense of autonomy in psychoanalysis and the sense of autonomy in politics.

Left-wing culture has often criticized analysis as a practice particular to a bourgeois society, because it is essentially based on a private contract of sorts. Above all, during the 1960s and 1970s, a certain segment of the left proposed substituting psychoanalysis with a social treatment of personal problems, reducing psychopathological disturbances to social alienation. What is your opinion of this left-wing, Marxist criticism of the psychoanalytical ethic?

That was a radical leftist exaggeration of the 1960s and 1970s, which drew motivation from certain aspects of establishment psychoanalysis. Every psychoanalytical process necessarily involves two persons: an analysand and an analyst. There cannot be a transference and a working through of the transference outside this relationship between analysand and analyst. There is, however, an aspect which is extremely difficult to resolve and to which no one has yet provided a solution: the financial aspect. On the one hand, the psychoanalyst has to make a living. On the other, as experience proves, even for the analysand an unpaid analysis is not psychically tolerable (because the debt he contracts with the analyst is enormous), and it will inevitably be ineffectual since the analysand can prattle on interminably, because the time of the session costs him nothing. There is in any event a problem: the enormous inequality of the distribution of wealth in today's society places psychoanalysis out of the reach of most of those who need it, unless they are reimbursed by the national health system. This could be resolved effectively only within the framework of a general social transformation.

What then are your practical, political suggestions for countering the classic criticism against analysts: that they only treat the idle rich, and usually too few patients in ratio to the average population?

This is not necessarily true. Of all the patients I have treated over the years, practically none have been rich. Some have made enormous sacrifices in order to go into analysis. I adapt my fee to the patient's economic possibilities. There are also those who cannot pay anything. But practically no one has come to me for analysis in order to be able to say at a fancy dinner party, 'I am in analysis'.

The financial question is, however, a real problem, and it would be good to attempt to eliminate this great inequality of income in today's society. However, from a theoretical standpoint, we cannot stay stuck at Freudian theory as originally formulated. Freud was an incomparable genius, and to him goes the credit for a wealth of ideas. But there is a blind point in Freud: the imagination.

There is a considerable paradox in Freud's works, in that everything recounted by him points to formations of the radical imagination of the subject. Of fantasies. However, Freud, who was formed in the positivist spirit of the nineteenth century, neither sees, nor wants to see, these formations. For this reason, initially, he believed in the reality of the scenes of infantile seduction his hysterical patients described. He believed that the subject was ill because of something which had created trauma.

In recent years, there has been in the United States the tendency to return to Freud's initial belief in the real seduction of children on the part of adults...

These are political idiocies, created by the faddishness of the politically correct. The patient, when he says that his mother, father, nurse or neighbor seduced him when he was a child, is always necessarily right. But that is not the problem, because the basic response is that for any traumatic event, the event is real in that it is an event, while it is imaginary in that it is traumatic. There can be no trauma if the imagination of the subject does not give a certain meaning to what has occurred, and that meaning is not determined by what's politically correct but by the meaning given to the fantasy by the subject and his radical imagination. Now, Freud does not want to acknowledge this basic concept. Currently, in the United States, we see an attempt to go back in time. It is touching, and even funny, to see that during the analysis of the Wolf Man, Freud long believed in the reality of the primary scene which the Wolf Man described: namely, that he saw his parents making love from behind. It was not until the end of the analysis that Freud acknowledged in a footnote that maybe that scene was only a fantasy of the patient's. However, the matter is of little importance. Freud did not account for the role played by the imagination in what he called fantasmatisation. He attempted to attribute phylogenetic origins to these fantasies, and then tried to locate them in the origin myth of *Totem and Taboo*, which is patently absurd.

To explain the origin of society, Freud created a myth. At the outset, he posed the problem of the origin of society as simply negative, as the problem of the origin of the two major interdictions: that of incest and that of intra-tribal murder. Not murder in principle, because nowhere is murder forbidden in principle; if you kill the enemies of Italy or France, you have done well and are decorated, but one must not kill within the community. You can kill within only if you are an executioner, or a policeman on duty. Freud did not see that the problem of the origin of society is not exclusively the problem of the creation of two interdictions. It is the problem of the creation of positive institutions: the creation of language, norms of behavior, religions, meanings, and so on. Freud's myth explains the creation of the two major prohibitions during the course of history of the primitive horde, where a father had all the women and castrated or drove out his sons in order to continue to reign over his harem. One day, the brothers killed the father and divided up the women of the tribe. Then the brothers entered a pact stipulating that on no one would attempt to take the woman of another or to commit murder. And so they portrayed their father as the tribe's totem animal. And every year they would prepare a sacrificial meal, during which an animal was sacrificed and eaten, thus repeating symbolically in the true sense of the term the murder of the father. From an anthropological point of view, the myth does not hold, although it is a very significant mythical construction, to the extent that it reveals the workings of Freud's mind as well as the thought of his time. But psychoanalysis didn't need *Totem and Taboo* to establish the Oedipus complex, that it had already done. Ultimately, the myth only represents that which instead it should explain, because it represents the brothers' capacity for socialization on the very day they joined forces to kill their father. That is already a social action, which presupposes the existence of language. Therefore, to explain the origin of society, Freud presupposes that society is already there; he presupposes that the brothers could converse among themselves, conspire and maintain a secret. Animals have never been seen to conspire.

However, because Freud totally dismisses the creative role of the radical imagination, of fantasmatization, he remains something of a reductionist or determinist. He tends to find causal links in a subject's psychic life to explain a symptom, neurosis or particular evolution. He carries this attitude to an extreme in stories like *A Childhood Memory of Leonardo da Vinci*, in which he attempts to explain one of Leonardo's paintings and his creative life on the basis of a single childhood incident: which here too is presupposed as something mythical and which, even in holding all the pieces together, still fails to explain Leonardo's art, why his painting is great, or why we experience pleasure in looking at it. Also when it comes to explaining the evolution of a singular subject – to demonstrating, for instance, the reasons for a certain neurosis and not another – Freud finally admits that it is impossible to know, and invokes 'the choice of the neurosis'. An individual chooses his neurosis, and by two or three years of age she has already embarked upon the road to obsession rather than, say, hysteria...

But is not the expression 'choice of neurosis' contrary to what you assume to be Freud's determinism? Because, evidently, to speak of choice is in itself to repudiate determinism, and consequently to admit that there is no relation of cause and effect between the history of a person and his psychopathology.

That is what I said. Freud inevitably attempts to find a connection between cause and effect. For example, in his case studies of the Rat Man and Wolf Man, he says that a certain symptom exists because a given thing has occurred at a given moment. However, in the first place, he does not see that the thing which has occurred at that moment has played this role only because the patient attributed to it a certain fantastic meaning. And secondly, Freud does not explain that which has occurred, and is consequently forced in the end to say that there is a choice of neurosis that he cannot explain. He often refers to constitutional factors, but constitutional factors are like histories (heredity) in old medicine, or the soporific virtues of opium, as Molière said. Saying that there are constitutional factors does not constitute an answer. Here, once more one must be fair: when Freud spoke of constitutional factors he was not completely mistaken; for example, with infants, from the outset there is a considerable difference in their tolerance of frustration. Some infants, given the breast or the baby's bottle, remain calm for six hours until they are once more hungry, while others very quickly begin to cry, scream, demand the breast or the bottle, or do not accept the mother's going away. Then, constitution implies something innate. However, any effort at psychoanalytical determinism fails.

Freud said much the same thing in the 1930s, as regards female homosexuality, when he stated that a girl, during adolescence, could make one of three 'choices'. She could become a woman who loves men and wishes to have children, a dried-up old maid who detests sex, or a tomboy in whom, even if it remains latent, there will be a tendency towards homosexuality. Why does she choose one alternative rather than another? One could point to factors which have led to a given choice or inclination, but ultimately it can never be determined.

Are not the problems Freud poses concerning the 'choice' of neurosis, or ways of being a woman, linked to problems inherent in all historical reconstruction? There has always been this oscillation between determinism and in-determinism in historical reconstructions.

Yes. It is precisely for that reason that determinist and scientist reductionism is false; one can never demonstrate the totality of necessary and sufficient conditions. That does not necessarily mean that there is an absence of any form of determinism; there are certain connections of cause and effect, but not always and not essentially. It is a question of domains.

But in analytical treatment, does one act on the causes or something else?

That is the most important and the most difficult question. Psychoanalysis attempts to transform the way the patient sees his world. In the first place, it attempts to make him see his world of fantasies. That is, it attempts to make him understand that the way in which he sees the world is a way which, for the most part, depends on his own psychic constructions and fantasies. Secondly, it attempts to lead him to an adequate relationship with his fantastic constructions. If you are dealing, for example, with someone who is on the paranoiac side, first of all he must be made to understand not by logical persuasion, but through the analytical work that it is not true that everyone wants to persecute him, but that, essentially, his view is his own fantasmatization, and that one might even say that when he actually does encounter persons really intent on persecuting him, it is he who has chosen them. He chooses the woman who will persecute him. I have chosen an extreme example, because with a delirious paranoiac there is practically nothing to be done. There are, however, other cases where a patient can be helped to live more or less peacefully and reasonably with his fantasy world, as well with his new fantastic productions. The way in which that occurs is also one of the mysteries of analysis. Freud never succeeded in explaining why a real interpretation has an effect. And I cannot explain why a true interpretation at times produces an effect and at other times produces none. A dyed-in-the-wool analyst will tell you: 'If an interpretation does not produce any effect, this is because it is not true'. That is not exactly the case.

Apropos of the effects of analysis, in recent years there has been considerable criticism by a certain epistemology of the validity, the scientific truthfulness, of psychoanalysis. For example, Popper, Grünbaum and Eysenck have criticized the scientific plausibility of psychoanalysis. Grünbaum in particular has said that analysis sometimes simply creates placebo effects. What is your opinion of these criticisms which consider the effects of analysis as being no different than the effects of magical cures? Because, at times, a magician can also cure...

But how does he do it? Mr. Grünbaum, Mr. Popper and even Mr. Lévi-Strauss have no explanation for that. Lévi-Strauss says that psychoanalysts are the shamans of modern times, and shamans the psychoanalysts of primitive societies. But why experiments in double blind? Why is there a placebo effect? Because there is suggestion. But why is there suggestion? Psychoanalysis responds that all suggestion is the result of transference. The patient to whom the physician gives a medicine is very likely to believe that that medicine will be beneficial, and for that reason there is a placebo effect and that faith can produce effects on the psyche. Secondly, it is for that reason that one makes experiments in double blind, and to say that the fact that someone goes to a psychoanalyst three times a week and that that is beneficial due to a placebo effect, is saying nothing at all. Why is there a placebo effect?

Yes, but you say that epistemology and analysis both admit to the existence of suggestion. I cannot believe that any analyst would be content to admit that the effects that he produces are due to suggestion, even if suggestion is explained in a psychoanalytic way...

Psychoanalysis can explain suggestion, but suggestion cannot explain psychoanalysis. Because psychoanalysis is essentially, I do not say exclusively, the work of the analysand. These philosophers, perhaps because they often live in America, have in mind a psychoanalyst who says to the patient: 'If you think that, it is because your mother did that'. However, other psychoanalysts worthy of the name would never say anything of the kind. Now, one has more sophisticated forms: one says that the patient who knows what the analyst thinks attempts to say to him that he knows what the analyst will think, and so on. But if one is experienced in analysis, nothing of the sort holds. It is a question of authority, but in the end I have an experience which Grünbaum has not. If one wishes to, one believes me, and if one wishes to, one does not. One sees how a patient changes in the course of a treatment, and one sees that he resists. How can Mr. Grünbaum explain why a resistance at a certain point gives way? Why does a patient for two years make no progress and then suddenly something moves and he shifts to another speed?

All these criticisms, beginning with Popper, compare psychoanalysis to an idea of science identified with positivism. But anyone who expects psychoanalysis to be a positivist science is a fool. Popper struggles against that fool. By Popper's own reasoning, one could say that there exists no history, because there is no possibility of falsification in history. That is possible only as regards concrete facts. If someone says 'there is no Parthenon in Athens', there is a falsifiable aspect of that thing because one can take him to Athens and show him the Parthenon. But if someone says, as Burckhardt did, that for the ancient Greeks the athletic element – that is, competition and the struggle against the opponent – was very important, that is an interpretation and not refutable in Popper's sense. Popper, with his would-be criterion, says that there are positive sciences in which there is experience, measure, etc., and all the rest is literature. That may be so, but this literature is more important, perhaps, than the positive sciences. History, society, the psyche, our lives, are at least as important as molecules and atoms.

Translated from the French by Joan Tambureno

Selected Bibliography

The Castoriadis Reader (1997, ed. David Ames Curtis). Oxford: Blackwell Publishers.

World in Fragments (1997, ed. and trans. David Ames Curtis). Stanford, CA: Stanford Univ. Press

Philosophy, Politics, Autonomy (1991, ed. David Ames Curtis). New York: Oxford Univ. Press.

Political and Social Writings (1988, trans. and ed. David Ames Curtis, 3 vols). Minneapolis: University of Minnesota Press.

The Imaginary Institution of Society (1987, trans. Kathleen Blamey). Cambridge, England: Polity Press and Cambridge, MA: MIT Press

Crossroads in the Labyrinth (1984, trans. Martin H. Ryle and Kate Soper). Brighton, England: Harvester and Cambridge, MA: MIT Press.

III

CLINICAL PRACTICE AND SOCIETY

THE MIRROR'S CHILD

Françoise Dolto

FRANÇOISE DOLTO, MD (1908–1988) remains, even after her death over twenty years ago, one of France's most popular and beloved psychoanalysts. A pioneer in child psychoanalysis, she was a founding member of the Société Psychanalytique de Paris (1939), and co-founder, with Jacques Lacan, of the Ecole Freudienne de Paris. A paediatrician and educator as well as a brilliant psychoanalyst, in the 1960s and '70s Dr. Dolto extended the public reach of psychoanalysis via a series of very successful radio programmes, broadcast live, during which she would engage directly with both children and adults, or would reply in detail to their letters. Her many books – on topics ranging from religion to female sexuality, from child-rearing to a remarkable autobiography, *Autoportrait d'une psychanalyste*, published soon after her death – influenced a generation of practitioners and parents but remain inexplicably untranslated into English (while otherwise known throughout Europe and in countries as far as China, Russia and Korea).

In this conversation with Lacanian psychoanalyst Juan-David Nasio, Dr. Dolto develops some of the concepts first put forth in her book *L'image Inconsciente du Corps* (Paris: Seuil, 1984; Points Seuil, 1992), emphasizing similarities and differences between Lacan's notion of the 'mirror stage' and her idea of the body's unconscious image. For Dolto, the actual mirror experience marks a wound for every child, a symbolic hole from which derives the impossible fit of the body image to the body pattern. Astounding clinical accounts of her work with children and young adults also intersperse the text, highlighting Dolto's contention that the unconscious image of the analyst's body in treatment serves as one of the consolidating points of transference.

This conversation, which took place during a seminar held by Nasio in Paris on January 25, 1985, was originally part of a longer discussion published in a book by Nasio and Dolto titled *L'Enfant du Miroir* (Paris: Editions Rivages, 1987; Editions Payot & Rivages 1992, 2002). It first appeared in English in the *Journal of European Psychoanalysis* n. 1 (1995) under the title 'The Mirror's Child', and is here reprinted courtesy of Editions Payot & Rivages, in conjunction with Dr. Nasio and the heirs of Françoise Dolto.

Juan-David Nasio

Françoise Dolto, your concept of castration is not of a mutilation of the code of the body's unconscious image but, on the contrary, an épreuve *[ordeal] to be experienced and overcome…*

Françoise Dolto

That is correct. Castrations are mutating *épreuves* – sometimes successful, sometimes not – having either promotional symbolic or pathogenic effects.

In this regard, one of the most stimulating ideas in your book, L'image Inconsciente du Corps (The Unconscious Body Image) *is the elevation of castration to the rank of an operation generating positive and socially humanizing effects on the child's body. Of course, all this depends on the manner in which the subject overcomes this ordeal of castration ...*

Yes, but it also depends on who the castrating agent is, and above all on how the child is helped throughout his ordeal, because this passage entails a decisive factor: the 'Ideal Ego' (*moi-idéal*) represented by the person assisting the child. It is clear that any adult, any 'other', who accompanies the child during his ordeal, must himself have undergone and overcome the same ordeal. The adult will thus gain the child's trust, and will represent for the child someone who has succeeded in overcoming the hardships of the ordeal. Nevertheless, it will still be necessary that the adult know how to assist the child during the ordeal, situating himself on the same level as the child. How is it possible, being an adult, to enter into the painful experience of the child?

When the infant is recognized as a subject overcoming castration, you use the expression 'accompanied by an ideal', by a moi-idéal *(Ideal Ego)…*

The *moi-idéal* can be a person or an animal, but not always the same one. For example, it can be a dog or any other domestic animal – or sometimes even a wild one – before which the child recognizes himself as a person. It is necessary that the *moi-idéal* be represented by someone or something real, whose experience the child admires. These can also be fictional images – why not? – such as Ninja Turtles, etc., which take on the value of real people. These are all very counter-phobic *moi-idéals*. While for adults these characters might appear phobogenic, for the child they constitute formidable, permanent and indestructible objects which are, as a consequence, very counter-phobic and protective; plastic or metal figurines, having never been born, are neither sensitive nor mortal, and in identifying himself with them, the child will not easily succumb to phobia. You see, the *moi-idéals* are the real sustainers and guarantors of basic security.

Discussing the nature of the psychoanalyst's intervention, you once stressed the importance of telling the child his sexual identity, and even of spelling out a prohibition – not in the sense of an authoritarian prohibition, but more along the lines of a reminder of Oedipal law. Would an intervention of this type mean a symbologenic castration inherent in the transferential experience?

Exactly; that is castration. But on the condition that the child feels that the adult telling him his sexual identity by spelling out 'You may not desire me', is someone who loves him. What is love, if not a sublimation of desire and not its satisfaction? It is not necessary to embrace the child to make him feel loved; the 'right word' suffices. It is love mediated by speech which will permit the child to blossom and become a source of desire for others. This is a general principle for all our patients, because we would not know how to listen to an analysand if we were not also capable of loving him. But I repeat, it is loving through speech – speech which remains with the patient throughout the ordeal. That is Freud's great discovery: castration is given, accomplished and overcome through the right speech.

In your book there is a very important chapter on the mirror, where you develop an extremely original concept regarding the mirror's function in constituting the unconscious body image. In 1949, one of your earliest works, an article published that same year in the Revue Française de Psychanalyse *titled* Cure Psychanalytique à L'aide de la Poupée Fleur *[A Psychoanalytic Treatment by Means of a Flower Doll], was the focus of a lively debate with analysts such as Lacan, Nacht, Lebovici and yourself among others. From the transcript of that debate, here is a summary of what Lacan had to say: 'Dr. Lacan has the strong impression that Mrs. Dolto's flower doll fits in with his own research on the mirror stage, the body image and the fragmented body. He considers it significant that the flower doll has no mouth and, after having noted that it is a sexual symbol and that it hides the human face, concludes by saying that he hopes one day to come up with a theoretical commentary on Mrs. Dolto's contribution'. You responded to Lacan, 'Yes, the flower doll relates to the mirror stage, if one understands the concept of the mirror as an object reflecting not only the visible, but also the audible, sensitive and intentional worlds. The doll has no face, hands or feet, no front, back, joints or neck'.*

I am sure that everyone, and you in particular, will appreciate not only the value of this text as a document and the richness of this exchange, but also the gap evidenced between Lacan's mirror stage and your understanding of the mirror; which for you constitutes the unconscious body image. Already in 1949 your singular conception of the mirror as an all-reflective surface of all perceivable forms (and not exclusively of visible shapes or forms), could be distinguished from Lacan's theory of the mirror stage. If I understand you correctly, what was important for you then – and still is today – was neither the specular character of the mirror nor the scopic image therein reflected, but the relational function of a completely different mirror of a completely different nature: the mirror of the subject's being reflected in the other.

In a very schematic distinction, I find three essential differences between Lacan's mirror stage and what we might call Dolto's 'mirror of primary narcissism'. The first difference concerns the visual, reflecting character of the flat surface in Lacan, as opposed to the psychic surface mirror reflecting all perceptible shapes in your theory. Of course, you also refer to the flat mirror, but you quickly relativize it as one instrument among many contributing to individualize the body in general (along, say, with the face, or the difference between sexes). In your theory, the mirror's reflected image is just one stimulus among any number of other perceptual stimuli in the shaping of the unconscious body image.

The second, more essential, difference has to do with the relationship of the child's actual body and the reflected image. We know that in Lacan's theory the image of the 'mirror stage' anticipates, on an imaginary level, the later unity of the symbolic Je *[I], and that this image is above all a mirage of totality and of maturation, when confronted with the dispersed and immature reality of the child's body. Thus Lacan's mirror stage is an introductory and primary experience. In your book, you place the problem in a completely different light. First of all, the child's body which experiences the impact of the mirror is neither a dispersed nor fragmented 'real', but cohesive and continuous. Instead of opposing a fragmented body with a totalizing mirror image, as in Lacan's theory, you juxtapose two different but complementary images: the mirror, or scopic, image and the unconscious image of the body. In other words, you displace the constitutive contradiction of Lacan's mirror stage. For him, confrontation of the real body with the mirror image is the decisive factor; for you, as the real body is already a continuum, the decisive factor is the play between two images: on one side the unconscious image of the body, and on the other the mirror image which contributes to shaping and individualizing this same unconscious image. If you accept these theoretical distinctions, then Lacan's mirror stage marks a beginning, while Dolto's confirms an original moment of narcissistic individuation dating back to the primary narcissism.*

The third and last difference regards the affective nature of the impact that the mirror image produces on the child. Lacan calls this impact 'jubilation', while you recognize in it the painful experience of castration. Lacan conceives of the jubilation as an affective agitation which signals the infant's acceptance of his image. You, on the contrary, find in castration the infant's painful acknowledgment of the gap which separates him from his image. One could summarize this by saying that in your view the primary narcissism is essentially the child's overcoming his ordeal of no longer being the image of himself reflected by the mirror.

Thank you for this recollection of my beginnings and for having succeeded in making so clear a presentation of the numerous questions posed by the difficult problem of the mirror. Paradoxically, the children who taught me the most about mirrors – and about primary narcissism – have actually been those who could not see: children blind from birth who had never experienced the effect of a visible image, but who nevertheless conserved intact a rich unconscious body image. Their faces are usually so movingly authentic as to give the impression that the body image within them shows through.

The reference to blind children is particularly interesting because it raises the problem of the formation of the unconscious body image even in the absence of the mirror ordeal…

This might seem odd, but I am sure that the body image of the blind remains unconscious for a much longer time than for those who can see. Therapists treating personality disturbances in children with congenital blindness frequently hear recounted Oedipal stories full of expressions that refer to sight. Blind children will always say, 'I see', which would prompt me to ask them, 'How can you see if you are blind?' They'd respond, 'I say that 'I see' because everyone around me speaks this way', to which I'd reply, 'Everyone says 'I see', but what they mean is 'I understand''. Blind children are gifted with a remarkable sensitivity. When, for example, they shape a piece of sculpture, the hands of the sculpted figure take on an inordinate importance. For instance, they don't make anything like a preliminary drawing on paper, but actually 'draw' by etching into the modeling clay itself. And they obtain, with the same mastery as sighted children, real body shapes in their sculpture. Now, in their sculptures, the hands are much larger than in those of sighted children, and the reason is obvious: it is with their hands that they see; it is in their hands that they have their eyes. You can understand why the designs are more etchings than drawings. It is very interesting to analyze a person lacking one sensory register, because to the extent that he is a subject of language, he has had to reorganize the symbolization of the other registers. In this case the psychoanalyst becomes aware that he concentrates his attention on the missing sensory register, while the same register passes unobserved under ordinary analytical circumstances.

So, if the blind child has his eyes at the tips of his fingers, the psychoanalyst of this blind child should have his eyes in the depths of his listening. But let us come back to the experience of the mirror, and to your observations on castration. Why must we consider the mirror experience a castration?

Because that experience is certainly an ordeal. Consider a child who suddenly sees his reflected image emerge in a mirror, an image he had not previously noted. Children, you know, are extremely sensitive to sudden impacts. The child joyfully approaches the mirror, and happily exclaims: 'Look at baby'. Attempting to play with the 'baby', he ends up bumping his forehead, and no longer understands. If the child is alone in the room, without someone to explain to him that it is only an image, he becomes very confused. This is the turning point in the ordeal. For this ordeal to have a symbologenic effect, the adult present must give a name to what is happening. It is true that many mothers at this moment commit the error of saying to the child, while indicating the mirror, 'You see, that's you'; when instead it would be very simple and correct to say 'You see, that's your image in the mirror, just like what you see next to you is my image in the mirror'. Lacking this essential word for the symbolization, the child will certainly have a 'scopic' visual experience – witnessing, for example, that his image disappears when he is no longer in front of the mirror, and that it reappears when he returns – but it will remain, in the absence of a response or of communication, a painful visual experience.

It is a very trying experience for the child if others are not in the same room with him in front of the mirror: not only to speak with him, but in order that the child also observe in the mirror the adult's image, different from his own, so that he might 'discover' that he is a child. A child does not know he is a child and that he has the size and appearance of a child. To know this, it was necessary to look at the mirror and notice the difference between his image and that of the adult. Consider also that when the same child is with a smaller child, he suffers from the feeling that his identity as a child is no longer stable.

Children want neither to be in front of a mirror with a smaller child nor to be in a communion of identities. This is one of the reasons why, as children grow up, they shove around the younger ones. In fact, a child may no longer be content with simply taking a smaller child's toy, but must knock him down too. One must explain to him that if he has knocked down his playmate, it was to assure himself that he had not become identical to him, for fear of losing his identity. After the adult's explanation the child is reassured and no longer needs to push around smaller children. You see how these exchanges among children are determined by the mirror which contaminates their entire reality.

You qualify the mirror experience as a wound, a symbolic hole, and define it in your book as follows: 'One can call this irreparable wound of the mirror experience the symbolic hole from which derives, for all of us, the impossible fit of the body image to the body pattern'. Thus, this wound determined by the visually reflected image is necessary for the child to be assured, in a way, that his image is well-regulated with regard to his being in relationship to others: in other words, for him to defend his own identity.

Yes. The best illustration is the case of a little girl who could not swallow well because she had lost her 'hand's mouth'. This healthy and wonderful child became schizophrenic at the age of two-and-a-half. I didn't have the opportunity of observing her for long, as she was in Paris with her American parents for only two months. While her parents toured the city, the child remained in the hotel room, watched over by an unknown person who spoke Cockney rather than American English. Thus, the little girl had no occasion for communication. The walls of the room were lined with mirrors and most of the furniture was glass. In this room of mirrors and without attentive company, she lost herself and fragmented into pieces of her body which she saw everywhere. Furthermore, the presence of a small baby who took most of the nurse's attention left her even more confused. On her return to the United States, she underwent treatment. Later, I received a letter from her mother containing some superb photographs of the child taken two months before the crisis for which they consulted me. It was terrible to see how the mirror experience had dissociated and scattered her being. And to think that the parents had been happily convinced that the mirrors in the room would amuse her… they had not the slightest idea that their little girl was falling into madness.

This moving case brings to mind your insistence on the deadly fascination of the mirror. One sees how the mirror image can both integrate and abolish the unconscious…

Absolutely. From the point of view of the body image, the child is never fragmented; it is others who are fragmented. But he can still fragment himself imaginarily through identification with others or with imaginary representations of others, just as in the case of the little girl who identified with multiple fragmented visual images. Children who suffer from this type of imaginary identification can be observed even in everyday situations. For example, some children are embarrassed at the sight of their parents in bed with only their heads showing from beneath the covers, or even in front of the television screen. The television is very fragmenting because the torso images which move around lead very small children to believe that these people are cut in two. Another trick effect of the visual image is when the child, facing the mirror, believes he is dealing with his double. At this moment – again I emphasize – it is necessary that someone older speak to him to help him distinguish between the warmth of a real relationship with others, and the trick relationship with the image. Yet it is also because of this imaginary trickery that children play at making faces, or at returning faces to the mirror. In this way the child learns to smile and to finally use the lying image to make his link with others less threatening, or by contrast, to separate himself from others.

Is this why in your book you maintain that the reflected visual image is refoulante *[repressive]?*

Exactly. The visual image is *refoulante* of the body image.

It is refoulante *because it distorts...*

Yes. It distorts insofar as the visual reflective image shows only one side of the subject, when actually the child feels complete in his being; as good in his front as in his back. Nevertheless, the influence of the image and of the scopic, visual drives is such that one pays almost exclusive attention to the front of the body. Think of what it's like going down steps in the dark. The caution we take shows that, despite the darkness, we descend with our eyes, and not only with our feet. Our feet are also in our eyes. In other words, in difficult real conditions the visual reflected image takes the place of the unconscious body image. If we could always have eyes in our feet, like children or tightrope-walkers, it would be fantastic! We live so much on the appearances we display, that the deep perception localized in the body image – which is not seen – remains generally negated by the mirror image.

You see, the visual reflected image is nothing compared to feeling. And the wound or, if you prefer, the castration of the mirror experience, is the child's shock at realizing that the mirror image, a purely inanimate reflection, is a very different image from the body image. My book contains an observation on twins, for which I am grateful to their mother – a woman I did not know – for having provided me with the following documentation: 'No one, not even their relatives, is able to distinguish between the twins, who are never separated, with the exception of their mother and a baby born after them, who already calls them using distinct phonemes, never failing to distinguish one from the other'. It is interesting to note that the baby never fails to recognize his older twin brothers, when even the father fails. This means that the baby is sensitive to the body image and not the visually reflected image.

But to get back to the story... 'One day the mother decides to leave one of the twins at home as he has a cough, and takes the other to school (the two were already in nursery school). She returns home and is going about her business when she hears the child playing alone in his room, complaining. The child's pleas become louder and more anguished, yet he is not calling for his mother. She approaches the door which is ajar, and sees the boy, mounting his wooden toy horse, as he appeals to his image in the wardrobe mirror. The anguish in his voice increases. The mother then enters, shows herself and calls to her son, who falls into her arms and says, in a complaining and depressive tone: 'X [his brother's name] doesn't want to play horse'.

The mother, troubled, understands that the child has mistaken his mirror image for the actual presence of his brother. She approaches the mirror holding him in her arms, taking the horse with them, and talks about the image the mirror shows, which is their image and not herself, the horse, or the absent brother. She reminds him that he felt a little sick that morning, while his brother did not; that she left him at home and took his brother to school, and that she will go back to pick his brother up. The child listens to her very attentively. In this case of twins who so closely resemble each other, the mirror, though placed on the wardrobe door in their room, had never before presented to that child a question regarding his appearance. When he saw himself there he undoubtedly acknowledged, as his brother had also (they were three years old), that he was looking at his brother, never wondering about his 'bi-location', that is to say, the capacity of his brother to be in two places at the same time. When his twin brother returned from school, the mother repeated this experience with both children, putting one on each side of her before the mirror and helping each one see his image as his own, and the image of the other as the image of the other brother. She explained that they resembled each other because they were twins born on the same day. This explanation, which they listened to attentively, clearly and silently presented a serious problem to her sons'.

This observation is extraordinary because this woman, who had neither heard me on the radio nor had anything to do with psychoanalysis, had felt it necessary to relate this experience to me. She concluded her letter by saying that, although everything subsequently went back to normal, it was important for her to tell me this upsetting story. This is an excellent illustration of the gap between the non-living visual image and the absolutely vital unconscious body image. The influence of the mirror, which reflects back to us and makes us continually aware of a person's face and genitals, is evidenced by the difficulty some people have in bearing the simultaneous view of both the sex and the face of someone. In front of one of his parents, the child has the alternative of seeing either the sex or the face; he ignores the sex if he sees the face, and he ignores the face if he sees the sex.

In this regard, you stress the importance of the first human face seen by the baby...

Yes. I have observed certain cases where a facial feature of the person present at the first moments of life remains forever present. For example, an infant cared for during his first days by a blue-eyed woman was troubled each time he saw a face with blue eyes. This case reminds me of the surprise displayed by the Vietnamese when first seeing Europeans with blue eyes. It was so anguishing for them to see blue eyes that the women hid their faces by putting their skirts over their heads. Why such anguish? Because they had never known anyone with blue eyes in whom to see themselves reflected. Because, as we have seen, there is not only the flat mirror but, more importantly, the mirror that the Other is for us. And, more particularly, the first person seen at birth; sometimes even the words heard during the first hours of life are like echoes of a sound mirror. I followed the treatment of a thirteen-year-old schizophrenic, who one day shared with me a dramatic event which occurred during the first hours of his life. No one knew about this except his adoptive mother, who had not even mentioned it to her husband, such was the shocking nature of the event. What cured the child was his recounting to me what had happened. I later learned by chance that he was definitively cured, had married and had a child.

A Participant

It seems that the question you pose concerns the articulation between trauma and fantasy. From what you have just said, the value of reconstruction can be questioned, as in the anamnesis of a 'first event'. How should a psychoanalyst approach a supposedly traumatic first event? Must he try to know it?

No one other than he who has experienced the trauma can *know* it; but one needs an analyst to let the original event emerge. Let us consider the remarkable story of a seriously phobic and schizophrenic adolescent suffering terribly from insomnia.

The boy in question feared all pointed objects, even pencils, which he considered a weapon capable of pricking and destroying. I was initially unaware of the fact that he was adopted. I later learned that his phobia of being pricked went back to something he heard someone say about wanting an abortion. I recall clearly one session when I convinced him to take a pencil and prick my hand to show him that I would not die. The session which followed was so important for the cure of this child, and such a trying moment for myself that it was as if all preceding sessions were nothing but a preparation for this crucial moment. That day, he was unable to sit down, he shifted from one foot to the other, and then suddenly began reciting a melodrama in two voices: one sharp and plaintive, the other aggressive. The first said 'Mummy, I want to keep it, yes, I want to keep it', and the other responded: 'No, you bitch! You dirty whore! You won't! If you keep it, I'll strangle it with my own hands'. I was shocked to hear these words coming out of a thirteen-year-old boy who appeared to be unaware of what he was saying. And swaying like a tree in an earthquake, I heard one insistent question: 'But how could this child live?' A few days later, I received a telephone call from the adoptive mother: 'Madame Dolto, it is urgent that I see you, because something quite extraordinary has happened. After my child returned from his session, he ate very rapidly and then slept uninterruptedly for thirty-six hours. I called the doctor thinking that he was sick or that he had taken some pills, but the doctor reassured me, explaining to me that there was nothing to worry about as long as he was sleeping'. She also told me that when the boy awoke, he was very surprised to have missed school, it was as though he had awakened from a timeless sleep.

I asked the mother to come and see me, and told her she had neglected to tell me something essential about her child. Gradually, she understood that the words exchanged during the last session were the source of this long sleep. I then repeated her son's words during the session. It was dreadful. Through her tears, she shouted: 'Don't tell me that, Madame! Yes, I lied to you, because if I had told you the truth, my whole life would have been ruined. Now I'll tell you: all our children are adopted, because I am sterile'. She then explained the circumstances under which she had adopted this boy, who was her oldest son. 'What I heard that day', she told me, 'no one in the world knows, not even my husband. How is it possible that my son, who was so little, understood these words?' When she had gone to the clinic to adopt the child, she had overheard from behind a screen a dispute between the child's biological mother and maternal grandmother. The child was only forty-eight hours old at the time.

You understand that it is necessary to have lived through such an experience to understand how the spoken word could have etched itself into the child – words with no meaning for him other than the *jouissance* of the death wish on his being. On the level of his body scheme he took *jouissance* from the prohibition of living, from the prohibition of developing the image of his fetal body in the outside world after his birth. These deathly words inscribed into his body scheme could only be displaced under conditions of transference, that is, through the words spoken by him and the emotion felt by me.

During the following session, the boy was completely calm. After he had told me that he was well rested, I asked him if he remembered what he had said during our last encounter. He responded: 'Madame, I didn't tell you anything'. Realizing that he recalled nothing, I decided to tell him – trying to imitate him – the quarrel between the two female voices. When the session was over, I had the impression, indeed the certainty, that he had let go of the entirety of his super-ego [*tout surmoi*]. Later he married, had a closely knit family, and established himself professionally. Wouldn't you know, he who had been so afraid of needles and scissors later apprenticed as a tailor. Here we have an experience which demonstrates how an early event can only be revealed through analysis. So, as to your question concerning the function of an anamnesis, this story shows how a very old event can emerge thanks to the conditions of transference.

A Participant

Yes, but weren't you still forced to form a reconstruction which remained hypothetical?

Actually, I reconstructed because I didn't understand why the session of the 'two voices' had produced such a strong effect of sleep on the child. During this deep sleep, the boy had found once more the peace of his death drive and could be secure. Until that moment, I could say that the words he had heard and registered when he was only a few hours old had so greatly marked his unconscious body image that he had remained fixed in a state of permanent phobia. Phobia of what? Precisely the phobia of the death drive.

After having said what he had to say, there was nothing left to threaten him. In the end, this child had four women who had suffered for him instead of ignoring him: the two women in the initial scene, his adoptive mother and then myself. Perhaps this is what it means to psychoanalytically treat a child: just as we support him in his speech and accompany him in overcoming himself and the ordeal impeded by resistance, so we pass through this ordeal ourselves and experience it within our own bodies. I could say that I experienced the ordeal of his speech condensed into a single moment of his entire existence. He was not the only child who made me feel physical emotions while he was speaking. These moments are always decisive, because they are evidence of the archaic re-living of the body image in a fusional transference.

One could also describe these moments by saying that the body image establishes itself as the transferential body image…

Exactly, it is the moment in which the body image of the two partners installs itself. It is like a fetal image where the child and mother simultaneously perceive an emotional drama. That is transference: a transference which is only possible if the analyst is counter-transferentially available for the patient. But it is never through anamnesis that the earliest event reveals itself. It is in the *après coup* [literally, *afterblow*] of a transferential dialogue. Children in analysis are often cured without our knowing exactly why. We go over our notes, try to understand, but the important thing is that they come out of it; that they have had the chance to speak the unsaid that until then was perturbing the good intersection of the body image and the body scheme.

A Participant

Do you think that articulating true speech suffices to produce an immediate effect on the subject?

When one calls a child by his name, this is already true speech. For example, in treatment, calling a child 'Mr. So-and-So' or 'Miss So-and-So' always produces unusual effects. You will see a smile appear in a profoundly depressive baby after you have called him by his name. You see, true speech, in the end, is respecting the other as much as oneself; respecting the child who does not want to speak or who is sad; respecting him while, at the same time, looking for the sense of his silence and asking, for example, 'Perhaps you want to die?' I once encountered in a hospital a fourteen-month-old depressive child who was apparently autistic. I asked him, 'Could it be you want to die?' He responded by nodding his head twice. 'You know, I myself would not prevent you from dying, but you know very well that in the children's ward you can't do such a thing'. While I was speaking, the child was constantly looking at the window. 'You're looking at the window because you would like to escape through it. But you can't because there are bars on the windows. If you want to die, you will have to get out of this children's ward. They have brought you to the hospital because they later want to put you in a psychiatric hospital, where there will be even more bars. I don't want this; I prefer that you explain to me why you wish to die. Once you've told me why, maybe you'll be able to live'. Here is an example of true speech addressed to a fourteen-month-old child who had already seen me in many sessions without apparently ever making contact.

I am deeply convinced that one cannot treat a child without speaking truly of what we feel and think in being with him. To 'speak truly' means considering the child before us as someone in the process of becoming a man or woman, who is completely language in his being, having the body of a child, but understanding everything we say. Whether we tell him of his desire for living in this particular body, or we tell him that there is no more room for living in this particular body, be certain that from the moment we say that he no longer has the desire to live, it will already constitute a beginning of desire. This is the function of language for all human beings, be they adults or children. Everyone has thoughts about suicide, but it suffices to put them into words in order not to be alone. Suicide is the call to solitude in order to rediscover an old body image, or the return to the freedom that the lack of a body can signify for the subject.

The question of the analyst's body in treatment is a path you've opened for clinicians, and which attracts people to your work. But what exactly do you mean by the 'analyst's body?'

During treatment, the analyst's body is constantly exposed to the speech of the other and is extremely sensitive to his presence. At the same time, this entity we call the 'analyst's body' – and which, to be more precise, we should call the 'image of the analyst's body' – constitutes one of the consolidating points of transference. Take the experience of working with children and psychotics: their presence often has the effect of making us miss a part of our own body image. We are literally dislodged from ourselves. As a reaction, we defend ourselves by relegating the child or the psychotic to the status of someone mad, denying him the role of a valid interlocutor. Since they do not speak, we assume they have nothing to say and, as a consequence, there is nothing to listen to. This is absolutely wrong: a child who does not speak is entirely language and entirely into language; all of this on the condition, of course, that you speak to him while trying to consider him as valuable a recipient as you can be for yourself. That is what is important. I am convinced that if you respect this condition, very small children understand everything you say to them. They understand not only the maternal language pronounced with a foreign accent, but even foreign phonemes. Now, think not about infants but about the analyst who listens. We were speaking about the psychoanalyst's body: the unconscious image of the analyst's body has the same receptive capacity as that of the infant when confronted with a foreign language.

A fascinating story told to me by the late psychoanalyst Muriel Cahen illustrates in an exemplary manner how a very small baby understands and registers the spoken words of an unknown language; how the same words can reappear years later in the child's now adult body; and how in the end the psychoanalyst of this adult can, in turn, collect these words and allow them to inscribe themselves in his image of his own analyst's body. Shortly before her death, Cahen asked me to make public the dazzling experience we shared; she as analysand and me as psychoanalyst. Aware that she was seriously ill with Hodgkin's disease and undergoing a trying cortisone treatment, she consulted me after her previous analyst preferred to discontinue the analysis. I saw her for six months, the last six months of her life. While aware of her illness, she was uninformed as to the fatal prognosis. With admirable strength and courage during this extremely painful period, she continued her activity as a psychoanalyst without respite.

During one session, she recounted a dream wherein some strangely pronounced words detached themselves neatly from the general context of the dream. Rather than words, they were a series of incomprehensible sounds. I recall well the exclamation following the recounting of her dream: 'I didn't know that it was possible to experience the happiness that I felt during this dream, hearing these meaningless words which had such a curious sonority'. I usually write down everything that happens and is said during an analytic session. It is comfortable for me to do so, because while my hand writes, I am completely free to think. On that particular day, I had written down everything Cahen said, including those words having that strange sonority. Before the end of the session, I remembered that Cahen, born in London, had lived in India for the first nine months of her life. Her father, an English civil servant, had hired a young Hindu girl to look after Muriel. Little by little, a strong affective bond developed between the baby-sitter and the baby, to the extent that the father considered taking the Hindu girl with him when they returned to England. This proved impossible and little

Muriel was separated from her beloved first nanny forever. To all appearances, this separation experience had not affected the child.

The memory of these first months of Cahen's life were associated with the words of the dream I had written down. At session's end, as she was about to leave, I gave her the piece of paper on which I'd transcribed these strange phonemes, and said: 'Here's the phrase as I understood it. It would be interesting if the sounds heard in your dream were words deriving from the language of the country where you spent your first months'. This idea pleased her very much, so much so that she went to a Hindu resident in the Cité Universitaire in Paris, who eventually put her in touch with a co-national of his who spoke the dialect of the region where Cahen's father had worked. Reading the words inscribed on the paper, the Hindu student burst out laughing and explained that they corresponded to a popular phrase used by nannies to cuddle babies: 'The eyes of my little girl are more beautiful than the stars'. But what was most surprising was what followed this unbelievable discovery. Some days later Cahen's illness worsened with the appearance of a painless paraplegia. Her legs no longer carried her, having become useless like those of a babe in arms. The baby walks by means of her mother's legs, and so we have to conceive the logic of the body image as being an image transplanted onto the body image of another: in order to walk, the upper part of the baby is fused to the lower part of the adult's body. In Cahen's dream, these strange-sounding words were just the representation of the bond linking the baby's body image (unachieved on the level of the body scheme of her legs and pelvis) with the supporting image of the young Hindu woman, the true holding mother of the child before she learned how to walk. So the unspeakable happiness experienced during the dream was nothing other than the return of that fusional tenderness between a holding mother who speaks and an immature baby who knows how to listen…

Translated from the French by Claudia Vaughn

MASOCHISM AND SEXUALITY

Jean Laplanche

JEAN LAPLANCHE, born in 1924, is a psychoanalyst, philosopher and professor emeritus of psychoanalysis at the University of Paris VII. General editor of the French translation of Freud's collected works, he has long been recognized as one of the most influential thinkers in contemporary psychoanalysis. In recent years, setting out from a critical reconstruction of Freud's terminology, he has developed a systematic rethinking of psychoanalytic metapsychology under the heading of a 'general theory of seduction' which hypothesizes the origins of the human psyche in the implantation, in the human infant, of the messages of its adult Other(s).

Here, in a conversation with French psychoanalyst Jacques André, Laplanche takes issue with Freud's theory of a primary non-sexual masochism and of a biologically given death drive. For Laplanche, masochism originates within the fundamental anthropological situation which places the infant face-to-face with an adult who has a sexual unconscious and is, therefore, active in his relationship with him. A sexual masochistic drive then results from the infant's attempt to translate the adult's overwhelming messages. As a result of this understanding, Laplanche situates masochism at the heart of the human sexual drive, insofar as it seeks tension without discharge and subsists as such in adult sexuality as well.

The following interview with Jean Laplanche, titled 'Masochism and Sexuality', is excerpted from the book by Jacques André *L'enigme du Masochisme* (Paris: PUF, 2000). First published in the *Journal of European Psychoanalysis* n. 16 (2003), the interview is here reprinted courtesy of Presses Universitaires de France.

* * *

Jacques André

You propose a generalizing movement for the theory of seduction based on the primacy of the adult other's unconscious, on the way this unconscious permeates caring gestures from the first moments of life. This generalizing movement brings with it masochism, that thus becomes coextensive with human sexuality: the movement of repression, which is constitutive of unconscious fantasy, the associated excitation, and drives. You say that this movement can only be experienced in a masochistic manner to the extent that the assault of drives, the assault of the ego by an internal foreign body, namely unconscious fantasy, can only be a painful experience on the part of a passive, traumatized ego.

My first question is the following: how does this generalizing movement differ from Freud's when he affirms, in the second part of his work, the primacy of masochism with respect to sadism, after having maintained the contrary position for such a long time?

Jean Laplanche

The difference is essential. Freud claims that primary masochism, a correlate of the death drive, is an *endogenous, non-sexual force, which is irreducible to anything else*. As for me, I spoke from the very outset of the 'originary position of masochism in the area of sexual drives'. However well – anchored it may be within the origins of human drives, this means that masochism, in my view:

- cannot be explained in terms of an internal biological force that's inherent to all forms of organization, which could be called the 'death drive';
- is linked to complex processes that give rise to sexual drives resulting from enigmatic messages from the other;
- is intrinsically sexual.

This ties in with my criticism of the 'death drive', which I do not consider as constitutional aggression or self-aggression, but as the 'soul' of human sexuality itself.

It's thus an implicit criticism of Freud's biological view of the death drive.

Yes. I've dedicated a number of books to criticizing the 'economic problem of masochism'. Freud presents the problem in the following way: if masochism really is basic in man, what then becomes of the pleasure principle, the 'guardian of life'? Is it not, as he says, 'anesthetized'? For me, this apparent impasse doesn't take into account an underlying difference in Freud, the difference between drive-based sexuality and instinct-based sexuality, or rather, between infantile sexuality, a sexuality that one can call preliminary or pre-and paragenital, on the one hand, and an instinct-based genital sexuality on the other. It's a topic that I was quite happy to find in a book by Widlöcher, called *Sexualité Infantile et Attachement*, in which he says quite rightly:

> Laplanche and I agree on this point, one needs to recognize that sexuality linked to fantasy, the sexuality that we mainly deal with in analysis, is not a sexuality that functions according to the pleasure principle, one which seeks discharge and a reduction of tension. It is, instead, a sexuality that seeks excitation.

Does this amount to taking a certain distance with respect to the economic point of view?

It would be an inverted economic point of view. Let's say that it amounts to taking a certain distance with respect to an economic point of view in which only biological aims come into play. It's the idea that human infantile sexuality goes against biology from the very outset. One finds traces of this in Freud, even if only regarding his reflections on the term *Lust*. In German, *Lust* means, on the one hand, 'pleasure', in the most ordinary sense of the pleasure principle; hence the pleasure of discharge, that is, the reduction of tension to an optimal level. But on the other hand, one encounters a series of terms in which the opposite notion is introduced; namely, the search for excitation. This is the case for *Schaulust* – one can't simply say 'the pleasure of watching' since there is no discharge in 'watching' – in which there is instead an increase of excitation. Here, one's forced to translate the term *Lust* by something that's either close to 'desire' or, if you will, 'pleasure-desire'. At times, Freud complained about the ambiguity of the term *Lust*, and at other times he was quite pleased with it. Thus the *Lust* in *Vorlust* ('fore-pleasure') and in the majority of infantile pleasures will be found once again in the fore-pleasures of the adult. Now, *Lust* is a pleasure of charge, a pleasure of tension, and not a pleasure of discharge. One finds the same nuance in *Berührungslust*, which is the 'pleasure-desire of touching'. 'Touching' of its own doesn't result in discharge; to the contrary, it's an attraction that feeds itself, that tends towards an ever-greater charge. This is clearly found in the fore-pleasures of adults. But in contrast to what occurs in the child, the adult's fore-pleasure desires are subordinated to pleasure in the biological sense of the term, that is, to discharge.

One must thus exclude Freud's biological objection regarding masochism. In fact, once one admits that there is a pleasure of tension, of charge, there is nothing surprising about masochism, except the fact that it acts against life. But there is nothing surprising in the fact that human beings act against life, to the extent that human beings can pursue their pleasure to the detriment of self-preservation.

But isn't this fundamentally surprising?

It's no more surprising than the human phenomenon itself. It's no more surprising than mankind in general, who's capable of any number of things, including committing suicide, sticking needles through his cheeks, or lying down on a bed of nails. It's surprising from a biological point of view. 'What the devil did he want on that galley?' Molière's question remains universally valid.

If masochism is at the basis of human psychosexuality, if it's present from the very first moments of life, how can one clearly define what's designated as masochism – masochism in the strict sense of the word – that which characterizes a particular psychosexual mechanism, whether it be perverse or moral? Would this mean, in light of your theory, that masochistic fantasy is nothing more than a simple derivation of originary masochism?

Between the two there is still considerable mediation. Originary masochism can be considered as a kind of general category that characterizes the birth of human sexuality. It's the fact that the small human being is, so to speak, attacked from the very outset by the other; the fact that he's very quickly attacked by inner fantasy, which one can consider as an enemy of the ego. Clinical masochism derives from this, but by way of complex mediations. Nevertheless, I think that in all preliminary sexuality, which is perverse in the Freudian sense, there remains a masochistic element.

It seems to me that you, more than Freud, insist upon the existence of masochism in fore-pleasure. Spanking can certainly be a fore-pleasure, but all the same it's not the kind of fore-pleasure that's best shared. Is it simply the idea of the increase of tension in fore-pleasure that leads you to speak of masochism?

I think that it's the rise in tension in itself and the search for this rise in tension that bear witness, like a kind of relic, or archeological ruin, to the exogenetic origin of sexuality.

It's the pleasure of making the tension rise and maintaining it without discharge?

Of fueling it oneself without discharge. And fortunately of its being fueled by the other, since the problem, of course, is relating the origin of this back to the other. There is a type of self-masochism or reflexive masochism in all fore-pleasures, but true masochism is one that seeks the other in order to increase tension.

So, following this movement, if one considers this infant from the beginning, premature, passive, overwhelmed by excitation, assaulted by fantasy... Is this young infant's masochistic position the correlate of the adult's generalized sadism, based on the fact that, to use your words, the adult implants, introduces the sexual, even if done in the name of care, with love, and with no awareness of the cause? In other words, does generalizing the seduction theory amount to locating a sadomasochistic pair at the origins of human psychosexuality? Some of your formulations tend in that direction; for example, when you say that the initial movement of sadomasochism is not centrifugal, but centripetal.

I'd have some reservations regarding your formulations: first of all, the notion of prematuration. I think that it's subject to certain qualifications. The problem doesn't have to do so much with prematuration as with the gap between the adult and child. It amounts to the same thing, if you will, but one's not obliged to include it within a model of maturity. The adult, who has an unconscious, is not for that reason more mature, he simply has something in addition.

To say that in the adult-child relationship, just because there is masochism, there is necessarily sadism in the adult, would be going too far. It's not a matter of sadism in the adult; one could perhaps say that it's a kind of 'sadism in itself', which is intrinsic to the situation. It's not an intended sadism, nor necessarily a perverse sadism. It's the fact that the adult's sexuality is necessarily overwhelming with respect to the message the adult transmits to the child.

Above you spoke of categories in relation to originary masochism, can the same also be said of the adult's de facto sadism?

Yes, but it's not a transcendental category. It's simply something that goes beyond the question of whether or not the adult is actually sadistic. The idea of implantation does not imply that the adult is *a* sadist. Objectively speaking, he is one, due to the fact that his sexuality necessarily overwhelms the abilities of the child who is passive. It's a category that one could call *situational*. Sadomasochism is located in the essence of the situation itself.

Despite these clarifications, isn't there still the risk of establishing a sadomasochistic pair at the origin?

The adult does not occupy a sadistic position. I'd speak in terms of masochism rather than sadism. I never spoke of an originary position of sadomasochism; I spoke of an originary position of masochism. There can be masochism without sadism. After all, someone who would go out and put himself at the risk of storms or volcanoes would risk suffering without having a sadist in front of him telling him to do so.

Masochism, therefore, on the part of the young child, but not necessarily sadism on the part of the adult. Is the term 'masochist' as applied to the child already the result of a translation, is it already an interpretation of what takes place?

It's my interpretation, or that of an analyst who thinks as I do, but it's not initially an interpretation of the child.

For the child, there is no 'masochism'?

For the child, there is masochism only when the first attempt at translation is made.

I have in mind a clinical example of masochistic fantasy, which is rather common among men: namely, being spanked by an older man. Underlying this patient's fantasy there was found to be a representation of the primal scene: noises from the parent's bedroom; the mother's laughter; the sound of a bottom being slapped. Doesn't the view that masochistic fantasy derives from an originary masochistic position, the idea that the foundational element of human sexuality is exacerbated, doesn't this movement give little weight to the Oedipal story? Doesn't the idea of originary masochism, which here precedes fantasy, contain some retrospective illusion, some reinterpretation of the beginning in terms of what follows? Doesn't one find at the basis of 'originary masochism' masochistic fantasy? Isn't it simply through fantasy that one is able to reread the beginning?

Your question contains a number of things. First, the reference to fantasy, and to something preceding fantasy. In the situation there is, of course, something masochistic 'in itself', something 'situational'. That's to say, the position of activity in the general sense of the term, of activity of the adult world with respect to a certain passivity of the child in the sexual domain. I repeat, though: not in all domains. But fantasy is born very early on; from the moment that the subject begins, what I call, to translate, there is necessarily something that passes by way of fantasy. Clearly, one can't say that masochistic fantasy exists in the first months; fantasy presupposes a certain ability to translate, which probably can't be traced to the very first months of life. But the question regarding the age at which fantasies appear remains open.

It's clear that I'm less Oedipal-focused than you. In particular, I don't think that it's necessary to include straightaway the primal scene within the Oedipal scheme. I think that the Oedipal scheme is a way of *interpreting* the primal scene, but that the primal scene itself, as a presentation of adult coitus and adult orgasm to the child, is something that's as much *pre-* and *para-*Oedipal as Oedipal. And the fact of presenting this orgasmic scene to the child seems to me to be itself a model of seduction. Thus, in my view, it's not a seduction that is in itself Oedipal. The Oedipal interpretation of the primal scene is a conscious-preconscious interpretation, that is, that mom and dad are making another baby. What arises from the unconscious is the fantasy of the parents joined. A fantasy that, in turn, becomes a fantasy of aggression, of exclusion, that is to say, of the passivation of the child.

Let's change to another type of masochism, assuming one can do so. One of the challenges for the psychoanalyst is moral masochism, something which is encountered fairly frequently among patients. Here, the pleasure of pain typically gives way to the pleasure of misfortune: the slightest threat of happiness promises ever-greater misfortune. Moral masochism presents a particularly well-entrenched obstacle to the dynamic of analysis. While it's already difficult to get the patient to recognize the pleasure he derives from his misfortunes, from the fact that everything goes wrong in his life, this recognition is not enough to remove the obstacle. Is one to consider moral masochism within the framework of the exacerbation of an originary masochistic position? If it's located entirely within that framework, that is, within the development of unconscious sexuality, how then is one to understand this powerful immobility that it sets up against the process of analysis?

I'll take up two points you mentioned: on the one hand, the question of misfortune; and on the other hand, the question of immobility. I'd say that the distinction between misfortune and pain seems to me to be just a secondary distinction, and perhaps a defensive distinction. That's to say, one of our tasks is to show that misfortune is a kind of pain, that behind misfortune is hidden a search for pain, indeed for a persecutor, a fate, which lies at the roots of this misfortune and hence provokes pain. This is true from the metapsychological point of view, and it's also true simply from the phenomenological point of view. It's rare that misfortune doesn't have some complicity with pain. When confronted with the moral masochist, our task is to locate together with the, obviously moral, pain – the exquisite and ultimately sexual pain.

As for the question of repetition, of immobility, I don't have any new insights to offer: it's at any rate ostensibly within the ego and the ego's mechanism that one need look for the origins, etc.

Is one to understand it as an intrication of masochism-narcissism?

Yes, possibly. Narcissism, of course, lies at the basis, but as part of the defense mechanisms, that's to say, as a kind of encapsulation, a block by the ego. The repetition of misfortune is a desire not to subject pain to a dialectic process.

Doesn't this more or less amount to relating immobility back to what, according to you, is also fundamentally sexual: namely, narcissism?

Yes, of course.

Doesn't the same problem remain, having only been shifted from masochism to narcissism? Sexual fantasy appears to essentially structure something that, however, cannot be dislodged, or only slightly so?

Yes. In fact, once sexual fantasy becomes narcissistic, it's much more difficult to dislodge it.

This shifts the question from immobility to narcissism?

It shifts the question. It doesn't resolve it from a practical point of view. A theoretical problem is one thing, a practical problem is clearly another. As for the theoretical problem, even if one can make out the first outlines of a solution, it does not necessarily provide a solution for the practical problem; it doesn't even prove that there is a 'solution' to the practical problem. Explaining a phenomenon doesn't necessarily give us the means for changing it. There are a thousand examples of this, in any number of different areas.

Translated from the French by Marcel Sima Lieberman

Selected Bibliography

Essays on Otherness (1999). London and New York: Routledge.
The Unconscious and the Id: A Volume of Laplanche's Problematiques (1999). London: Rebus.
Seduction, Translation, Drives (1992). London: Institute of Contemporary Arts.
Life and Death in Psychoanalysis (1976). Baltimore: Johns Hopkins University Press.
The Language of Psychoanalysis (1973, with J-B. Pontalis), New York: W.W. Norton.

NARCISSISM: THE AMERICAN CONTRIBUTION

Otto Kernberg

IN THIS SECOND INTERVIEW with Otto Kernberg narcissism is considered both at a theoretical level (as libidinal investment of the Self) and at a clinical level (as regulator of self-esteem). After exploring the preconditions of normal narcissism, Kernberg goes on to explore its distortions as well as the later determinants of narcissistic personality disorder, characterized by an overinvolvement with oneself and an inordinate envy of others. He then explains how, in such disorders, internal morality is weakened as a result of the super-ego's positive aspects being incorporated into the Self, while prohibitive ones get projected onto the environment (which thus becomes persecutory). Via an overview of so-called malignant narcissism, the 'psychopathic personality', and the ordinary borderline personality, readers get to see how Kernberg's approach to narcissism – involving a combination of object relations theory and ego psychology – differs from Kohut's, in that the latter's infantile grandiose self is taken to be rooted in normality. For Kernberg, instead, this is an adaptive strengthening of the pathological structure whose effect is the stabilization of self esteem without a deepening of object relationships.

This conversation between Otto Kernberg and Raffaele Siniscalco was originally published in Italian in the *Enciclopedia Multimediale delle Scienze Filosofiche*. It first appeared in English in the *Journal of European Psychoanalysis* n. 12–13 (2001) under the title 'Narcissism: The American Contribution', and is here reprinted courtesy of RAI – Radiotelevisione Italiana.

* * *

Raffaele Siniscalco

American psychoanalysis has made an original contribution above all in the definition and study of narcissistic personalities. First of all, what is a narcissistic personality?

Otto Kernberg

Narcissism refers to two kinds of concepts: one at a very theoretical level and one at a very clinical level. At the theoretical level – within psychoanalytic metapsychology – it refers to the libidinal investment of the Self. At the clinical level, it means the normal or pathological regulation of self-esteem. Those two definitions are related in the sense that a normal Self and its normal libidinal investment assure the regulation of self-esteem. Normally the regulation of self-esteem is assured by an integrated concept of Self in contrast to a split or disorganized concept of Self, that otherwise yields a general sense of uncertainty and lack of capacity for internal well-being and safety. So, an integrated sense of Self is a first precondition for normal narcissism. Second, we normally incorporate the images of those who are close to us, we internalize them, and develop an internal world where we feel surrounded by our friends and the people whom we love and who love us, and who support the representation of our Self that we have. So normal self-esteem is strengthened by an integrated representation of Self and by an internal world of significant others whose representations we have internalized. Third, normal self-esteem is also regulated by our internal consciousness: the super-ego and the ego ideal, in psychoanalytic metapsychology; that is to say an internal mental structure which tells us you are doing all right, you deserve to think well about yourself, you can be proud of yourself. Normal self-esteem is also supported by our expressing instinctual needs in an acceptable way, by our sexual and aggressive impulses. Normal self-esteem is finally and obviously supported by our being effective, successful in pursuing our tasks, ambitions and ideals. So, there are many sources that regulate normal self-esteem and protect it.

When everything is in order, we call it normal narcissism. There are many individuals whose internal value system, whose super-ego, has remained at a childlike level. They feel good not because they live up to adult values of maturity, intelligence, depth, compassion, friendliness, tact, and concern invested in others, but they feel good if they are beautiful, admired, have shining clothes, bright cars, in other words, ideals that are normal for a little child, but childish for an adult. We call this normal infantile narcissism, and it only becomes a problem if it persists into adulthood, which is the case when there is a general non-specific personality disorder or character pathology as a by-product of unresolved psychic conflicts causing a fixation of infantile values. For example, it is normal for a little girl to feel that if she is clean and doesn't touch her genitals in public, she is a good girl. But in general, this is not something that any woman of forty does, otherwise it may become a disaster, an unconscious repression of all her sexuality.

So the adult's super-ego creates unconscious conflicts. In other words, the absence of an adult super-ego and the dominance of infantile super-ego values create unconscious conflicts and symptoms, with a by-product being a fixation at the level of infantile narcissistic values. So, I have talked about normal adult and normal infantile narcissism, and a certain infantile narcissistic attitude in individuals who are stuck with unconscious conflicts.

The narcissistic personality disorder is the prototype of pathological narcissism. About 30 percent of all patients with significant personality disorders have such pathological narcissistic features. And this is an area where we have gained a lot of understanding in both diagnosis and treatment. It is one area where psychoanalysis has made a significant contribution to the understanding of personality disorders and their treatment, because the psychoanalysis of the narcissistic personality is capable of resolving them. Interestingly enough, the narcissistic personality was the only narcissistic pathology that Freud did not describe in his seminal article *On Narcissism* of 1914, where he initiated the whole study of normal and pathological narcissism. Freud described all other areas in great detail, except for the narcissistic personality. Abraham, in an article of 1919 on a particular resistance to psychoanalytic treatment, describes the characteristics of these patients, but without being aware that he was describing a major character pathology. It was only in the 1960s and 1970s that psychoanalytic thinking really developed a clear understanding of these disorders and methods for their treatment. What then is pathological narcissism and what are the problems of the narcissistic personality?

Clinically, these individuals show an abnormal self-love and way of loving others, as well as problems with their internal morality system and their super-ego. What is abnormal self-love? Individuals who are over-involved with themselves, who are grandiose, who have excessive ambitions regarding their capabilities, who are exhibitionist, self-centered, selfish and have great difficulty in depending on other people desperately need the admiration of others. They live on admiration, but not on real dependency. They tend to oscillate between a sense of grandiosity and episodes of severe feelings of inferiority and failure they develop when that grandiosity is punctured. There is a combination of grandiosity, over-involvement with themselves, sometimes to the extent of recklessness, arrogance and simply acting in inappropriate ways, which oscillates with feelings of insecurity. So, while they seem to love themselves excessively, it is in a frail way. With regard to others, perhaps the most important aspect is an inordinate envy of others, both conscious and unconscious. Oral problems predominate from very early stages of development, and particularly intense oral aggression derived from conflicts in the infant-mother and child-mother relationship is evidenced. And the form that this aggression takes is envy, the hatred of something that another person has: they want what they don't have, and so they try to spoil it, to destroy it in the other person. The envy of others leads to a number of severe problems: first, the need to devalue what others have as a defense against envy. They devalue that which they think is great, what they would like to have but don't. And that devaluation is an unconscious process which interferes with learning. For example, they may want to learn something from another person, but they can't because they envy the knowledge of the other person. Their incapacity to depend on others derives from that envy. To depend on somebody else, we have to appreciate that person, but that would generate envy. Such people cannot depend, they can only accept admiration. They tend to be exploitive of others, they tend to steal others' ideas, they have difficulty in accepting things from others because it gives them a sense of inferiority, and they are always so concerned with who is superior and who is inferior that it rules their significant relationships to others. So their relations with others are superficial, shallow; they lack empathy, and have difficulties in committing themselves. There are practical consequences: they fall in love, but envy the person with whom they fall in love, and so fall out of love as fast as they fall in love. There is a narcissistic form of promiscuity, traditionally seen only in men, but now also in women, as women's liberation facilitates women's imitation of men's behavior. Typically, a man falls in love with a woman, has sex with her, and then devalues her: she is no longer interesting, he has to go on to the next woman, and so the process repeats itself endlessly. Their difficulties in appreciating what they get from others also makes it impossible for them to enjoy what they themselves have, and there is a chronic sense of emptiness that they try to compensate for with exciting experiences, sometimes with drugs or alcohol.

I spoke about abnormal relations to others, to the Self and, thirdly, about abnormal relations to the internal *conscious* mind. What in psychoanalysis is called the Ego Ideal – ideals and aspirations incorporated into one's super-ego – is absorbed into their Self. They don't have a normal Self, they have an abnormal, grandiose Self, constituted by real self-representations, ideal representations of Self – as they would like to be ideally – and ideal representation of others. They incorporate what they see as ideal in others and see themselves that way. They live on the incorporation of everything that is ideal into a false self-structure. That, at the same time, implies a devaluation of others, so the internal world of representation of others does not reconfirm them, as happens in normal narcissism. The super-ego is weak because the ideal part of the super-ego is incorporated into the Self. What remains are the prohibitive aspects of the super-ego; and so the super-ego becomes so severe that, to protect themselves against their super-ego, they reproject it onto the environment, by seeing other people as critical and demanding; and thus they do not make demands on themselves. So, their internal moral structure is weakened. The price they pay is that they lose the normal regulation of self-esteem. The normal super-ego tells us 'you did well' or 'you didn't do well', so our self-esteem oscillates. But their weak super-ego can't perform that function, so they either feel great or, if the super-ego finally tells them 'you made a fool of yourself', their self-esteem collapses totally. Their self-esteem fluctuates widely because they don't have the compensating representation of significant others, nor a good super-ego. They have a sense of aloneness, they need others, but can't appreciate them.

Under mild circumstances this means severe mood swings, and a tendency to depression. They have a *shame morality*, not a *guilt morality*: this means that they don't do things they shouldn't do just because they are terribly afraid of getting caught and of being humiliated. They don't do bad things not out of a sense of guilt and morality, but out of a sense of shame. These are relatively mild phenomena, but severe cases have a severe deterioration of the super-ego, where you find a combination of severe narcissism, anti-social behavior, ego-symptomatic aggression, and severe paranoid features, suspiciousness and distrust of others. This forms the syndrome of *malignant narcissism*. And there is still the most severe form of narcissism, wherein there is a total destruction of the super-ego, that constitutes the anti-social personality or the psychopathic personality. Severe criminals, whether aggressive or passive – stealing, murdering, exploiting – have a total incapacity for any guilt feelings or concern for others, and are practically and unfortunately untreatable. So, the narcissistic personality operates on a broad spectrum. The typical case has an excellent prognosis for treatment, the most serious cases, with severe anti-social behavior, a bad one.

Now, in their psyche's structure, instead of a normal Self they have an abnormal grandiose one with a projection outside of all undesired, unacceptable parts of the Self, a weakening of the super-ego, and the absence of an internal world of object relations. It is a serious pathology of the psyche's structures. How does that look during treatment? First of all, why do these patients come to treatment? Normally they feel great, but if they have any symptom or difficulty, they feel like collapsing, because they have to be perfect to feel well, they cannot tolerate the normal weaknesses of life. The most severe cases appear already in childhood between ages five and ten;

these are children who become very dominant and controlling, who have to be number one among their friends whom they treat as slaves, who have difficulty at school, who don't have mutuality, who do not show gratitude, and who have difficulty with learning because of this process of unconscious envy for knowledge, so they have learning difficulties.

Later on, you find some cases in early adolescence, because of their arrogance, grandiosity and inter-personal difficulties. A very typical syndrome is that they are either the best students or the worst. If they are intelligent they are great because, when something comes easy, they love it because they are on top and they learn very easily. But they reject anything that is more difficult, because it would generate envy, and so they never learn it. All the brothers of a patient of mine learned to ski, but my patient never learned to ski because he couldn't do it immediately as well as his brothers, so he stopped. He became an excellent swimmer, since nobody in his family swam, but he could never learn skiing. This illustrates that many school failures are derived from narcissistic pathology. During adolescence, they may have many friends at school. But, as an adult, your friends depend on your personality, so they have more serious difficulties at work and with others, and come to treatment because they don't understand why others don't love them. They don't see that their arrogance, grandiosity and lack of consideration puts others off. Other patients come because in intimate relations they are terribly selfish. For example, a narcissistic man marries a beautiful woman because she is so stunning that everybody will envy him. But once married, because of his unconscious envy, he loses all interest in her and can't appreciate her. He feels her demands are terrible, and treats her as if she were willing to be a slave. If she is not, there is a terrible marital conflict. Later in life, those who have done well in the past come for treatment because with age they have lost their beauty, their attractiveness, their power, their health, and they have great difficulties in accepting these normal losses in life because their self-esteem is so frail.

What happens in treatment? The psychoanalytic treatment of these patients first of all permits us to see their incapacity to depend on the analyst. They treat the analyst either as if the analyst were the greatest man in the world and they depend on him, or as if they were the greatest patients and the analyst were their admirer. There is always a one-sided great admiration rather than any mutuality, and that has to be analyzed. These patients tend to exert omnipotent control on the analyst, the analyst must be as good as they, because if he is not, they feel depreciated. But he can't be better than they are, because they would become envious, so he has to be as good as them. So, they tend to be very controlling, and cannot imagine that the analyst might be interested in treating them for themselves, instead of for their prestige or the money. They project onto the analyst their own difficulty in investing in others. So in the transference, you analyze all these aspects and gradually undo the pathological grandiose Self, decomposing it into its component internal relationships that can be worked through in the transference. As you do that, these patients develop intense envy, all the unconscious comes out into the open, and they become – as they must – aware of their aggression and exploitiveness. They experience great suffering. But, as they learn to tolerate those feelings, they can gradually see the infantile origin of this, free themselves from it, and eventually establish an in-depth relationship, developing feelings of gratitude, and of guilt for their own aggression, which permits them gradually to incorporate what they receive from others, to not feel envious any more, and to be able to establish in-depth relationships and resolve their pathological narcissism.

What insights can an analysis of narcissism give to understanding syndromes like psychosis, criminal behavior, borderline pathologies and perversions?

I have already mentioned how criminal behavior may reflect the most severe types of narcissism with the most severe deterioration of the super-ego, so that the theory of narcissism opens out to an understanding of anti-social behavior and to the understanding of the psychopath. When Freud described narcissism, he also thought that psychosis developed from narcissistic conditions, because the libido was withdrawn from the environment. We don't think in that simple way any more. We think that psychotic patients are much more invested in their surroundings and that their conflicts have more to do with primitive aggression than with a pathology of the libido. And so the term *narcissism* is more and more used for narcissistic personalities, and less and less to talk about psychosis.

Regarding borderline pathology, when you analyze the pathological grandiose Self, you find underneath a lack of integration of the concept of Self, and of the concept of the significance of others. This is characteristic of borderline personality organization, and common to all severe personality disorders. In other words, underneath the pathological grandiose Self is a lack of integration of a normal Self, which underscores the diffusion of identity And when you dissolve the pathological grandiose Self in the treatment, the identity's diffusion comes to the surface. So, in the middle of the treatment, narcissistic patients look like borderline patients, already on the road to improvement. So, pathological narcissism is a secondary complication to borderline personality organization. Narcissistic patients may look better on the surface, because the pathological grandiose Self helps them to adjust better superficially, but paradoxically they are ill because there is a greater destruction of the world of internalized object relations than in the ordinary borderline case. The ordinary borderline case involves features like impulse control, anxiety intolerance, and chaos, yet it is better able to relate to people and to be clingingly dependent, in contrast to the narcissistic personality. Thus, the narcissistic personality is a secondary development out of borderline personality organization, and in the course of treatment, the borderline pathology emerges in the transference and can then be treated like any borderline pathology.

Our modern concept of perversion covers a broad spectrum of pathology. In DSM IV the term *paraphilias* replaces the word *perversion*. What is called perversion in the United States is sexual behavior restricted to one particular part of polymorphous perverse infantile sexuality, so that the patient can obtain sexual excitement and orgasm only if he performs that particular activity, in contrast to normal sexuality, which can integrate fetishistic, sadistic, masochistic, exhibitionistic, voyeuristic tendencies, with homosexual and heterosexual feelings. An exhibitionist must exhibit himself to be able to obtain sexual gratification. A shoe fetishist must have a shoe to smell and caress. Freud described the dynamics of these patients. But the personality structure of patients with perversions varies from normal or neurotic to borderline, narcissistic and psychotic. The study of narcissism has permitted us to better understand patients who have a perversion with a narcissistic personality structure which they need to resolve as a precondition to cure their perversion. Thus, an understanding of pathological narcissism has permitted us to make inroads in the treatment of those perversions that are based upon a narcissistic personality structure.

Can you describe briefly the most important approaches to narcissism today in the United States and abroad?

The psychoanalytic treatment of narcissistic personalities in the United States is probably dominated by the combination of ego psychological and object relations theory. I myself have tried to integrate British object relations theories with American ego psychology, and I have developed over the years some of the work on pathological narcissism that I have summarized here. This is probably the dominant approach to narcissism at present in the United States.

Another important current for the treatment of pathological narcissism is Kohut's Self psychology. In fact, Heinz Kohut's original contributions centered very much at first on the study of narcissistic personalities, which he then broadened into a general review of psychoanalytic theory. Kohut's approach differs from mine very markedly in that for him the grandiose Self is not pathological, but rather a normal archaic grandiose Self on which the individual is fixated. And in treatment, the patient must be helped to develop it and to mature, rather than to dissolve it in order to discover the underlying primitive conflicts. Kohut achieves this by managing the two dominant or major transferences, as he describes them in his patients. What Kohut calls *mirroring transferences* are seen to occur when the patient perceives the analyst and himself as one, when the patient needs to be mirrored, and when the analyst accepts and does not question the patient's grandiosity, but on the contrary helps him gradually to mature through the development of this mirror transference. On the other hand, what he calls *idealizing transferences* are when the patient idealizes the analyst, with the expectation that the patient will gradually internalize that idealized analyst who, at the same time, is the one who mirrors the patient. The patient's Self will become surrounded by what Kohut calls Self-objects, namely, the internalization of the idealized mirroring analyst. The analyst confirms the patient's grandiosity – disappointing it only bit by bit so that the patient can tolerate it – analyzing all the frustrations that he himself unwillingly, unwittingly produces while at the same time lending himself as an idealized figure to be internalized by the patient. This helps bring about the transmuting internalization of the ego ideal. The patient is helped to constitute an ego ideal, and at the same time to strengthen that grandiose Self that for Kohut is really rooted in normality. As you see, it is a very different approach, in which the management of mirroring and idealizing transferences leads to a very positive relationship in which the unconscious negative transference is not analyzed, and in which Kohut sees the emergence of aggression as derived not from unconscious drives, but from the temporary fragmentation of the grandiose Self that has been frustrated, because of its frailty. It is an approach that permits the patient to improve his view of himself and his relations with others, because the Self psychologist, in a very understanding, empathetic way, helps the patient to come to terms with himself and to mature in the process. For critics of Kohut, such as myself, it is a very sophisticated application of psychoanalysis to have a supportive approach that in fact strengthens the pathological structure while making it more adaptive, but that neglects the underlying conflicts surrounding both libido and aggression. In my view, the effect of Kohut's treatment is a stabilization of the patient's self-esteem, but not a deepening of object relationships such as that obtained by the more classical approach which I described earlier.

A third approach to narcissism is the classical Kleinian technique that has been applied to the treatment of the narcissistic personality by Herbert

Rosenfeld in England. I have incorporated many aspects of this extremely interesting technique, although there are differences between my approach and that of Rosenfeld, too detailed to specify here. Another different approach on narcissism derives from French psychoanalysis. There have been very important French contributions, particularly from Béla Grunberger, who described the narcissistic features of the various stages of development – oral, anal, genital – their manifestations in transference, and the importance of incorporating them in analytic work with patients. It is an approach that deals less with narcissistic personalities, but more generally with the integration of narcissistic tendencies. Another very important French contribution is that of André Green, who talks about *narcissisme de vie, narcissisme de mort*: narcissism of life, narcissism of death. He refers to a negative narcissism in which well-being does not derive from a grandiosity of being admired and at the center of attention; instead, it is a narcissism of total staticity, of negative entropy, of a radical discontinuation of all relationships and all connections, in which all anxieties and conflicts are eliminated by a total denial of one's psychic life. It is really a narcissism of death which underlies the most severe self-destructive tendencies. André Green has made a very important contribution for patients with very severe chronic, self-destructive and suicidal tendencies. In practice, the first approach, the combination of object relations and ego psychology, is probably the prevalent one, and also extends into psychoanalytic psychotherapies with narcissistic patients who cannot be analyzed because of various contraindications. It is an approach that helps to improve the narcissistic pathologies significantly, although it does not have the totally satisfactory result that one obtains with the psychoanalytic treatment of these patients. I believe that the ideal approach to very sick patients is to start out with a psychoanalytic psychotherapy and, when they are ready for psychoanalytic treatment, then continue with psychoanalysis, perhaps with another analyst to maintain an ideal analytic structure.

GROUP ANALYSIS TODAY

Diego Napolitani

DIEGO NAPOLITANI, MD, was a member of the Italian Psychoanalytic Society from 1963 until he left it in 1999. He founded and directed the first therapeutic communities for psychotic patients in Italy, inspired by those directed by Maxwell Jones at Melrose Hospital in Scotland, and by Thomas Main at Cassel Hospital in London. This experience led him to an ever-greater interest in group analysis, and in historicist-relational psychoanalysis. He was a member of the Group Analytic Society founded by S.H. Foulkes in London, and in 1980 founded the Italian Society of Group Analysis (SGAI). By 'group analysis' he means the substitution of the 'monadic' representation of the mind (psyche) with its structurally and dually relational configuration. He has published two books in Italian: *Di Palo in Frasca* (Milan: Corpo 10, 1986) and *Individualità e Gruppalità* (Turin: Boringhieri, 1987). Most of his work has been published in the *Italian Journal of Group Analysis* (*Rivista Italiana di Gruppo Analisi*).

In this conversation with Maria Luisa Tapparo, Napolitani looks at the 'state-of-the-art' of the theoretical model and practice of group analysis in Italy. In particular he underscores the various difficulties in maintaining and developing Burrow's and Foulkes's more innovative proposals, and outlines his own 'return' to Freud's metapsychological constructions. Napolitani goes on to consider the role of Bion's later thinking, of modern cognitive science and of the paradigm of complexity within his own theoretical model, and ends by explaining his conception of group analysis as an hermeneutic practice aiming at the construction of consistent meaning hypotheses for internal/external relational experiences.

The following interview with Diego Napolitani, originally titled 'Group-Analysis Today', was first published in the *Journal of European Psychoanalysis* n. 12–13 (2001).

* * *

Maria Luisa Tapparo

How do you view group analysis today?

Diego Napolitani

Group analysis plays an important role in the history of psychology and psychoanalysis. This can be very briefly explained in two comments by S.H. Foulkes. In the first, taken from the foreword to his book *Therapeutic Group Analysis*, he claimed the necessity of a method and a theory able to brush away false counter-positions – such as cultural versus biological origin, psychogenesis versus somatogenesis, individual versus society, fantasy versus reality – in an attempt to utilize concepts that from the start could set up an integrated vision. The second comes from his essay 'The group as matrix of an individual's mental life', and maintains that group analysis eliminates the need for usual concepts such as the unconscious, repression, defenses, etc., necessary to a psychoanalytic setting.

These two radical theoretical proposals highlight the profound revolution started by group analysis nearly a century ago, when it was founded by Trigant Burrow, in opposition to a psychoanalysis founded on Freudian metapsychology, whatever its endless re-elaboration in the history of the psychoanalytic movement may have been.

Today, there are two opposing trends within group analysis: one aims at developing the anthropological and philosophical arguments present in the thought of Burrow and Foulkes, to which I've made my own contributions; the other proposes rather a sort of integration between the classical psychoanalytic postulates relating to psychic monadism (drives and defense mechanisms) and a transpersonal vision of the mind. The latter trend is prevailing, even within the Italian Group Analytic Society to which I belong; and in the schools I run in Milan, Rome and Turin 'revivals' often appear (which I myself sometimes inadvertently occasion) of the so-called psychoanalytic *satanic jargon* (as Bion would later term it).

How do you view this revival? As something syncretistic, as a regressive weakness, or as grounds for further reflection?

We cannot speak of syncretism since there are two contrasting points of view (two anthropologies, two epistemologies). Nor would I call it 'regression', since this suggests a linear vision of development (whether individual, social or cultural), as well as related 'defense mechanisms' or 'resistances'. I rather think, congruent with group analytic speculation, that cultural matrices *sensu lato* play an important role in such a conservative phenomenology. Matrices lay a clear footprint for the thought formulation process, and no matter how rationally one might opt for logical and behavioral choices which differentiate themselves from biases originating in the matrix, the latter maintain their own vitality, like ghosts that haunt old manors. Yet I don't view this persistence, no matter how old the trend may be, as a 'pathological' event: the friction between past and future, between conservation and change, and between an *originary* cultural formation and the possibility of *original* transformation, characterizes the substantial ambiguity of human nature.

And what do you see emerging from group-analytic practice today?

Group analysis should first of all deal with its very cultural matrices. Burrow, who first coined the term 'group analysis', later replaced it with 'phyloanalysis': thus he not only saved his own philosophy and clinical practice from the misleading suggestion that they referred only to the 'group', in the sense of social organization, but with that term he also meant to emphasize the transgenerational and transpersonal *phylum* that was the privileged focus of both his observational and theoretical work. The *phylum* constitutes the *filigree* of every mental act and, as happens in clinical practice, so should group analysis permanently apply itself to itself, like a conceptual apparatus, in order to distinguish its residual and parasitical elements from its own origins. This parasitical element is embryonic, that is inconsistent, and awaits further development. In short, group analysis must lie down on the analytic couch (as Freud taught), in order to develop its full creative potential.

If one works from such a premise, then the most obvious applications are:

- Those referring to clinical practice with individuals, whereby the group is evidenced and analyzed as the 'inner *groupality*' [*gruppalità*] of both patient and analyst.
- Those referring to institutional groups such as companies, schools, medical and hospital organizations.
- Those referring to training experiences in large groups.

What are the most significant aspects emerging from present-day research being carried out on large groups?

In such settings one may experience a series of emotions related to the condition of belonging *statu nascenti* to a group of persons among whom interpersonal relationships are as yet unborn, or still lay hidden. This is a total sense of belonging at a stage, an embryonic stage, that Bion termed 'proto-mentality'. This state of non-differentiation releases anxieties related to the blurring of individual identities, to a sense of mental vacuum, to the loss of speech. To the fullness of transpersonal continuity there corresponds a sort of *horror vacui* that invades the individual mind when the clear borders of its self-identity are lost. On the other hand, full immersion in a large group releases emotions, visions and dreams that, for their surprising intensity and orientation towards the same horizon, constitute the typical phenomenology of a protomental state – transpersonal in the newborn stage – of individual minds. This phenomenology – with its double edge of anguish and of mystical ecstasy (I again refer you to W. R. Bion) – is as intense as in a one-on-one or small group experience; it represents the epitome of change felt as 'catastrophic', forming a nucleus around which develop processes related to *self-reorganization* (Edgar Morin) or *self-poiesis* (Humberto Maturana and Francisco Varela) of the cognitive system.

You have trained many group analysts. What do you see as the new trends related to the dual concept 'training/group analysis'?

Group analytic thought plays a significant role in the 'de-medicalisation' of analytic practice, and consequently in ridding it of the technological cages – of the diagnostic and therapeutic biases – that have confined psychoanalysis. Group analytic practice aims at transforming the relational stereotypes inscribed in the individual matrices by giving value to the dynamic matrix established during an analytic relationship. But this dynamic matrix also involves the analyst, with both his individual matrices and his professional abilities. Thus, training should not be viewed as a process by which the 'trainer' molds the mind of the person being 'trained', but rather as a *self-poietical* (self-productive) process of the dynamic matrix in which all parties play their part. In this perspective one can see a *continuum* amongst the processes of so-called therapeutic analysis, of so-called supervision, of experiential groups and, lastly, of the processes which show up in the (endless) research groups of the analytic discipline.

Is it possible to transfer the training experience acquired in supervision to other cases that cannot be examined under supervision?

Bion used to say of himself: 'I am an analyst in progress', an idea akin to the one expressed when he spoke of a sufficiently free man as *em-mature*, as someone who tends to maturity (a state never totally achieved). So not only can the training gained in a supervised case be applied to other cases, but it is precisely this pre-condition that allows other cases to provide the possibility of further training for the analyst. According to the standard psychoanalytic view, supervision is a practice that verifies the pupil's level of conformity to prevailing theoretical and methodological canons: not to psychoanalysis in general (which perhaps never existed), but to the particular interpretation which a 'training analyst' makes from within his or her own necessarily biased understanding of psychoanalysis. According to the group analytic view, which privileges a model of 'complexity', a better term might be *meta-vision* rather than *supervision*. That is, a condition wherein the more experienced analyst invites the less experienced one to see things from a different point of view starting with: 1) the relationship between the patient and his/her analyst; 2) the relationship between the two analysts; and 3) the relationship between the latter two and the theoretical model.

From a group analytic perspective, what changes have you noted in your patients over the last forty years? Can you help us highlight some of the changing trends in suffering, and in syndromes as well?

In his *Group Psychology and Analysis of the Ego*, Freud already maintained that individual psychology is indeed and always a social psychology: a concept that group analysis has totally absorbed by creating and focusing its attention on the keyword 'matrix'. Man's mental, behavioral and moral life is informed by values and models that derive from his world of relationships (i.e., the family as part of one's broader communal context). It is no wonder, then, that even in disruptive scenarios, and across a wide variety of phenomena, such a social imprint is invariably revealed. For instance, Freud, as an expression of his own personal and cultural history, maintained that sexuality was the specific ground from which sprung good and evil in human beings. But morals have changed, and sexuality can no longer be seen in the same terms as it was in Freud's day. For example, to reduce female problems today to a paradigmatic phenomenon like hysteria (which has practicallly disappeared), or to 'penis envy', would be like calling someone up from beyond the grave. The same can be said of the centrality of the father, that unchallenged *dominus* of family and social life, around whom Freud elaborately fantasized, on the basis of disconnected excerpts from the Oedipus myth.

Western culture has changed profoundly in the last fifty years, and now the future is no longer neatly separated from the present; it is no longer 'postponed' to some distant time, so that it can be only vaguely predictable. Our present no longer has that relative stability which characterized individual and social life for millions of years, because it is lacerated by a future that grasps at it from all sides. It is as though we were living in a seismic age whose tectonic plates were shifting and colliding with unprecedented frequency and intensity. To withstand change, man's 'constructions' must have the flexibility and elasticity equal to the geological upheaval produced by man himself. Even *tradition*, which gives the foundation of collective and individual identity, runs short of breath; even the past is traversed by the future, because every agreement, rebellion, and every past construction with meaning for the individual as well as for the community is an integral part of one's projections into the future. And if the future does not appear sufficiently stable, then any plan will seem hazardous and precarious, and thus the past, traditions and matrices will seem either the only possible worlds wherein to find certainty (e.g., religious fundamentalism, or nationalism), or, on the contrary, they will pale in favor of an empty and frantic consumerism.

The contrast between these extremes, to which individual conscience and interpersonal relationships are deeply exposed, causes the so-called new pathologies manifested in individual behaviors. To use Bion's enigmatic metaphor, we can say that modern man has no 'memory of the future', and that this particular form of *dementia* (insanity) reduces man to either a skeleton of his past (the rigid fossils of tradition), or to a totally empty present (as evidenced by the pervasiveness of depression); or else it leaves him in the vicious spiral of eating disorders or drug and alcohol addiction.

Group analysis, then, can be grasped as a means for reading and deciphering social phenomena in today's complex society...

A sociological or cultural-anthropological analysis cannot suffice today to account for the relationship between social morals and the peculiarities of individuals. It is necessary to find the link between macro- or micro-social phenomena and the individual's cognitive and affective aspects; a link which in some way recreates, in the mind's complexity, the recursive circularity between the individual and society. I have found this link joining together what I call the *matrix* and the specifically human capacity for self-reorganization, or *self-poiesis*. The matrix is the transgenerational component of individual identity and is from its origins exposed to an incessant reorganization of the self-poietical device; *idem* is the term I use to define an individual's identity so constituted and in some way definable at every instant, whereas *autòs* is the undefinable author of every transformation process of the *idem*. Between these two polarities there occurs a dialectical relationship, such as that in the *polis* between conservatives and reformers.

I would compare *idem* and *autòs* to an inner parliament, that is, the place which gives rise to the Speech/Law that legitimizes the experience of the individual's autonomy.

Moreover, the family institution has lost much of its power in recent decades, due to its progressive extroversion into a wider social web. A child's education is increasingly entrusted, and already at a very young age, to figures outside the family; moreover, the intrusion of consumer and mass-media idols, combined with the relativism of ideals and values (all as fleeting as fashion trends), have all marginalized family ties. In such a context, family is no longer the privileged place of the transgenerational transcendence of beliefs and morals, but gets replaced by multiplying ephemeral aggregations of youth within which is rife a certain *mal de vivre*.

To whom is group analysis suited?

If by 'whom' one means the individual as a whole and not a 'patient', my immediate response would be: whoever asks for it. During the first session, there is a mutual introduction, in the sense that our 'histories' meet: obviously, not in the sense that I recount my life story, but in the sense of where I am now in my cultural and professional experience. So when a patient complains of some distress, I make it clear that I have no cures, simply because I think that the patient's discomfort is not 'caused' by an agent that I can neutralize. Using the elements relayed by the patient, I sketch a picture that represents, in various ways, my cited metaphor of the 'inner parliament'. The need for change and the need for conservation come face-to-face in such a tumultuous way that no Speech can emerge: what I can offer is to help the patient with this 'parliamentary debate', which is in some way blocked or severely distorted. Were the patient to ask me for some salvational intervention, and were I to think that I could give it, I would but ratify the failure of his/her 'parliamentary' effort. Basically, I try to offer the patient a pathway, offering myself as a 'skipper', to use an image provided by one of my patients at the end of his analysis. I know well that such a statement is no definitive solution, and that at any moment, a request for analysis can be motivated in the interest of conservation or of change: the analysis could be group-analytically defined as an analysis of the *questions* incessantly asked by one of the many components belonging to the 'inner groupality'. If the patient perceives our mutual introduction as a 'starting point', the adventure begins, otherwise it does not.

Group analysis, then, is much more than a mere technique. Might it perhaps serve as a model for thought or action?

Any human practice derives its legitimacy from a theoretical, ideal or ethical basis. I construct my group analytic thought and practice on the basis of an *hermeneutic psychogogy*. I do not propose any models, at least not intentionally, but rather try to arouse in the patient a loving curiosity for his or her own history which, no matter how painful, is still the only one a person has. And that history provides the only experiences available to that person: experiences from which to plan new constructions, informed by individual taste and *genius*, within the limits of individual autonomy.

Translated from the Italian by Valentina Tenedini

PSYCHOANALYSIS AND HOMOSEXUALITY

Elisabeth Roudinesco

IN THIS 2001 CONVERSATION with François Pommier, Elisabeth Roudinesco discusses the consequences of Freud's reclassification of homosexuality in terms of sexual choice rather than degeneracy. She does so by tracing the changes in attitudes towards homosexuals and homosexuality within psychoanalytic institutions, moving from the IPA's official exclusion of homosexuals in 1921 to their 'outing' at the Barcelona Congress of 1997. Prof. Roudinesco also considers here the accusations of homophobia made against Lacan, arguing that his portrayal as a reactionary defender of traditional patriarchy is based on a misreading of his texts. While Lacan considered homosexuality a perversion, he nevertheless saw it as part of a universal structure of personality: indeed, Lacan saw homosexual love as the prototype of love. Roudinesco goes on to claim that the homophobia that still characterizes the psychoanalytic community is a reaction, not to the 'perverse' desire of homosexuals, but to their desire for 'normalization', seen by many as an attempt to 'homosexualize' society: much like the emancipation of women was once seen as a threat to feminize society by undermining the paternal figure.

A longer version of this interview, originally published in French in the journal *Cliniques Méditerranéennes* (n. 65, 2002), appeared in the *Journal of European Psychoanalysis* n. 15 (2002) under the title 'Psychoanalysis and Homosexuality: Reflections on Perverse Desire, Insult and the Paternal Function'. It is here reprinted courtesy of Prof. Roudinesco and the editors of *Cliniques Méditerranéennes*.

* * *

François Pommier

Freud reconciled a structural conception of homosexuality with anthropological facts. One of his greatest struggles was to clear homosexuality of the notions of defectiveness and sin, to show that it's a sexual choice like any other. He didn't consider it a drama, and he withdrew it from the category of illness only to place it into that of tragedy. Is one thus to consider Freud as belonging to a long line of defenders of homosexuals?

Elisabeth Roudinesco

Freud was an emancipator of man in general and of women in particular. Of course, he couldn't imagine what the fate of men and women would be in the twenty-first century. Yet, in meetings of the Wednesday Psychological Society, which took place at his home at the beginning of the 1900s, Freud condemned the misogyny expressed by some of his followers. In a conference in 1907 dedicated to the question of 'women doctors', one finds some eccentric views put forward. Fritz Wittels, for example, stated that a woman who wants to become a doctor, and hence work in a male profession, seeks in fact to leave her 'natural' condition. She thus risks doing harm to herself: she's necessarily 'hysterical', and ought never to be allowed to pursue her studies. For Wittels, a woman's only role is to reproduce. In his view, even if a woman became a psychiatrist, she'd never be able to understand the psychology of men. Against this, Paul Federn proposed the idea that, while women certainly have the right to work, a woman doctor should never be allowed to palpate a man's genitals. The discussion shows the extent to which Freud's early followers were divided on the question of the emancipation of women, and how naive they were. Freud, however, was decidedly modern. Having criticized Wittels for his lack of gallantry, he went on to note that civilization had placed a much heavier burden (i.e., reproduction) on women than on men and, while remaining convinced that women couldn't equal men in the sublimation of sexuality – and hence in creativity – he denounced misogyny as an infantile attitude among men. He would, however, later change his mind on the possibility of sublimation for women, developing a lifelong admiration for exceptional women, due as much to their intellectual acumen (Lou Andreas-Salomé) as to their 'virile' virtue (Marie Bonaparte).

Freud adopted the same attitude towards homosexuality. He took a great step forward in refusing to classify it as a sexual 'defect' or 'anomaly', unlike many sexologists of his time. He didn't believe that homosexuals committed 'acts against nature' and he refused all forms of stigmatization based on the notion of 'degeneracy'. He didn't separate homosexuals from the rest of humanity, but thought that everyone is potentially faced with such a choice because of the existence of psychic bisexuality in each of us. At times Freud didn't exclude the possibility of a biological predisposition that might lead to homosexuality, although he was convinced that being raised by women favored the development of homosexuality in both men and women. If the human being, in the Freudian sense, is marked by the tragedy of desire, then the homosexual, with respect to this general tragic figure, is simply a more tragic subject than the ordinary neurotic, since he's ostracized from bourgeois society as a result of his choice. His only recourse is to become a creator in order to assume his own drama. One finds this argument in Freud's work on Leonardo da Vinci. And in this 1910 booklet he refuses to use the term 'inversion', opting instead for the term 'homosexuality'.

Freud did not classify homosexuality *as such* as belonging to the category of sexual perversions, and he condemned all forms of discrimination against homosexuals. Freud universalized the category of perversion by not restricting it only to homosexuals, even though he often considered homosexuals as perverse. The category applies to both sexes since it is not limited to sexual perversion. Freudian universalism is thus much more progressive than the differentialism of sexologists and psychiatrists at the end of the nineteenth century, who treated homosexuals as 'abnormal' or mentally ill, extending in this way the Christian category of sodomite – the damned of the damned, who bear the guilt of all sins.

The Freudian homosexual is a civilized subject, needed by civilization since he is, in a certain way, the embodiment of the sublime. Freud here returns to a Greek conception of homosexuality – in this sense he's an emancipator. But he clearly couldn't have imagined that homosexuals would one day want to 'become normal' to the point of no longer suppressing their desire to have children, imagining themselves within a bourgeois family model that was once scorned. It's possible that Freud, today, would probably reject several of the theses he had once accepted, in particular the thesis that being raised by women encourages homosexual tendencies in children. Experience shows that this isn't so, and Freud, who was always quite attached to a certain conception of (non-experimental) experience, would have taken into account the actual experience of homosexual couples who raise children.

In 1920, referring to the case of a young girl from Vienna[1] whom he had treated because her parents were forcing her to marry, even though she was in love with a woman, Freud proposed his canonical definition of homosexuality which challenged the theses of sexologists regarding 'intermediate states', the 'third sex' or the 'female soul in a male body'. For Freud, homosexuality is the result of human bisexuality, and exists in a latent state in all heterosexuals. In the case of girls, infantile fixation on the mother and disappointment

1 See Freud's 1920 article 'The Psychogenesis of a Case of Female Homosexuality', *SE* 18, pp. 147–172.

with respect to the father eventually lead to homosexuality, which becomes an exclusive object choice. In this text, Freud brings a certain clinical clarity to the question by showing that it's futile to try to 'cure' a subject for homosexuality when this is already established, and that psychoanalytic treatment must not, in any event, be carried out with such a goal in mind.

In his 1921 study *Group Psychology and the Analysis of the Ego*, Freud provides a clearer definition of male homosexuality. Here, he claims that homosexuality arises after puberty where, during childhood, there was an intense bond between mother and son. Rather than renounce his mother, the son identifies with her, transforms himself into her, and seeks objects that can stand in for his Ego and that he can love just as his mother loved him. Finally, in a letter from April 9, 1935, to an American woman distressed over her son's homosexuality, Freud writes:

> Homosexuality clearly is not an advantage, but it's no cause for shame, it's neither a vice nor a disgrace, and it can't be called an illness; we consider it a variation of the sexual function, which results from arrested sexual development. Several highly respected individuals, from ancient to modern times, were homosexual, and among them one finds some of the greatest men (Plato, Michelangelo, Leonardo da Vinci, etc.). Persecuting homosexuality as a crime is highly unjust and cruel. If you don't believe me, read Havelock Ellis's books.[2]

He notes once again the futility of wanting to transform a homosexual into a heterosexual.

In the psychoanalytic movement, it was Ernest Jones and Anna Freud who, in contrast to Freud, held the most regressive attitudes towards homosexuality. But why did Freud's daughter defend a position so opposed to her father's, reclassifying homosexuality as a mental illness and going as far as claiming that a well-conducted analytic treatment could result in curing the homosexual of his homosexuality? Anna herself was accused of being homosexual because she was a single woman who had never had a physical relationship with a man and sought, above all, female friendship. Thus a kind of 'self hatred' is shown in her condemnation of homosexuality, a rejection of what was for her, perhaps, a source of guilt.

As in any number of families in nineteenth-century bourgeois society, Anna occupied the role of 'old maid', the daughter who must take care not only of

---

2 See *Letters of Sigmund Freud 1873–1939* (New York: Basic Books, 1960).

the father, but also of the patriarchal legacy. In this sense, she was a replica of Antigone. Freud was extremely fond and protective of her. He jealously kept her to himself, warding off any of his students who may have wanted to court her – Jones in particular. He even insisted on analyzing his daughter (in 1921–1922), which was seen by his followers as an incredible transgression, a type of Oedipal appropriation. But at the same time, he pushed her to take on the modern destiny of an intellectual woman. Anna completed her studies and succeeded in establishing herself as the head of her own school of thought within the psychoanalytic movement. She was a pioneer in the psychoanalysis of children and set the basis for what was to become known as Anna-Freudianism. Anna Freud was, in a manner of speaking, a *fille au père*[3], a daughter dedicated to her father, keeper of the legacy and tradition, and hence necessarily conservative on matters of sexual mores. She was an orthodox follower of the doctrine. There existed between her father and her a passionate love story to rival Greek tragedy.

1921 is the same year when, under the influence of Jones, and against Freud's advice, homosexuals were banned from practicing psychoanalysis…

Beginning in December 1921 and for an entire month, the question divided members of the famous committee that secretly directed the International Psychoanalytical Association (IPA). The Vienna group turned out to be much more tolerant than the Berlin group. Supported by Karl Abraham, the latter thought that homosexuals were incapable of being psychoanalysts, since analysis had not 'cured' them of their 'inversion'. Backed by Freud, Otto Rank opposed the Berlin group. He stated that homosexuals ought to be able to enter the psychoanalytic profession like anyone else on the basis of their ability: 'We cannot distance ourselves from such people without a valid reason, just as we cannot accept that they be persecuted by the law'. He reminded his opponents that there are different types of homosexuality, and maintained that one needed to examine each particular case. Jones refused to consider this position. He backed the Berlin group, and declared that for the rest of the world homosexuality was 'a repugnant crime: if one of our members committed it, we would be seriously discredited'. It was then that homosexuality was banished from the Freudian empire, and came to be considered a defect once again.

Over time and across over fifty years, the IPA reinforced its repressive arsenal under the growing influence of North American psychoanalytic societies. After having turned away from the Freudian position favoring

[3] A pun, because *fille au père* sounds like girl *au pair* [*Editor's Note*]

the access of homosexuals to psychoanalytic training, the IPA, moving once again against the Freudian current, classified homosexuals as sexual perverts, judging them at times unsuited for psychoanalytic treatment, at others curable, provided that the cure was aimed at orienting them towards heterosexuality.

Was this decision made under Anna Freud's influence?

No, under Jones's. Anna Freud came in later. And she played an important role in misappropriating her father's theses, campaigning against any possible access of homosexuals to analytic training. With the support of Jones and the North American societies of the IPA, she had considerable influence in this area, which was not offset by the Kleinian school. Although the latter was more liberal, it viewed homosexuality (whether latent or manifest) as an identification with a sadistic penis in the case of women, or, in the case of men, as either a schizoid personality disorder or a means of coping with excessive paranoia. As a result, homosexuality was treated as a borderline pathology, which made it possible to dissolve it while continuing to classify homosexuals as patients suffering from serious pathological disorders of a psychotic nature.

In her practice, Anna Freud always sought to transform her homosexual patients into good fathers of heterosexual families, which led to a clinical disaster. In 1956, she asked journalist Nancy Procter-Gregg not to publish her father's famous letter from 1935 in *The Observer*. As for Jones, his repressive attitude can be explained in several ways. He himself was accused, in a Victorian and puritanical England, of pedophilia simply for having talked about sexuality with children he was treating in an hospital. In Canada, where he later emigrated, he was denounced by the Puritan leagues because he was living with Loe Kann. One needs to understand what the beginning of psychoanalysis was like: the first Freudians were constantly being accused of seeking to corrupt society with their sexual theories.

Wanting to mainstream the IPA and rid it of its most 'deviant' practitioners (in particular psychotics and perverts), Jones, who was himself a seducer of women (unlike Freud), thought that the psychoanalytic movement needed to train 'irreproachable' clinicians – whom no one could attack for so-called deviant sexual practices. Jones acted against himself in wanting to mainstream the IPA, just as Anna Freud struggled against her guilty desire by establishing repressive rules against homosexuals. Freud, the great discoverer of sexuality, was neither libertine nor transgressive. He didn't have sexual relations with his patients and was not known to have a mistress. As a result, he was more liberal on matters of sexuality. He didn't have to defend himself against himself. His blind spot in this area was his daughter, for whom he felt an immoderate love to the point of being jealous of her potential lovers.

However, the British Psycho-Analytical Society, founded by Jones in 1919, included among its ranks some rather non-conformist clinicians. James Strachey, for example, the famous translator of Freud and brother of the well-known Lytton Strachey, was an avowed homosexual. He practiced psychoanalysis as a member of the society before marrying Alix Strachey, with whom he fell in love because she resembled a 'melancholic boy'.

Only recently has the famous unwritten rule established by the secret committee in 1921 been gradually 'erased' (and not abolished), coinciding with increased protests from the American gay movement and especially the coming out of certain American psychoanalysts – members of the IPA who have begun to openly acknowledge their homosexuality, most notably at the International Congress in Barcelona in 1997. Such was the case of Ralph Roughton, training member of the Psychoanalytic Society of Cleveland, and member of the powerful American Psychoanalytic Association (APSAA), which is affiliated with the IPA. In a brilliant account, Roughton described the struggle of American homosexual analysts who finally succeeded in being recognized by the IPA, while outlining the conditions for a clinical approach that would take into account the 'undeniable existence of healthy and mature homosexual men and women'.[4]

By drawing on the work of Freud as well as that of the great Robert Stoller, a psychoanalyst from California specialized in perversion and transsexualism, homosexual psychoanalysts were finally able to show for the first time, using concrete cases, that homosexuality was a sexual orientation, that in no way ought to be qualified, *as such*, in terms of pathology. In other words, this thesis made it possible to reestablish the link with Freudian universalism according to which a homosexual is a subject in his own right, one who may also have neurotic, psychotic, perverse or borderline disorders, just like any other heterosexual individual. It was thus a matter of finally erasing homosexuality from the category of pathology or sexual perversions, such as fetishism, sadism, transvestitism, pedophilia, etc.

The courage of these psychoanalysts needs to be applauded. Their struggle, however, is not yet finished. They succeeded not in eradicating homophobia within the IPA, but in changing its repressive strategy. Today, no one in the IPA dares admit to being homophobic in public. Yet hatred towards

---

4 See Roughton's article 'Psychanalyste et Homosexuel?' *Revue Française de Psychanalyse*, 63.4, 1999.

homosexuality certainly persists with the same violence: it's only assumed a new face. It's expressed in the form of denial, a bit like the anti-Semitism of today's democratic societies. 'No, I'm not against homosexuals', say homophobic psychoanalysts in the IPA, 'and yes, I condemn homophobia, but still, one can't accept that homosexual psychoanalysts campaign for the gay cause'. It was in this way that the French psychoanalyst Gilbert Diatkine responded to Roughton, accusing the latter, in the name of the alleged neutrality of psychoanalysis, of a 'militant, proselytizing' attitude. One finds the same argument of denial in César Botella[5], another French psychoanalyst who claims that militancy is most likely a 'denial of the personal drama of the homosexual', who probably suffers from a 'narcissistic pathology' that psychoanalysis cannot, in any case, resolve. Why shouldn't persecuted psychoanalysts thus have the right to be activists? Why would being an activist indicate a lack of psychoanalytic ethics? What's more, if psychoanalysis is unable to resolve the question of homosexuality, as notes Botella, it's in any case able to treat certain narcissistic pathologies that are not specific to homosexuality.

Compared to its earlier form, the IPA's new homophobia, besides being unreasoned and pathological, is characterized by a lack of any theoretical basis. The usefulness of the gay movement's struggles is quite clear: it's made the public expression of homophobia 'shameful'. This isn't surprising, and it's why laws against discrimination are indispensable. They force homophobes to use other tricks, and that's progress.

I'd like to move on to Jacques Lacan's position. Beginning in 1945–1946, he underwent a radical change of perspective…

Yes. In the years immediately following the war, the American societies became more repressive than ever, adhering to the guidelines of psychiatry which classified homosexuality as mental illness. As for the English school, whether geared more towards Kleinism or Anna-Freudianism, its attitude towards homosexuals was terrible. In the case of Kleinians, as I mentioned earlier, homosexuality was considered a schizoid disorder, a 'means' of coping with paranoia and thus, once again, a perversion of a sadistic or masochistic nature. Homosexuality practically didn't exist for Kleinians. It was a variation of a mortifying and destructive psychotic state. It's not included in dictionaries of Kleinian thought, which amounts to keeping homosexuals within the category of 'deviants', of those who are ill, and hence to denying

[5] Both Diatkine's ('Identification d'un Patient') and Botella's ('L'homosexualité(s): Vicissitudes du Narcissisme') responses to Roughton appeared in the same issue of *Revue Française de Psychanalyse*, 63.4, 1999.

them access to the psychoanalytic profession. At the time France followed IPA rules and homosexuals were banned from professional training. As patients, they were considered ill before being reeducated to become heterosexual. In this context, homosexuals wanting to follow analysis fled the couches of the IPA, except if a particular 'perversion' led them to hate their own homosexuality to the point of wanting to eradicate it. Others, often from an intellectual or artistic milieu, preferred less repressive couches. A number of them found themselves in analysis with Lacan, who never sought to transform them into heterosexuals.

Lacan not only accepted homosexuals into analysis without ever trying to reeducate them or prevent them from becoming psychoanalysts if they so desired, but when he founded the Ecole Freudienne de Paris (EFP) in 1964, he even accepted the principle of their integration, whether as analysts of the school or member analysts of the school. I myself was a member of the EFP and can say that in this respect there was considerable tolerance, even if, of course, a number of psychoanalysts hated homosexuals. 'Private' and personal homophobia is one thing, establishing discriminatory rules is another. It was because such tolerance existed that homosexuals, who wouldn't have had any future in the societies of the IPA, flocked towards the EFP. In my book *Jacques Lacan & Co.* I discuss the career of Robert Lander. As for François Peraldi, who went to Montreal, he was more readily accepted by Lacanians than by other Freudians, even though he carried out his analysis within the Paris Psychoanalytic Society[6].

That said, Lacan didn't share the same conception of homosexuality as Freud. In Lacan's view, homosexuality is not at all a sexual orientation. A highly transgressive character, his reading of de Sade and his contact with Georges Bataille did indeed have a certain effect on him. His fascination with Greek homosexuality led him, on the one hand, to see the perverse figure as the embodiment of the highest intellectuality – though it be damned – and on the other hand, to consider all forms of love, indeed of desire, as something perverse. Just as Lacan 'psychoticized' the clinical handling of neurosis, he also tended to see perversion in all manifestations of love. It's in this context that homosexuality, *as such*, is a perversion and not a sexual orientation. In order to understand how Lacan reinserted homosexuality into the category, not of sexual perversions, but of perverse structures, one must take into ac-

6 François Peraldi (1938–1993) underwent a training analysis with Simone Decobert, an analyst with the Paris Psychoanalytic Society, which later rejected him. He was accepted by Lacan's École Freudienne where he completed his training. In 1974 he emigrated to Montreal, where he practiced until his death at the age of fifty-five. Peraldi claimed that what he called the 'intellectual terrorism' then practiced in France had driven him from the country. As regards Robert Lander, see Roudinesco's cited *Jacques Lacan & Co.*, pages 455–56.

count this underlying premise. He never reestablished the former frameworks of sexology, psychiatry or the theory of degeneracy. In fact, he wasn't that far from what would later be the positions of Michel Foucault or Gilles Deleuze. Perversion occupied an important place for both Foucault and Deleuze, since they saw it as a way of radically contesting the bourgeois social order characterized by the Oedipal family inherited from Freud.

But there is a fundamental difference between Lacan and Foucault: the former made of perversion a universal structure of personality, of which homosexuality was the purest embodiment, while the latter favored the study of concrete practices of perverse sexuality without worrying about fitting them into any particular structure or category. For Lacan, the homosexual is an example of sublime perversion in civilization, while for Foucault the homosexual is a figure who must escape, by a subversive or inventive practice, from the degrading label that normative discourse has placed on him. One sees how Lacan's position differs radically from that of homophobic clinicians in the IPA. Lacan links homosexuality (both female and male) to perversion, but rejects any kind of discriminatory attitude.

In his discussion, the recognition of homosexuality as perversion leads neither to intolerance nor to segregation. And Lacan, for the same reasons, did not condemn homophobes. It's difficult to understand at times his tolerance of behaviors considered the most 'deviant', offensive or virulent. It's undoubtedly the result of the violence he carried in him. One will never be able to say enough about how transgressive a teacher he was, sensitive to all of the most extreme manifestations of madness, mysticism and *jouissance*, while harboring no illusions about human depravity. Because Lacan considered homosexuality a perversion, he believed that homosexuals were not 'curable'. He distinguishes female homosexuality, which he places near hysteria and sexual rivalry, from male homosexuality, in which he finds the bases of the social bond. In his seminar on *Les Formations de L'inconscient*, he states that if one values his position as a homosexual, it's because for him the mother sets down the law in place of the father, or rather, she 'sets down the law for the father'. Lacan here takes up the Freudian theme of the inverted Oedipus complex, but he situates it within the context of his own topography (imaginary, symbolic, real).

In short, Lacan would make perversion into a kind of prototype of sexuality. But then, you say that one can't interpret his comments on Plato's Symposium, *which he describes as a 'gathering of old fairies', as homophobic.*

A lot of ink has been spilled regarding that passage from the seminar[7]. Let me say that Lacan, as early as 1953, considered homosexual love the prototype of love. Now, since in his view homosexual love is a perversion, there is necessarily, according to him, a perverse tendency in love generally, which he expressed in the unforgettable maxim: 'Love is giving something one doesn't have to someone who doesn't want it'. What's more, the 'perverse desire' that for Lacan characterizes, but isn't limited to, homosexuality, is based only on an 'inexhaustible appropriation of the desire for the other'. By way of showing that the perverse desire characterizes homosexuality just as much as heterosexuality, Lacan draws on Proust: 'Consider the extraordinary analysis of homosexuality developed by Proust in the myth of Albertine. It doesn't matter that the character is female – the structure of the relationship is eminently homosexual'[8].

It's in this context that one needs to read Lacan's comments on the *Symposium*. He compares the role of homosexuality in Greece to that played by courtly love in medieval society. Both most likely had a sublimating function that made it possible to perpetuate the ideal of a master within a society constantly threatened by the havoc of neurosis. Courtly love placed the woman in the same position as that attributed to the master by homosexual love in Greece. As a result, the perverse desire, which is present in the two forms of love where sublimation and physical sexuality come together, is identified as being highly favorable to art, creation, and the invention of new forms of social bonding. Lacan lamented the fact that this love no longer existed in the homosexuality of the 1950s, a period when 'education turns acne-covered high school students into imbeciles'. I don't think one can treat Lacan as a homophobe on the basis of a few offensive phrases against 'fairies'. Lacan insulted everyone. In his seminars, he never ceased to insult his opponents, curse his grandfather, or treat those he didn't like as 'imbeciles'. It's even worse in his personal letters. Even his compliments often came with insults. When he favorably described Melanie Klein as a 'brilliant meat butcher', the insult was all the more erroneous since Melanie Klein was in no way a butcher. One could offer any number of examples. The vocabulary of hatred is part of Lacan's discourse.

Nor is Lacan homophobic when he considers homosexual love a perversion and perverse desire the quintessence of sublimated love. In his speech, the term 'perversion' is not used in a degrading or pejorative manner. Like

[7] Lacan's remark translates as follows: 'Regarding the banquet, I spoke in passing of a gathering of old fairies, seeing that they're no longer in the bloom of youth and fit, besides, a certain mold'. See Lacan's *Le Séminaire, livre VIII. 1960–1961, Le Transfert* (Paris: Le Seuil, 2001, p.163).

[8] See Lacan's *The Seminar, Book I. Freud's Papers on Technique, 1953–1954* (New York: W. W. Norton & Co, 1988).

Freud, Lacan uses this word while ridding it of its defamatory content. For Lacan, more than for Freud, perversion is given a certain standing. In this respect, as I mentioned earlier, he's more the heir of de Sade and the contemporary of Bataille than the upholder of the Freudian doctrine. Except for wanting to empty perversion of any trait of human passion, I don't see how one can view Lacan as a homophobic reactionary. His view of homosexuality is similar to Proust's, who considered the homosexual as a sublime and damned character, a pervert of civilization.

Lacan, in his practice and dealings with psychoanalytic institutions, was in a concrete way both an emancipator and a man of progress. I repeat, he was the first to allow homosexuals to become psychoanalysts. As for his view of homosexuality, it doesn't deserve so much opprobrium. It of course excludes the idea that homosexuals may want to become 'normal', to the point of imitating the most bourgeois models, and hence the most neurotic structures of family relationships. But it has the merit of honoring the role occupied by the homosexual figure in Western society: a figure that's both damned and sublime. Lacan would have been quite distressed by the fact that homosexuals today no longer want that role, and choose instead to imitate those who have never stopped persecuting them since the beginning of time. But he would never have adopted, under the current circumstances, the homophobic discourse. I think instead that he would have been surprised, as we all are, by the desire for normalization that's expressed today among homosexuals.

What do you think of the Catholic hatred of perversion that Michel Tort discusses in relation to Lacan?[9]

Tort's argument isn't limited to this accusation of homophobia. The argument claims to provide a theoretical and anthropological basis for it. He turns the Lacanian conception of the family, as formulated in *The Family Complexes*[10], into a kind of fanatical theology, a Catholic fundamentalism, which seeks to deny homosexuals basic rights: civil solidarity pacts, adoption, etc. But worse yet, according to Michel Tort, Lacan is guilty of sympathy for the Vichy government even before it was established, since the thesis of family neurosis and patriarchal decline is only 'the etiology of social symptoms in the 1930s, which would assume their ideological

[9] Tort's argument was articulated in two separate articles. See his 'Homophobies Psychanalytiques' in *Le Monde*, 15 October 1999, and 'Quelques Conséquences de la Différence 'Psychanalytique' des Sexes' in *Les Temps Modernes*, 609, June, July and August 2000.

[10] Lacan's 1938 article 'The Family Complexes', first published in *L'Encyclopédie Française*, only appeared fifty years later in English. See *Critical Texts*, 5.3 (1988).

importance during the Vichy period in the figure of the *maréchal* [Pétain] – followed by the *général* [De Gaulle]'.

Beyond this absurd comparison, which places in the same category of 'fathers of the nation' two radically different figures (Pétain and de Gaulle, a traitor and a hero), one is stunned by such falsehoods.

In my book on Lacan I remarked that he was the first, even before the specialists in history from Vienna (Carl Schorske and Jacques Le Rider), to be struck by the fact that psychoanalysis was born out of the decline of the patriarchal family in the West. In light of this decline, symbolized in Vienna by the fall of the Hapsburg monarchy, Freud pointed out a new form of subjectivity, comparing twentieth-century man to Oedipus and Hamlet, that is, to the solitary actor of a drama of conscience, condemned to continually reenacting the scene of an original murder in order to undo his genealogical lineage.

If psychoanalysis attributes a central role to the father within this configuration, it's not done in order to claim for itself the caricatured position of the criminal and tyrannical leader of a horde – as the fascist regimes and Nazism would later do – but in order to symbolically emphasize the importance of a paternity that has come apart, and that's always in search of itself.

For Freud, the father is a figure weakened by the emancipation of women, and Lacan draws on this tradition. In 1953, with his so-called Name-of-the-Father theory, Lacan placed the symbolic position of fatherhood at the center of the family constellation. Far from being an advocate of fundamentalism, attached to a false patriarchy, and far from turning the symbolic function of the father into an 'essence', Lacan takes himself to be an Enlightenment thinker, detached from his Catholic culture but capable of integrating it in his work, just as Freud did with Judaism. It's for this reason that he would later borrow Lévi-Strauss's notion of the symbolic function (of the father, of paternity), clearly stating that he had no intention of using it in a nominalist or essentialist sense.

It's true, there is in Lacan a constant reference to Christian theology. But to make him out to be a rigorous, orthodox representative of the Roman Catholic Church, means forgetting that he was an atheist, a Nietzschean, a Spinozist, an Hegelian and later a structuralist, and that he referred to himself in his youth as an 'antichrist'. His baroque and flamboyant 'Catholicism', tinged with a hatred of the sacred, is closer to that of Salvador Dali or Luis Buñuel than to the precepts of the good fathers. And even if the notion of the Name-of-the-Father was borrowed from theology, it also has its basis in the modern anthropological categories of Durkheim, Mauss and Lévi-Strauss. In this respect, there is no confusion for Lacan, contrary to what Michel Tort (2000, p. 213) claims, between an anthropological law (the incest taboo) and a 'paternalist' family structure. Likewise, there is no contradiction in principle between the Oedipal model developed by Freud (and taken up by his successors) and the liberation movement of homosexuals initiated at the end of the nineteenth century with the decline of patriarchy. If in Western society the father was gradually dispossessed of his traditional authoritarian functions, the family is not for that reason any less indestructible today than it was in 1938. Whether it be 'natural', 'reconstructed', 'single parent' or 'gay parent', the family resembles this Oedipal tragedy reinvented by Freud. Provided it doesn't turn the tragedy into a simple 'complex'. The family is as much a crucible for the assertion of a symbolic and social normality as for the growth of the greatest criminal impulses or the development of transgressions and all types of conscious and unconscious pathologies tied to the construction of human subjectivity.

In listening to several members from various psychoanalytic schools, I've noted that there is no common position regarding the question of homosexuality. Analysts willingly speak of very different personalities among homosexuals. Some prefer to avoid the subject of gay or genital homosexuality altogether, talking instead of psychic homosexuality. Thus Thierry Bokanowski speaks of 'primary homosexuality', of a 'structuring' or 'inverted' Oedipus complex, or of an 'inversive' type. Other psychoanalysts adopt more clear-cut positions, such as Charles Melman in the Encyclopédie Universalis[11]*, as much with respect to male homosexuality – I'll pass over the clinical aspects and details of his article – as to female homosexuality, itself apparently not exempt from perversion. This is what he said in 1990. In a text published in* Cliniques Méditerranéennes, *Melman writes that in his opinion today, if male homosexuality constitutes a perversion, female homosexuality, on the other hand, could not be so considered, to the extent that it doesn't exist. It would be a kind of 'accomplished hysteria', he says. What do you think of this?*

All this 'theorizing' seems to me to be, once again, the expression of a masked homophobia. Why not call things as they are? We know quite well that 'psychic' homosexuality exists or that latent homosexuality is present in heterosexuals. We can also assume, as Lacan did, that female homosexuality is more 'hysterical' than male homosexuality. Or perhaps that... we know nothing about it! And Lacan never said, unlike Melman, that 'female homosexuality doesn't exist'.

---

[11] 'Homosexualité', an article Melman wrote in 1976 and since reprinted unmodified.

In fact, beyond the clinical questions of this nature, it's not the definition of homosexuality or homosexualities that obsesses the psychoanalytic community today, but rather, its 'real' (in the Lacanian sense) as well as its social reality. What bothers them, makes them at times paranoid, violent, and offensive, is that *practicing* homosexuals, that is, same-sex couples having sexual relations, want to behave like ordinary neurotics: to have children and live as a family; enjoy rights, etc. This is unacceptable to homophobic psychoanalysts. They in some way fear that a sexual act, which differs in nature from coitus between a man and a woman, will take the place of *their Freudian primal scene*. They're afraid that the primal scene, based on the anatomical difference between the sexes, will be replaced by a real and practically 'monstrous' stranger. As if this anatomical difference ran the risk of being erased or might disappear under the weight of the alleged 'homogenization' of the sexes. What a curious fantasy! This sexual difference is not about to be abolished, and it doesn't risk being covered up by other differences.

But luckily not all psychoanalysts are homophobic and many are by now able to listen *differently* to what these new homosexuals have to say, a group that has brought disorder to the Freudian community due, not to their perverse desire, but to their desire for 'normality'. I'm also shocked to see that this community is more tolerant of psychotic psychoanalysts or perverse heterosexuals than of 'ordinary' ('neurotic') homosexual psychoanalysts who demonstrate no particular pathology. Within the Freudian community there is the desire to retain the idea that homosexuality is, in itself, the essence of perversion.

The new reality will one day have to be accepted since it exists, and since new laws will soon be passed legalizing the desire of homosexuals for normalization. One has to reflect upon and take into account this reality, without being afraid of completely reviewing our psychoanalytic categories. It's also necessary to defend homosexuals against all forms of discrimination. If psychoanalysis wants to remain Freudian, it must pursue the civilizing and emancipatory task that first characterized it.

In this respect, the Lacanian conception of homosexuality is not appropriate for the analysis of homosexuals today, since the homosexual, considered as embodying the damned raced of the sublime pervert, is disappearing. Contemporary homosexuals can no longer be universally categorized as perverts. Likewise, *neurotic* homosexuality today is not, as such, a perversion: neither a sexual perversion nor a perversion in the structural sense. On the other hand, what remains of Lacanian theory is the quite brilliant idea that love in general has a component, indeed a structure, of a perverse nature, a 'sublimated homosexual' structure common to both homosexuals and heterosexuals. And if the Lacanian thesis regarding the necessary existence of a real that's irreducible to the norm is correct, then there is good reason to believe that the figure of the damned and sublime pervert will continue to exist within our society under new forms.

We must be on guard against an upsurge of homophobic violence by psychoanalysts. Concerning Lacan's work, we're still making our way through his legacy. One needs to make a choice and not endlessly dwell upon the master's quips. He has bequeathed to some of his disciples, luckily in the minority, both a pronounced taste for insult as well as a dogmatic reading of his Name-of-the-Father theory and of the symbolic function, which rightly deserves the criticisms made by Tort and others. More than Freud, Lacan provoked, indeed favored, a regressive reading of his work.

Charles Melman and Jean-Pierre Winter, who launched a real media crusade against homosexuals in the name of Lacanism and psychoanalysis, use the Lacanian notion of symbolic paternity in order to reestablish the lost figure of the authoritarian father which, in their view, is threatened by the new homosexual order. But this attitude only serves to recreate a hostile and conservative feeling of terror at the very idea of 'progress', similar to that which invaded Viennese society at the end of the nineteenth century. One finds traces of it in the books by Otto Weininger and Bachofen, but never in those by Freud. Strangely conservative and nihilistic, these authors feared a generalized feminization of society following women's emancipation. And even today, homophobic Lacanians, joining their IPA colleagues, are victims of the same terror. They're scared stiff that a kind of apocalypse will destroy all society to 'homosexualize' and 'homogenize' it.

They express their terror in the form of insults, affiliating themselves more with a kind of 'Mosaic' authoritarian patriarchy than Christian paternalism. Thus Winter invoked a caricatured Judaic order so as to stigmatize homosexual women who adopt children. He essentially said that such women represent a maternal Christianity since, like the Virgin Mary, they made the error of bringing forth a child without having heterosexual intercourse.[12] 'Christians', as it were. Here, the anti-Christian insult is like the Judaeophobic insult; it assumes that the 'Jewish' paternal function could reestablish the psychoanalytic 'Law of the Father' in light of the decline of Christian paternalism. In the same context, Winter accused homosexual couples of wanting to make 'symbolically modified children'.[13]

---

12 This accusation was made in my presence on February 2, 2000 during the radio broadcast of *France Culture* (*La Suite Dans les Idées*), with Geneviève Delaisi and Martine Gross, president of the *Association of Gay and Lesbian Parents*.

13 See Winter's 'Gare aux Enfants Symboliquement Modifiés', *Le Monde des Débats*, March 2000.

For his part, Charles Melman condemned Martine Gross, accusing homosexual parents as participating in a kind of primary narcissism that excludes the possibility of any real relation with others. In his view, children of these couples would only be 'stuffed toy animals, destined to satisfy their parents' narcissism'. He went on to add that it's impossible to view such a project as 'honorable'. As for Melman's definition of the so-called normal family, it's quite peculiar: 'By a normal family I mean one that allows the child to confront real problems'. When one considers that Lacan showed in 1938 that the worst depravities and the greatest anomalies arise in the most apparently normal families, one is able to see what separates the teacher from his homophobic disciples. In my opinion, they dishonor Lacanism and psychoanalysis.

I don't see how homosexuals' desire for normalization could endanger democratic principles. That these are based on the difference between sexes, and hence on heterosexual marriage, is clear. But precisely because homosexuality today takes it as a model, it doesn't endanger democracy. To the contrary, it asks even more of democracy. What's acted against democracy so far are the barbaric and authoritarian forms of an archaic patriarchy. On this point, Freud's conjectures regarding the primal horde and Lacan's analysis of the family come together. For now, the only apocalypse that seems to threaten Western society – and Islam as well – is radical Islamic fundamentalism disposed to terrorism. Islamic threats are made by extremist bearded and barbaric polygamists who constrain women's bodies and spit invectives against homosexuals, whom they hold responsible for weakening the masculine values of God the father. And finally, homosexuality cannot be likened to the sadistic or 'hedonistic' practices of SA or SS soldiers. Homosexuals, considered an 'inferior and degenerate race', were exterminated in concentration camps, and like Jews and Gypsies, marked with the badge of infamy. Today, they're killed in Saudi Arabia and tortured in Egypt, without the least bit of protest from the psychoanalytic community.

A few words regarding homosexual psychoanalysts. At the end of an interview you gave to the journal Ex Aequo *in April 1999, you say that homosexual analysts ought not to reveal their sexuality, for the simple reason that rules require that patients don't know about their analyst's private life. What do you think of this idea and of the creation of a network of homosexual psychoanalysts?*

As concerns treatment, I think that one needs to apply universal rules. We know that patients, in transference, quickly learn about their analyst's sexual orientation. But the rules proscribing analysts from sharing with their patients information about their 'private life' need to be retained. Homosexual analysts must also avoid a 'ghetto' mentality, and treat both homosexual and heterosexual patients. If a patient tells his or her analyst that s/he knows or thinks that the analyst is homosexual, and this is indeed the case, the analyst must not, in my view, deny it. All the same, analysts needn't detail their sexual choices. A lack of response to this type of question can be a *de facto* response in the form of interpretation.

A number of questions will have to be raised in the future, following the transformation of homosexuality in our societies. For example, how ought an analyst proceed in the treatment of a child who shows signs of premature homosexuality? Ought the analyst proceed in such a way that the child evolves towards another sexual choice? I think so, if it's a matter, for example, of a prepubescent child subject to his mother's fetishization. But how will the analyst be able to do so, in a world in which homosexuality is considered as ordinary sexuality and no longer as pathology? Where then will the boundaries be drawn, between the normal and the pathological?

Translated from the French by Marcel Lieberman

CONTRIBUTORS

THE FOLLOWING LIST comprises the names of people responsible for the interviews not conducted by the editors of *In Freud's Tracks*. In parentheses and italics is the name of the person interviewed.

Jacques André (*J. Laplanche*) is a psychoanalyst and member of both the Association Psychanalytique de France and the International Psychoanalytic Association. Editor of the series 'Petite Bibliothèque de Psychanalyse' at Presses Universitaires de France (PUF), he teaches psychopathology at the University of Paris VII and is the author of books on fratricide, masochism and the feminine origins of sexuality.

Marco Francesconi, MD (*J. Cremerius*) is a neurologist, psychiatrist, and psychotherapist, and an associate member of the Association of Psychoanalytical Studies in Milan. Professor of dynamic psychology in the psychology department of the University of Pavia, he has studied and written extensively about the construction of identities within gender differences, parental functions as interpersonal and intrapsychic dynamics, unconscious problems underlying bioethical decisions and developmental thought models in precocious mental states and during adolescence.

Maurizio Meloni (*R. Girard*) is a Girard scholar whose research focuses on the therapeutic-affective aspects of various ideologies, with particular attention towards religious ideologies. He has written on globalization for numerous Italian magazines, newspapers and anthologies.

Juan-David Nasio (*F. Dolto*), psychiatrist and psychoanalyst, is director of studies at the University of Paris VII (Sorbonne). The author of eight books on psychoanalysis, Dr. Nasio is a former member of the Jacques Lacan's Ecole Freudienne and served as editor of the Psychoanalysis Series at Editions Payot.

François Pommier (*E. Roudinesco*) is the author of an important study on psychoanalysis and AIDS, *La Psychanalyse à L'épreuve du Sida* (Paris: Editions Aubier, 1996).

Raffaele Siniscalco (*O. Kernberg*) is an Italian journalist working in New York for RAI (Radiotelevisione Italiana). He is the author of many programs about American and Italian culture.

Maria Luisa Tapparo (*D. Napolitani*) is a psychologist, psychotherapist and group-analyst. A member of the Turin-based APRAGI (Association for Research/ Training on Individual/Group Psychotherapy and Institutional Analysis), she leads groups in several Italian institutions. She has worked in a camp of Kosovar refugees in Tirana (Albania) and oversees volunteer youth groups for VIDES (International Volunteers for Women, Education and Development).

* * *

The editors of *In Freud's Tracks* would also like to thank the following translators for their assistance in transcribing and translating the interviews not originally conducted in English.

Tristram Bruce *(Henry; Fachinelli)*
trisbruce@katamail.com
Marcel Sima Lieberman *(Roudinesco; Laplanche)*
marcel_lieberman@hotmail.com
Joan Tambureno Mosconi (*Stengers; Castoriadis*)
g.mosconi@agora.stm.it
Gianmaria Senia *(Stengers)*
gianmaria.senia@fastwebnet.it
Valentina Tenedini *(Napolitani)*
Claudia Vaughn (*Dolto; Kristeva*)
pugwash@iol.it

ABOUT THE EDITORS

SERGIO BENVENUTO

Is the founder and longstanding editor-in-chief of the *Journal of European Psychoanalysis*. A researcher in psychology and philosophy at the National Research Council (CNR) in Italy and member of SGAI (Italian Society for Group Psychoanalysis), he is also a contributor to cultural journals such as *Differentia* and *Telos* (New York), *Lettre Internationale* (French, German, Spanish, Hungarian, Rumanian and Italian editions), *Texte* (Vienna), *RISS* (Basel), *Journal for Lacanian Studies* (London) and *L'évolution Psychiatrique* (Paris). He has translated into Italian Jacques Lacan's *Séminaire XX. Encore*, as well as works by Françoise Dolto, Paul Feyerabend, Richard Rorty, and others. His books include *La Strategia Freudiana* (Naples: Liguori, 1984); with Oscar Nicolaus, *La Bottega Dell'Anima* (Milan: Franco Angeli, 1990); *Dicerie e Pettegolezzi* (Bologna: Il Mulino, 1999); *Un Cannibale alla Nostra Mensa* (Bari: Dedalo, 2000); *Perversioni. Sessualità, Etica, Psicoanalisi* (Turin: Bollati Boringhieri, 2005). His most recent work is *Accidia: La Passione Dell'Indifferenza* (Bologna: Il Mulino, 2008).

Email: benvenuto.jep@mclink.it

ANTHONY MOLINO

Is a practicing psychoanalyst and award-winning translator of Italian literature. Based in Italy, he was awarded a doctorate in anthropology from Temple University in 1998, and is a member of the National Association for the Advancement of Psychoanalysis (NAAP), the United Kingdom Council on Psychotherapy and the Italian Society for Psychoanalytic Psychotherapy. He is best known for the books *Freely Associated: Encounters in Psychoanalysis* (London: FAB, 1997) and *The Couch and the Tree: Dialogues in Psychoanalysis and Buddhism* (London: Open Gate Press, 2001), for which he won a Gradiva Award from NAAP in 1999. He has also compiled the two-volume *Squiggles & Spaces: Revisiting the Work of D. W. Winnicott* (London: Whurr,

2001) and, with Christine Ware, edited *Where Id Was: Challenging Normalization in Psychoanalysis* (Middletown: Wesleyan University Press; London: Continuum, 2001). His most recent work is *Culture, Subject, Psyche: Dialogues in Psychoanalysis and Anthropology* (Wesleyan/Whurr, 2004).

As a translator, he has published works by poets Antonio Porta, Valerio Magrelli and Lucio Mariani, as well as by playwrights Eduardo De Filippo and Manlio Santanelli. His translation of Porta's *Kisses, Dreams & Other Infidelities* (Riverside, CA: Xenos Books, 2004) was also awarded a Gradiva Award in 2005.

Email: tonymolino@hotmail.it